THE LOST COAST

Books by Tim Bowling

Low Water Slack (poetry, 1995)
Dying Scarlet (poetry, 1997)
Downriver Drift (novel, 2000)
The Thin Smoke of the Heart (poetry, 2000)
Darkness and Silence (poetry, 2001)
Where the Words Come From: Canadian Poets in Conversation (editor, 2002)
The Paperboy's Winter (novel, 2003)
The Witness Ghost (poetry, 2003)
The Memory Orchard (poetry, 2004)
Fathom (poetry, 2006)
The Bone Sharps (novel, 2007)

the Lost Coast

salmon, memory and the death of wild culture

TIM BOWLING

Nightwood Editions · Gibsons Landing, BC

Published by Nightwood Editions
773 Cascade Crescent
Gibsons, BC, Canada VON 1V9
www.nightwoodeditions.com

Edited by Silas White.
Cover design by Anna Comfort.
Photos courtesy the Bowling family. Title page: Nola, Heck and Tim; page 8: Heck.
Printed in Canada on 100% recycled paper.

Nightwood Editions acknowledges financial support from the Government of Canada through the Canada Council for the Arts and the Book Publishing Industry Development Program (BPIDP), and from the Province of British Columbia through the British Columbia Arts Council, for its publishing activities.

LIBRARY AND ARCHIVES CANADA CATALOGUING IN PUBLICATION

Bowling, Tim, 1964–
The lost coast : salmon, memory and the death of wild culture / Tim Bowling.

ISBN 978-0-88971-211-9

1. Bowling, Tim, 1964– 2. Salmon–British Columbia. 3. Salmon
fisheries–British Columbia. 4. Biotic communities–British Columbia. 5. Human ecology–British Columbia. 6. Fishers–British Columbia–Biography. 7. Authors, Canadian (English)–20th century–Biography.
I. Title.

SH349.B68 2007 C811'.54 C2007-903873-5

for my brothers, Rick and Bruce, and my sister Nola
who will remember all this with differences
but with an equal amount of love

What I will never see again I must love forever.
–Yehuda Amichai

You must grieve for this right now
– you have to feel this sorrow now –
for the world must be loved this much
if you're going to say "I lived" . . .
–Nazim Hikmet

I think we're going to the Moon because it's in the nature of the human being to face challenges. It's by the nature of his deep inner soul. We're required to do these things just as salmon swim upstream.
–Neil Armstrong

Splendour without diminishment
–British Columbia's motto

HEATING

The author wishes to thank the BC Arts Council for its financial support of this manuscript. Several individuals, as well, supported *The Lost Coast* in various ways. My gratitude to the following: Helen Maxwell, Ann Robertson, Russell Thornton, Curtis Gillespie, Norm Sacuta, Jacqueline Baker and Silas White. And, as always, I owe so much to my family, who keep me from being lost.

I

IN THE ORIGINAL TOWNSITE of Ladners Landing, at the corner of Georgia and Chisholm Streets, under the wasp-yellow glow of the single streetlamp, a middle-aged, unshaven man in rubber gumboots pauses to adjust the pressure in his shoulders. He's carrying two large spring salmon, each of his index fingers hooked under a gill. A rich, almost black blood trickles down the sides of each silvery slab and makes a perforated line along the clamshell-coloured pavement, leading back a half-block, up the crushed gravel dyke to the government wharf where the *Rona*, the man's twenty-eight-foot wooden gillnetter, rests gently at moorage.

It's May, still early in the season. Blossoms on a nearby row of wild cherry trees sweeten the briny air. Several drift down. One lands on the man's blood-stained white T-shirt and blends in. The touch, subtle as a child's look in a world of working adults, normally goes unnoticed. But tonight the man is particularly sensitive to, and grateful for, his place in these surroundings. No clock but his own and the river's has told him to stop work, no man holds power over him, he's looking forward to a meal of fried hamburger patties, potatoes and onions, all slathered in ketchup and salt. In an hour or so, when the tide has turned, he'll return to his boat with another full thermos of milky, sweet Red Rose tea, a brown paper bag of bologna sandwiches, and a new pack of Player's cigarettes. The springs, laid in a wheelbarrow in the sideyard and covered with a burlap sack that once held potatoes, will be picked up in the morning by Mrs. Nakatani. She will pay cash, over a dollar per pound, such an astonishing amount of money that the man feels guilty taking it and so charges thirty cents per pound less than the going rate. Even though the extra money is welcome, he sells only the occasional spring privately. The rest of his catch, he turns in to the cannery with whom he has a working relationship: they advance him the money for gear each season, and therefore the man feels obligated to give them his fish. Still, every now and then, if he catches such beauties as these . . .

With pleasure, he recalls making a small cut in the hard flesh beneath each gill to determine that the springs were red and not white – people want the coloured flesh, and will pay more than double for it compared with the white, though the difference in taste is marginal. The man smiles. Himself, he doesn't care for fresh salmon, no matter what the colour. If he has to eat salmon, he prefers the canned variety, the store's even more than his wife's.

A dog emerges from the surrounding dark. It's Pepper, the family springer.

"Down boy," he says gently, and lightly swings one of the fish away from the dog's sniffing nose.

The interruption breaks his reverie. He looks up the empty street. His small, modern bungalow, dwarfed on each side by tall Victorian houses going to ruin, will be warm and bright and smelling of fried onions. What time is it, he wonders, and thinks suddenly of his two youngest children. Will they be up? Did he promise Nola that he'd take her with him tonight, even though tomorrow is a school day? And Tim? Will he beg to go again, though at only five, midnight will see his eyes closed as surely as a high tide follows a low?

He thinks, how strange to be the father of a small boy once more. He had not expected it. Almost twenty years have passed since Rick and Bruce were that age. Now they are men, Rick still on the river at this minute, fishing his own boat, and Bruce, engaged to be married, apprenticed to the plumbing trade, following in his late grandfather's footsteps.

As for his youngest, who could tell? The boy loved books, happily played alone. How different his life would have been had the baby before him survived, a brother strangled by the cord. But then, if that child had lived, perhaps he and Jean would have had no more.

The man sighs. He is not often given to such musings, the patterns of his or any human life being so much more difficult to understand than those of the salmon. But the salmon are mysterious too, perhaps more so. He looks down along his arms to the wide dime-sized eyes. Living or dead, the eyes are the same – open, hungry. The man feels the tug in his shoulder blades. The dog flows around him like a current. Overhead, a bat's flitting warps the air. The man gazes up. Scudding clouds peel blackly off a full moon not much larger than one of the salmon's eyes, and he wonders again if it can be true, that the Americans will soon put a man on the surface. It seems impossible. But then, most amazing things seem impossible. Having children, for instance, or the salmon's return to the very stream of its birth. Of course, those are natural events, meant to be. Walking on the moon, though? That's just . . . well, it seems wrong, arrogant somehow. The whole idea saddens him. He sighs as the clouds slide over the moon again, grateful that for now at least, it's the same as it's always been: untouched, pure, mysterious.

The man rejigs the knuckle of each index finger and walks the remaining half-block home. The broken line completes itself, even the blood of the dead salmon driven to fulfillment.

* * *

The kitchen is silent but for the little clicks of dishes in the soapy water and the occasional string of whispered words from down at the linoleum floor. The woman glances at the clock, a large sun with brass rays of differing lengths shooting out in all directions – a Mother's Day gift from her eldest child. Thinking of him, she worries, shuts her eyes. The boat he is fishing is too small and fragile. Imagine. A boat named the *Driftwood.* No cabin, no protection from the weather, the sides almost at water level. And no drum! He has to pick up by hand, piling the net in the stern, leaning too far over, the tide fast and . . . she opens her eyes. But he's young and strong, and Heck watches out for him. Even so, things happen fast on the water. She wipes her hands on her flower-print apron and, by instinct, comforts herself by looking at her children who are still children.

Nola sits at the kitchen table, writing a book report, long black hair framing her pale face. She wants so badly to go out with her father tonight, and thinks that if she finishes her homework, she'll be allowed. Well, perhaps. But not without a lifejacket. The woman doesn't care what the children of other fishing families are allowed. The river is not something to be trifled with. She shudders, recalling how frightened she'd been when Heck had first started fishing, and she'd gone with him a few times, the boys barely out of diapers then, staying with their grandmother. Oh yes, the river was beautiful, but a seal pup had become tangled in the net and Heck had had to club the poor thing with a gaff until it was dead. He hated to do it, but he'd had no choice; the tide was running so fast and the net had to be brought in quickly. That had been enough for her, seeing those wet eyes reflecting moonlight, then hearing the mother seal cry in the sloughs all the rest of the night and into the next morning. Of course, if Heck had wanted her to keep coming out with him, she would have. But it was so much easier for her to stay home with the boys. And Heck had never minded being on his own.

The woman looks at the clock quickly. He ought to be home any time. She should start slicing some onions. But first, she looks down.

Her youngest is on his knees, head bent, whispering names half-familiar to her from Saturday night television. Some she knows well: Howe, Delvecchio, Hull, Keon. But others surface like the names of people from her childhood in Toronto, remembered but without detail: Nolet, Hicke, Rochefort. How intensely yet softly he utters the names as he picks up the cards he's positioned into teams on the floor and uses two at a time to pass a marble back and forth before shooting it at one of the nets he's removed from his brothers' old table hockey game. Where has this idea come from? There are no other boys near his age on the street. And his sister, though she likes to watch hockey, never bothers with the cards. Well, he has a good imagination, probably because he's been left on his own so much, Nola off at school. But he'll start grade one himself before too long, and make some friends. No, she has little cause to worry about her baby. He seems so serious at times, scowling and quiet. But he's here, at her feet, safe. Hull, Mikita, he shoots he scores. It's easier when they're young.

The woman steps carefully across the cards to the fridge and takes out a ceramic bowl of leftover boiled potatoes. Then she crosses back, removes a frying pan and a wooden cutting board from a cupboard, a knife from a drawer. The onion comes from a mesh bag hanging off a cupboard doorknob. When she slices into it, the air sharpens, stinging her eyes. The tears come slowly and do not fall, as the stars have come to the darkness that presses against the house, to light her husband's way up the gravel drive.

* * *

The kitchen door opens. River, salmon, brine, blood, blossoms, earth: a tidal wave of wild whelms the domestic, the hockey players collapse from my hands, I am looking beyond my father's salmon-clad figure to the life-swollen black of tides and fathoms washing against his shoulders, whispering my name in a thousand different voices. My mother and sister are exclaiming over the springs – "How big are they? Are they red?" – there's a clamour in a drawer as the little black hand-scale with the pewter hook is produced and yesterday's newspaper is spread on the floor to catch the slime and blood. But my father does not lay the fish down. When I finally break free of the night's swirl, I look up to see the familiar laughter in his blue eyes. He knows what I'm seeing in the darkness out of which he's emerged. Why, then, won't he let me go with him?

The fish keep me from asking. My father has lifted them.

Their eyes are at the level of my eyes. As always, I open mine wider, try not to blink, try to hold their intensity. The clotted blood at the gills draws me in, it's so thick and crimson, with dark, coagulated bits, as if blood has been poured over chunks of soot. The trickle down the scales is straight and a lighter, thinner red; cherry-coloured, it drips at intervals of a few seconds on the round braided mat. I think the blood should make some kind of noise, just as I think the dying salmon should cry out when they die, but my father says they don't. Nola says that they cry like babies, and sometimes she says they cry, *Please let me go, please, please.* But she grins as she says this, and I suspect she's just teasing. Dad is telling the truth, but I can't quite believe it. They must make some noise, their look is so fierce when they're dead. He says they fight a lot in the net and that they kick in the stern for several minutes after he's untangled them and tossed them under the drum. It's hard to imagine that now. Their blood falls quieter than the rain.

The hook is hooked under a gill. My sister asks for our father's guess, our mother's, then gives her own. She doesn't ask me because I always guess what Dad guesses. I am not so interested in the weight. They're big enough. Instead, I'm waiting for Dad to let me cut below the gill to see if the fish are red or white. I can never believe the fish aren't exactly the same. It's a thrill when, his hand firm on the back of my hand, we sink the blade into the gumline and pull back the little flap to see the colour.

The door is still open, like a gill through which we're all breathing. The sun-clock ticks. The spring hangs like a still pendulum. Its eyes are open. But Nola says you can't see anything once you're dead. Dad agrees. Mom says she doesn't really know, but I think she's thinking about God, whom I understand a little because I've heard about him from books: *I see the moon/ and the moon sees me/ God bless the moon/ and God bless me.* I touch the wet scales of the one on the newspaper. Soon the scales will be sticky and dry. The paper will come up with the fish when it's lifted. Outside, a burlap sack soaked with hose-water will be kept over them, and rocks placed at the edges of the sack to foil the cats. Now, however, the kitchen belongs to the salmon and their death and the terrible salt longing of the night to possess them again. Why can't I go? When can I go? I want to see what the salmon were seeing before they stopped seeing forever, what the rest of my family has seen. I lean towards the door. My body is knife-sharp against the dark. I've begun the cut into which all my bloodsoaked words will pour.

II

My father said, "It's best he didn't live. The doctor told me he would have been a vegetable." My mother says, "His name was Christopher." My father said, "I saw him. Your mother didn't. It was good she didn't." My mother says, "I told Verna the week before, something's wrong with the baby." My father had to arrange to dispose of the corpse. Someone from the hospital phoned to say that he needed to come and collect it. Arrangements were quickly made. As Ladner, so marshy as to be almost underwater, had no burial ground, Christopher was buried in an unmarked grave in Boundary Bay Cemetery in neighbouring Tsawwassen. My mother visited a few times, took flowers. But she was the daughter of a woman who'd lost several children at birth and several in infancy, and she had living children to raise. Her memory of the gravesite has been gone for decades. Does she ever think about him? How does she think about him? I could ask, but it's akin to saying, *Why didn't you die from grief?* or, *At seventy-nine, you ought to cry every day. How can you not cry every day for all that is gone, and going?*

And then I realize, again, as if for the first time, as if all the slowly accumulating knowledge between the ages of five and twenty happened in a single burst, "But we don't cry every day." Nothing, not even the salmon's remarkable journey home from the sea to the inland waters of its birth, is as mysterious as our adaptability to the conditions of greater and greater loss. My parents, to use one of my mother's favourite verbs, "coped" – just as their parents coped – with poverty, war, the death of children. How different, then, were human eyes from those of the salmon? To the boy I was, to any child, the degree of difference matters less than its mere presence. There was something in the look of the wild that hinted at cold and depth and vastness – the salmon's pupil was made of the space between stars. The salmon were different, yes. We killed them to make a living. I knew that, even at five. I also knew they were gods.

Death and again death, Walt Whitman wrote of what the sea whispered to him. *Death, death, death.* The salmon in the Fraser River whispered the same to me, by the millions, but in one voice. The sound was the wind howling between stars. It shook every cell in my body when, at last, one warm night in the year of the moonwalk, I followed my father in darkness along the clamshell road, through a shower of light, into the beginning of knowledge.

* * *

Five of the six species of Pacific salmon return to the Fraser River (the sixth, the masu, returns only to Japanese waters): chinook, the largest (commonly known as springs, and by fishermen sometimes as smileys); sockeye; coho (also blueback); chum (commonly known as dogs); and pink (commonly known as humpback or, to fishermen, slimeys). By the age of ten, I had watched thousands of each species die, had handled them, thrown them, carried them, gaffed them. I had eaten springs, sockeye and coho, but dogs and humpies were not, as my mother said, "good eating." Each species, however, shone with the same power of returning; each left its inland waters of birth, travelled for between two and five years (depending on the species) and thousands of kilometres – down the Fraser and out at sea – then, suddenly, as if a switch had been flicked on in the brain, began the furious dash for home, for the exact waters of its origins ("exact" meaning right down to the same little patch of gravel on a creekbed).

As a boy, I learned three things from the salmon that would greatly influence my understanding of life: the knowledge of man is limited and even miniscule in the face of the natural world; death is not an aberration to shut our eyes and minds against; and, rich patterns exist everywhere. But anyone picking up an encyclopedia can deduce these truths from the scientific evidence. The fact that so many don't, even on the west coast with salmon swimming gloriously past them, eventually taught me the great gift of hands-on sensory involvement with the world. When I went out that first night with my father, and he set his gillnet across a muddy side-channel of the Fraser River's mouth, and I hung over the stern in the dim pick-up light, I didn't know that I was being taught anything important. I doubt my family really thought about it in those terms. Certainly the greater human culture around us put no value on such lessons, and puts even less value on them now. It was the only education that mattered, however, the only one that sustains me as I move closer towards my own death and there is still no one to answer the real questions.

* * *

Beyond the streetlamp, we walked fifty yards along Chisholm, the darkened office and store of Buckerfields Feed and Seed on the land side, and on the river side at the top of the paved, slanting ascent to the dyke, a high, long, inverted-V-roofed barn that extended out over the channel itself. Supported by dozens of creosoted black pilings, this structure – its grey paint was mostly flaked off to reveal equally grey planks – was a century-old architectural marvel. Its roof beams, running from one end to the other of the building, were unjoined, meaning they had been fashioned from giant cedars several centuries old at the time of felling. Now my father's shadow lapped at the base of the two tall sliding doors. Behind them, the barn was partially filled with other products that Buckerfields sold to local farmers: bags of fertilizers and chemicals, sheep pellets, salt licks, barbed wire, bales of timothy and alfalfa and straw. A small forklift also crouched in there under the swirling chaff, waiting to slam into the stacks of empty and loaded pallets.

Once, not long before, I had taken Rick his lunch at work

and was told to find him in the warehouse. From broad daylight and flocks of pigeons and sparrows, I stepped cautiously into the half-light of the nineteenth century and gazed up. There seemed no roof at all, just a few lengths of sisal rope hanging from the musty darkness like fishing lines. But what could live up there, and what did it hope to catch for food? I hovered, then tried my weak voice against the silence. The echo took forever to bounce back, as if it had had to wrench itself free of some great spiderweb. I tried again, louder. Way at the far end of the barn, in the deeper dark, a thin shaft of daylight widened with a scrape, and a wall of sunlight collapsed inward, soundlessly. Sliding doors! Over the river! Before I could take in this surprising fact, my brother strode towards me. Grinning, he swooped me up, messed my hair, and gave me a quarter for my trouble.

His full, bushy beard, grown for Canada's Centennial (the town held a competition), was like a chunk of the chaff-laden dark. He smelled of sweat and hay. I turned from him reluctantly, but was relieved nonetheless to enter the daylight again.

Between the barn and the entrance to the government wharf were thirty feet of blackberry bushes. To my right beckoned the swing in the abandoned, tin-roofed Home Oil shed. Someone had looped a thick rope to the rafters when two of the shed walls had been removed. It dangled there, its fist-sized knot some kind of monster spider that feasted on oily flesh. Shuddering, I looked ahead. A dim lightbulb threw a sandy light on a narrow path of wooden planks running between the high blackberry bushes and a netshed the colour of dried blood. We took the path. At the corner of the netshed, we turned right. Here was a large square of wharf. Four standing net-racks, like giant sawhorses only with rounded backs, covered most of the space. A sea-green net hung hammock-style between two of the racks, its corks bunched at one end, its leadline coiled at the other. No one was mending the net, however, and no one stood in the netshed either, though the wall fronting the river was wide open. An empty cardboard beer case sat near the edge of the wharf, and there was one stubby bottle perched on a piling head, its brown glass flickering dully. I stared at the river, my eyes opening in a long swallow.

High tide. The water dark and oily, slippery-looking like salmon guts. And the smell that rich too: muddy, briny. The air like a black Lab's fur after it's been retrieving ducks in the marsh. I could hear the current lapping at the pilings that supported the main wharf and at the series of smaller floats at the bottom of the gangway.

My father told me to go first. The grade of the wooden plank was not steep, the tide being high, and there were little ribs of wood hammered in sideways all the way down to help with footing, but there was no railing and the viscous slop of the river seemed filled with intent. I descended with caution, my hand clutching the brown paper bag of sandwiches I'd been deputized to carry. From the bottom of the gangway to my father's tie-up spot, we walked another fifty yards over six mossy floats connected by thin plywood boards. The floats shifted slightly with our weight, like lily pads under a frog's leaping. Each float contained a pair of net-racks and a heap or two of nets covered with burlap tarp. More empty beer bottles, some pop cans, spare engine parts, and a hairless doll lying on her back on the bare planks. I shivered as her blank eyes met mine.

Across the harbour channel, no wider than an older boy's best stone-throw, hung a dimly lit row of tin- and cedar-plank-roofed netsheds as old as the Buckerfields barn – there were six of them, each fronted by a small wharf. There, and along our series of floats, shimmered a ghostly absence. All the men and boats had vanished, but for my father and the *Rona.* My senses flowed into the empty spaces and tried to fill them. But the spaces slid inwards, the way the sand of a sandcastle does at the advance of the tide. We were alone.

My father swept me aboard the *Rona* in one swift, sure motion, helped me into the bulky, padded lifejacket that my mother had insisted on, over and over, and then disappeared through the skinny doorway of the cabin to start the engine. It coughed once, twice, a third time, before catching and idling smoothly. I saw the net wrapped around the drum – it was still wet and dripping. I bent down a little to see better. Something flipped up with a thump. I almost fell backwards. Was that sweet, gassy smell actually blood? Exhaust quickly overwhelmed it.

My father emerged from the cabin, smiling. He stepped back onto the float and undid the stern, side and bow ropes, then pushed us off. We swung a lazy circle around, the tide doing the work. I breathed deeply. My father, at the deck-wheel, lit a cigarette, cupping the wooden match as if in prayer, then flicked it into the river. Not far off, a dog barked. I wondered if it was Pepper, if he was worried about me and had run up to the dyke for a last look. But I couldn't see him at the black end of our street as we drifted past, the streetlamp glow like the sun's an hour after setting. I couldn't see anything.

We chugged west out of Ladner Harbour in darkness, with a low-treed, uninhabited silt island to the near north and a high gravel dyke to the near south. Along the dyke's bank were weathered netsheds on mossy, collapsing wharves, rotted pilings from a century-old cannery, and several wrecked gillnetters lying on their sides, ribs showing. Above, along the dyke itself, were equally blackened houses, small and briny, their properties cluttered with old engine parts and heaps of net and cork; usually the grass was uncut, strafed with buttercups, and blackberry prickles hung over everything. Skinny, untrustworthy-looking wooden gangways angled down to tide level.

Now the desolation was even greater. No one was around. The dim wharf-lights touched only a disturbing absence. We idled past, my father smoking at the deck-wheel, me at his side, still clutching the brown paper bag, my big, orange lifejacket hanging like lungs of flame over my chest. Suddenly the silt island ended and there was another channel of river leading north. We turned slowly, and I felt the town drop off the earth. The darkness deepened, the wind picked up and blew in our faces, there were masses of deadheads surfacing and vanishing along both sides of the channel. Now the musky, oily tang of salmon rising off the planks of the *Rona* charged itself again, the way the rhododendron at the foot of our driveway gave off a sweeter scent at nightfall. I looked around wildly. Why did I want to come? Terror lapped at my eyes. I wanted to go home, but I couldn't say anything; I knew my father wasn't going back until morning. I pressed closer to his leg, but the lifejacket wouldn't allow any comfort in. Once past those deadhead masses, tiny and dark as rectory graveyards, the *Rona* hugged the eastern bank. Something rose up from a little slough mouth with a tearing squawk and flapped away with large, slow wingbeats. I knew it was only a great blue heron, but I couldn't stop my eyes from widening.

More deadheads, just single ones now, rising as if to look at us, and behind them the bulrushes of the marsh into which the silt island had dissolved. The tide, running out, pulled chunks of mud off the bank. I turned to face the river. The channel was much broader than the one that made the harbour, and completely dark. No, not quite: a small yellowish light right on the surface was drifting past us, and in the distance another small light, higher, hung in midair. Scared though I was, I knew the first light marked the end of a net, and that the second was a mastlight. Those tiny illuminations in the wind-whipped dark steadied me. I could not see where we were headed. I would have had to step to one side of the small cabin and lean out a little, which I could not bring myself to do, nor would my father have allowed it. He had told me to "stay put."

In a matter of moments, though, when we had passed another pair of lights, the *Rona* turned on the breeze, its bow pointing to the west, and I could look easily to the north. Up there, I knew, was the "main river," the deepest channel of the Fraser's south arm, so deep, my sister had told me, that killer whales could chase seals there all the way to New Westminster. I was sufficiently awed, though I didn't know how far New Westminster was, nor did I realize the depth a killer whale required to transport itself. For now, the information just made me happy that we didn't fish the "main river." I stared to the north. A clutch of lights, like a pearl necklace bunched up, hung way above a smattering of lights almost at river level. I knew there were mountains beyond Vancouver; we could see them clearly from our kitchen window. But I had forgotten they would still be there in the dark. And what was that necklace? Could it be a low constellation? I looked up. The rest of the stars, glimpsed through scudding black cloud, were much higher.

I didn't have time to wonder. My father turned and ordered me to sit down on the cover of the main hatch and not to move. He'd come and get me when he could. "Stay away from the sides of the boat," he repeated, in that tone he used for the most important instructions. I was happy not to move. I wasn't liking this experience nearly as much as I'd expected. Everything was darker and colder than I could have imagined. And soon we were going to try to catch those big fish whose eyes were so haunting? Those fish covered in blood? I didn't want to do it, and yet some part of me yearned to discover how it was done. A net, of course. But how did they get out of the net?

The *Rona* pointed north again and I looked west across the channel. Bathed golden as a nativity scene, another fisherman's stern drifted slowly away from us, the man's head bowed, his hands releasing a long horse's tail of web, another, another, another, endlessly, as the engine pulled him across the river and the tide pulled him down. Before he became just a faint glow below us, our own drum – a kind of giant spool laid sideways in the stern – began to turn. I focused on the near glow.

My father was "making a set." We were at the top of the "drift," at the "towhead." This particular section of the rivermouth, dropping south off the "main river," then veering sharply west through a narrow slough between two low-treed silt islands, and blending into another section, was called the Prairie Drift. To this day, no one really knows why – either because some loner from Saskatchewan made it his personal set way back in the Dirty Thirties, not minding the terrible "snags," or because, on a calm day, the water and the low bulrush marsh resembled a prairie wheatfield.

In any case, we were fishing the Prairie, an unglorified side-channel to where the real money was made, and drifting towards the Port, so named because it hugged the bank of Port Guichon, not an official town, but a part of the delta first settled by the Guichons, who'd come to the Nicola country of BC's Interior from the Savoy Region of France, and then to the delta in 1883. I would know nothing of local history for decades – only a few names and some living descendants were left as signposts for the disregarded origins of heritage (just as a totem pole or two, a reservation near the BC Ferries Tsawwassen terminal, and some all-but-invisible living descendants, suggested the much older aboriginal presence in the area). At five, I was just coming into the marriage of language with work, place and history, easing naturally into it, not knowing how rare the marriage was nor how rapidly it would begin to break up: Set. Drift. Snag. High boat. Berrypicker. Scotchman. Hanging bench. Sockeye. Wingdam. Saltchuck. Humpies. Hole in the wall. The Pass. The Brunswick. Smileys. Blackfish. Fire in the water. The Rice Mill. Gaff. Forty mesh. Sixty mesh. Oilery Slough. Indian candy. Highliner. The Adams. The Stuart. Smokers. Packer. Tenderman. Pike pole. Hooky-kacky. Low water slack.

I wasn't standing merely on the scuffed hatch-cover of a salmon gillnetter; this was a threshold to a world that extended beyond one place and one language, reached out to a world of similar small and unsung places and of huge, much-chronicled cities, of thousands of languages, billions of people, the living, the dead, the not-yet-born, whole civilizations I could participate in simply by virtue of having a tongue and a portion of the loved earth in which to sow desire.

My father set his net. Bending at the waist every half-minute to use the stern wheel, he turned the *Rona* in large half circles, so the meshes of the net would hang loosely, making it harder for the salmon to snap through. Sometimes, when he reached a section of net that had been snagged and quickly mended, he had to chuck the leadline and loose webbing over the wooden rollers so that they wouldn't catch on the planks of the stern and cause him to stop the drum. More commonly, it stopped on its own due to a hook-up or hooky-kacky, which occurred when the net was restricted from flowing smoothly off the drum by a small stick or other tiny object that had not been picked out of the net the set before. I would soon learn how shredded the nets of the river fishermen could become and how difficult just getting the net on and off the drum would prove. I would soon learn too the violent colour of the response to such difficulties, but never from my father. He let the net slide through his fingers, going and coming, with the same easy concentrated rhythm he employed brushing my sister's long hair in living-room lamplight. Never did he swear or slam things down or show any signs of panic. This made him as much, if not more, of a novelty than did his obstinate refusal to fish anywhere other than the Prairie Drift.

Of the three dozen or so gillnetters fishing out of Ladner, only six regularly made sets on the Prairie – two belonged to older fishermen who didn't really need the money, one to a moody, wild loner in his late twenties who lived year-round on his black-painted boat, one to my Uncle Earl, one to my older brother Rick, and one to my father. At forty-six, with two children still to raise, he had the greatest need of money, yet he would not venture even to a nearby "hot spot," much to the delighted teasing of several others, those who, week after week, challenged for the title of "high boat" (most fish caught). The reasons for his loyalty to the Prairie were complex and had mostly to do with his unease in competitive situations, his taproot desire to be left alone, a desire I've inherited and which, as much as anything, turned me towards writing as a way to live.

We idled, looping, across the black channel to the unlit, bush-hung bank of Wilkies Island. The drum, empty now, stopped turning. Only a bare length of thin corkline attached the boat to the 160 fathoms of forty-mesh deep net wound snakelike across the current. I stood as still as the constellations clustered above me, but the boat drifted downriver at a steady clip, and would pick up speed, set after set, as the tide dropped. My father lit another cigarette, then stepped lightly alongside the drum and into the cabin. A second later, the engine cut off. Silence washed in on its invisible tide. What was there to hear?

That faint creaking – stars rubbing together? I looked over my shoulder at the island. A tiny float, a single piling, and a wooden skiff, all in black outline. I blinked, not sure I was seeing them. Did somebody actually live in that dark, lonely place?

"Listen," my father said, inclining his head slightly towards the net. "Hear it?"

I shook my head.

"There."

What had I heard? A splash in the distance, yet close too. Like hearing water slosh in my ear. I didn't need to ask to what it was.

Five minutes. Ten. A few more splashes. My father started the engine. He tied on his long, shiny apron by making a bow at the small of his back. Against the far bank, the mast light of another boat slowly climbed, like a lit reed in a back eddy. It passed the cherry-pit-sized light I knew marked the end of our net; the light bobbed with the boat's swells, blinked off, on, off, on . . . then finally stayed that way. I went into the stern with my father. He positioned me against the empty drum, its circular sides protecting me like the wings of a cemetery angel. He asked if I was enjoying myself. I nodded. He took a long drag on his cigarette and resumed watching the end of the net. If he hadn't set too close to the far bank, or if the net didn't snag, or if the current didn't play any unexpected tricks, the night-light would swing neatly inside the slough at the far point as our boat swung neatly in at the near bank. Only once, in the ten years I fished with my father, did the end of his net ever "wrap the point" – but set after set, in fog, rain, wind, blazing heat, he worried quietly at the prospect. Unlike the highliners, those fishermen who chased the salmon up and down the coast using the most modern electronic fish-finding technology, he didn't have many extra nets – perhaps one old one in the backyard shed, or a small section of a newer one. He couldn't afford disasters.

I had never smelled such richness. Mud off the banks, the wet, blooming bushes, gasoline, the brininess of the still-gasping fish – which turned out to be a sturgeon – somewhere near my feet. I didn't even notice that I was getting cold. It must have been hours past my bedtime, but I wasn't at all tired. Who could ever fall asleep out here?

"Time to pick up," my father said, gently placing me to the starboard side of the stern. "Don't reach your hands out. And don't lean over the side." He smiled, knowing how long I'd been waiting for this moment. Gloveless, he lightly fingered a piece of leadline, feeling for pullers, as he explained. Then he stepped onto the bar at his feet, the drum turned, and the first corks – yellow, green, black, white, ochre – bumped over the rollers. I could just see the net as it came into the yellowish glow of the pick-up light. Meshes were spread out and glistening like a geisha's fan dipped in dew, then quickly snapped together as they rose, squeezed between the corkline and leadline, to slip between my father's hands. He eyed the fathom nearest the boat, then the end of the net, a sequence repeated for the next twenty minutes, with the same non-expressive rapt attention.

But first, he told me to look. Out on the river, in the glow, two corks were missing and a third bobbed violently every half-dozen seconds. My father took his foot off the bar. The tone of his posture changed, tightened. He held the net bunched in both hands and pulled slowly, dropping the corks, leadline, and meshes softly to the stern. He leaned his upper body over the rollers, a puppeteer intent on the strings of a marionette. Everything slowed down. Without looking, my father reached and found the gaff-hook leaning against the port side of the stern. I didn't think he could move any slower, but he did. The net in his left hand, the gaff held shoulder-high in his right, he hovered.

A second passed. A summer. Ten summers. Thirty-five years. I couldn't see for the salt in my eyes. Then it cleared, a black shape flickered, my father's right arm plunged down. The gaff held fast. My father's arm jerked from side to side, as if he was carving frozen meat with a dull knife. After one fierce splash, the scene fell quiet. My father stepped on the drum pedal to pick up the slack (the net bunched at his feet). Seconds later, a yard-long, thigh-wide hunk of silver swung into view. It seemed to expand at the end of the hook like a glassblower's glass before it thunked to the stern and thrashed violently for a few seconds, a single mesh in its gill. My father slid his finger into the gill, removed the mesh, then retracted the now-bloody hook. With the blunt end of the gaff, he bashed the fish twice, stilling it. An even richer smell, like fresh mint snapped and held to the nose, washed over the stern. One blank eye gazed past me, only it wasn't blank like the doll's on the wharf; this eye, while motionless, pulsed with life. Yet there'd been no scream. Spring. Chinook. Smiley. But I wasn't smiling, nor was my father. We looked across the fifty pounds of rapidly dying flesh for a second, then he neatly slid the fish under the drum with his boot and resumed picking up.

The net rolled in, dripping, drenched with mudsmell, frayed in places from earlier snags. There weren't many fish – a few springs, less dramatically gaffed, and a half-dozen small, sharp-spined bottomfish called bullheads, a combination Chinese dragon and monarch butterfly which my father picked out with painstaking patience and tossed back in the current as the river carried us into the slough and we drifted towards the Port. Also problematic and worthless were the branches like candelabra, the driftwood gnarled and smooth, and the slabs of cedar bark – I especially grew to love these, with their outsides like crocodile skin and their smooth insides the colour of salmon flesh. I would hold them, rubbing first the rough side, then the smooth, and imagine the huge trees they'd been torn from somewhere upriver. In no way did the bark or the denuded ancestral trees disturb me; the former was attractive and manageable, while the latter was invisible. Mostly. It wouldn't be long before I learned that anything dying or being killed near or on the river belonged by rights to the sea – and our net hung in the path.

We finished picking up, our night-light bobbing into the glow. It was a coal-oil lantern mounted on a painted triangle of wood. Within a year or two, this type of gear would be obsolete, replaced by a spear-long, styrofoam-girded and plastic-headed battery-operated light that didn't flick out with such maddening frequency. My father, typically, resisted the change longer than most. Eventually, however, he gave up his coal-oil lantern just as he'd given up linen nets in favour of the stronger, synthetic nylon variety.

To the end, though, he could not give up his strict adherence to the fishery's unwritten code of etiquette. Even as the behaviour of others became less gentlemanly and more cutthroat, even as the lust for salmon rivalled the lust for Fraser gold of the 1850s, my father would not "cork" another boat (make a set, out of turn, immediately below another fisherman), nor would he "open it up" (travel at full throttle) past an anchored or drifting boat in order to reach the top of the set sooner, nor would he stop coming into harbour in the evenings for supper. Instead, he chose to get out of the business. Nothing ever pained him so much as a lack of courtesy due to greed.

Now the net was on the boat, the lantern-glow puddling our feet. My father reached under the drum and pulled out the spring. It was white, he said, because of the snout and the size of the teeth. He put my hand on them. They were fine, pointed, closer together nearer the back of the jaw. But you couldn't always be sure of the colour, which was why you had to make a cut in the gumline.

Blood trickled down from where the hook had pierced the head. The scales, packed tight, shone dully. The gums of the jaw were blue-black, the tail was speckled, as if brandishing the sky's tiniest constellation. And the eyes were dead and seeing everything I saw, and much that I didn't see.

My father opened the side-locker and laid the big spring and the smaller ones inside. He fitted the wooden cover over the locker again, so we could walk across it to the deck. Once more, I stood beside him as he turned the small, metal wheel. The night was blackberry dark and we had no spotlight. The tide was running faster. Our progress against it, along the bank to the top of the drift, was slow. Halfway up, emerging from another, narrower slough that lay parallel to the one we'd just drifted down, we came suddenly upon a flat, short skiff without lights. My father cut the engine and let us drift. He announced our catch into the stillness. A familiar voice flowed back. It was my brother's. I couldn't see his face, but I could hear the smile in his words. Eventually, I picked out his standing form, and understood why our mother worried about the boat he was fishing. The *Driftwood* looked to have no sides at all. Rick might have been standing on a sheet of plywood. But he didn't sound the least bit worried.

"Just a handful, but Timmy got to see a big white," our father said.

"Hey, way to go, bud. I knew you'd be lucky. When you going to come onto my boat?"

I was strangely shy, a little anxious. I couldn't go on that boat! It was scary enough being on the *Rona.*

They exchanged information on the tide and the wind. We drifted below Rick because we had no net in the river to hold us back. My father didn't have to raise his voice, though. The words just carried. Finally the engine rumbled to life and we continued up the channel, oxen slow, ploughing the black water into long, buttery furrows.

* * *

When did the spring fishing end? When did the federal government, recognizing the depletion of the runs, shut the river down until the early sockeye runs in June? And when did the government shut the river down for the early sockeye runs? For each of the past ten years, the commercial salmon fishery on the Fraser has been limited to a handful of twelve and twenty-four hour openings in late July and August – in some of those years, the river has not opened at all. The most active vessels in Ladner Harbour are the yachts and kayaks piloted by the residents of condominiums built over the marshes where I once collected mud-filled beer bottles for the two-cent deposit. Can it be only twenty-five years since my father and I last idled past the end of Georgia Street towards the Prairie, and only ten since Rick and I did the same, closing our family's forty-year chapter in the annals of one of the world's great fisheries?

But even by the time of my father's retirement in 1980, the fishery was unrecognizable from when he and my uncle started out in it in the early 1950s. Gillnet fishing was almost a full-time job in those days. The river opened in March and did not close until almost Christmas; often, my father fished three days a week for that whole period, scratching out a bare living. Springs in March to dogs in December, thin fog to heavy fog. And in between, the violent redness of the sockeye summer, the glory months, those eight tense weeks, often boiling down to a few good tides at the height of the big runs, when the season was made or lost, just as it had been made or lost since the 1870s when the first canneries were built along the Fraser's banks.

That feeling of inheritance was potent in my childhood: no one talked about the nineteenth century or all the blackened remains of the pioneer canneries shut down in the delta at the turn of the twentieth century due to declining salmon stocks, but the ghosts were palpable presences. And they had seen what I was seeing. In summer, especially, they had stood, as I did, calf-deep in slippery, writhing silver as the hour gutted the sun and the river slowly bore their burdened skiffs into the crimson. Greek, Japanese, Finnish, Norwegian, Chinese, Austrian, English, American, Coast Salish: the hands of the world closed when my hands closed, the eyes of the world saw the same glut and, in the end, the same numbing diminishment. It is the history of my place, of North America, writ dramatically into the flesh of the wild. Yet the Pacific salmon has not quite gone the way of the buffalo or the cod. And the south coast of British Columbia flourishes in the modern economy. Few of the two-million strong population of the Lower Mainland cry for what's vanished, or even know about it at all. Loss doesn't require tears to be loss, however. In a powerful way, the lack of public awareness of and mourning for the destruction of the salmon culture on the southwest coast makes the destruction all the more heartbreaking. But perhaps some losses are beyond the ken of human grief.

III

IT'S JULY 2005, in Gibsons Landing, an hour and a half by car and ferry northwest of Vancouver. With my wife and three children, I've moved here after ten years in Edmonton – to be closer to my mother, to give my children a taste of a more rural experience, and, in a way I can't even articulate to myself, to claim what is mine.

I phone my brother Bruce. He still lives in Ladner, in semi-retirement at age fifty-eight, having left his job of twenty-five years as the chief plumber for BC Ferries. I've always envied his uncomplicated relationship to the dying culture of the coast, his ease with the practical, hands-on business of our inheritance. Simply put, he once dwelled in the salmon fishery much more potently than I ever did. He fished with a young version of our father on a much more powerful, dark and silent Fraser, he fished his own gillnetter while still in high school, and in his early twenties, he was the skiff-man on a seiner up the north coast. He's closer to the flesh of the ghosts of home than I am, but while he's fond of his memories, he's also casual about them. "Things change," is his motto, spoken with a shrug that conveys only a mild regret. If I quoted Faulkner to him – "The past isn't dead. It isn't even past" – he'd look at me cock-eyed and say that I'd been reading too many books. We're brothers, we love each other, but the almost twenty years between us, the parenting we knew, the cultures we grew up in, have fashioned us differently. I hunger for the tiniest details of irretrievable Time, convinced I can retrieve something; Bruce tosses me details the way he'd toss bread crumbs to the tame mallards in Chilukthan Slough behind the strip mall.

"When did Dad sell the first boat?"

"Hell, I don't know. But he never sold the *Rona*, anyway. Just the licence."

"What happened to the boat?"

"It was rotting. That's why he had to get a new one."

"But what happened to it?"

"To the *Rona*? It just rotted on the banks. There's probably still pieces of it out in the marsh somewhere."

I'm astonished, yet I shouldn't be. This is the history of the Fraser River delta. In 1904, there were fourteen salmon canneries operating in the few miles between Canoe Pass in the west and Annieville in the east. A decade later, most were abandoned. By 1970, all that was left of them were the black, rotted pilings. Still, the idea that a plank or two of my father's first gillnetter might still be riding the high and low tides of the rivermouth overwhelms me into silence. For the sad fact is, we have hardly any physical evidence of either of the family boats, nothing more than a few partial photographs. Our record of the entire fishing past is slim. There are no old gaff-hooks or hanging benches or scotchmen left in the backyard shed. And, after hanging onto them for years, Mom finally threw out all of Dad's tally books, his year-by-year record of the numbers, weights and kinds of fish he delivered to the cannery packer each opening, a record going back to the early 1950s. So, to think that there might be an actual piece of the *Rona* in the marsh!

A crazy notion slides salmon-quick into my thoughts. I could conduct a search. Perhaps there's a whole chunk of the bow or stern stuck in the mud. It's possible. The banks of the Fraser are dotted with skeletons of abandoned vessels. But how would I know a piece of the *Rona* if I found one?

"She was square-ended," Bruce says, as if reading my mind.

"Square-ended?"

"And flat-bottomed. A real riverboat. The second boat was a double-ender. You know, rounded at both ends."

Well, yes, I guess I did know, now that he mentioned it. My memories of the *Rona*, I'm beginning to suspect, have blurred into my memories of the *Nautilus*, renamed the *Nola J* after my sister. That boat was bought sometime in the early seventies. Which boat am I remembering when I remember my first trip to the Prairie?

"Bolton Trim built the *Rona* just after the war. Auntie Mary-Helen's dad. Uncle Earl bought it off Ronnie Johnson. Dad bought it from Earl."

Wait, wait. The information is coming too fast. "Auntie Mary-Helen's dad built boats?" I say. "I thought he was a farmer."

Bruce sighs. "He was. But he built boats too."

"Where? Where did he build them?"

"Right there by the farm. On Westham Island. Just over the bridge..."

I can fill the rest in. Just over the bridge, on the bank near the black pilings of the old cannery, one of the fourteen that thrived at the turn of the twentieth century. I'm touching the cycle again, of time, history, work, place, all limned by a faith in the salmon's endurance. And like the salmon, the *Rona* began and ended its life in the delta. Successive phone calls reveal that the gillnetter got its name, as so many salmon boats did, from combining or rearranging syllables from the names of the owner's relatives. My mother tells me that Ronnie Johnson's sister was named Nora.

And there's the *Bev-Mark*, she says. Edgar Birch's boat. Named for his daughter and son. Or Harry Maxwell's boat, of course. The *Halary*. For Helen, Alvin and Larry.

Yes, of course. Harry Maxwell's widow, Helen, still lives along River Road west, in Port Guichon, in a small house under a great weeping willow. Her middle son, Larry, still makes his living in the fishery, selling smoked salmon. Each Christmas over the past decade, he's given my mother a side, which she would then pass on to me as a treat when I visited from Alberta. I've known Helen all my life. I sometimes played with her youngest son, Mick. Helen's mother, a notorious character, had been the local bootlegger and driver of the town's one cab back in the thirties. Her late husband's brother, Rene, was for many years the collector on the salmon grounds – my father delivered his catch to him, but that was before my time. Of Helen's husband, I knew little. He didn't come around to our house, nor did I often go to the Maxwells'.

Putting the phone down gently, remembering, thinking of the *Rona* out there in the marsh, daydreaming about finding a plank of it and having a skilled woodworker friend of mine incorporate it as the base for a desk or table or chair, I suddenly recall the sad details of Harry Maxwell's death. Now the cycle chills as it sustains, as the eyes of the salmon both terrify and comfort, as memory destroys and creates, or perhaps destroys to create, the way a fire in the forest clears ground for new growth.

Like so many others in the industry, Harry Maxwell retired from fishing when he could no longer handle the physical demands. After a few years, he was stricken with Alzheimer's and his memory began to go. So far, this is a sadly common story. What I recalled about Harry Maxwell, and what gave me such a chill in relation to my daydreams, was not his illness, but rather the death it fashioned for him. In brief, he took to wandering the dyke, searching desperately for his first boat. He would disappear, and either his family, the police or friends of the family would find him down at the wharf, searching for a boat he could never find – it had long before gone the way of the nineteenth-century canneries. Eventually, he lost even the ability to locate the harbour; he'd walk in the wrong direction, south over the farm fields towards the coalport, or west towards Westham Island. This went on for months. Then winter came.

He vanished. No one phoned to say they'd seen him. A patrol car didn't bring him home. Searches turned up nothing. His wife knew he wasn't well dressed, and the nights had been cold for the coast, below freezing. Family and friends searched day after day, concentrating their attention near the river. Perhaps he had fallen in and been swept away. Perhaps he had enough spark of awareness left to jump in and end his undignified suffering. Somehow, there was comfort in the idea that he could gain some last vestige of the vigour and control that he'd needed to work so effectively in the fishery his whole life.

I wasn't living in Ladner then. I'd moved to Edmonton, where I'd started a master's degree in English literature at the University of Alberta, simply because I needed an income and the English department had offered me a scholarship. Even better, I could take regular literature courses instead of creative writing classes and submit a manuscript of poems for my thesis. I was happy. My first book, *Low Water Slack*, a collection of poems based on my experiences in the salmon fishery, had just appeared. Life was wonderful. If anything troubled me, it was a mild homesickness. After all, I had lived in Ladner and fished for salmon all my life. Like the Scots poet George Mackay Brown, who rarely ventured out of his native Orkney, I knew I was destined to try to write books from "right under the parish pump." This destiny no doubt explained my dreams. They weren't disturbing, just consistently concerned with salmon.

In the most vivid and striking one, I step out of my Edmonton apartment to find myself in the middle of Georgia Street. It's dawn, there's dew on the grass in the sidewalk cracks. Suddenly the heads of a thousand sockeye salmon silently break the surface of the concrete. In a moment, I'm surrounded, and realize I'm in a skiff, holding a handful of net – corkline, leadline and web.

But I always woke before anything else happened and fell easily back asleep, pleased that my connection to home remained so vital. Casually, I was comforted by the presence of such an odd, visceral image sequence, thinking perhaps it would lead to a poem. At the very least, I thought my parents would get a kick out of it. But when I phoned to tell them about the dream, my mother had other news.

"Remember I told you about Harry Maxwell going missing. Well . . ."

A farmer found him. Lying on the frost-crusted potato

furrows, equidistant from the river and the Gulf of Georgia (in other words, as far from water as you could be in that part of the delta). His weakened physical condition, and the cold, had combined to stop his heart. He'd been missing for three months.

That was over a decade ago. Of course, I was sorry, but my own life, then, was just opening up. I had little time for the past, or rather, for how the sorrows of the present wash backwards and forwards on tides half-fresh and half-salt.

Fortunately, the intervening years have curbed the innate selfishness of ego that accompanies the hunger for love and success. I'm a wiser man now, and particularly to the extent that I constantly question whether I have any wisdom at all. Why else should I think of Harry Maxwell at almost the exact moment I begin to daydream of finding a piece of my father's first boat in the marsh? And think of him wandering the familiar dykes and fields of home, the syllables of his own blood on his lips, until the familiar is stranger than the deepest dark and the blood explodes in his chest?

It means this much: the search for the past is always doomed and always urgent to the point of desperation. What is native in the salmon is native in us – memory's mysterious and even destructive pull. Perhaps we can't go home again, as Thomas Wolfe famously wrote, but perhaps it is natural, in extremity, to risk our lives to get there. And what is more extreme on this earth than the always-approaching truth of our leaving it?

* * *

Ladner lies along the south bank of the south arm of the Fraser River, in the ever-lengthening shadow of the ever-more cosmopolitan and sophisticated city of Vancouver, much the same way history lies along the curbside of an increasingly amnesiac North American culture. Few people stop to muddy their shoes in the marshy slop of stumps, fish blood, opium smoke and oat chaff on which the global citizen's pretensions and privileges are built. Yet I make no romantic appeals on behalf of the town fathers of Ladners Landing, those dark-browed, vested Victorians who never saw an opportunity they couldn't exploit. It is the worst kind of falsehood to believe that the movers and shakers of the nineteenth century aren't the ancestors of today's most rapacious capitalists. The Englishmen, Scots and Americans who largely pre-empted and developed the marshy south section of the Fraser delta came for fortune; they weren't escaping religious or political persecution, nor were they in rebellion against the status quo of the societies they left behind. Utopia was simply home with a greater chance to accumulate dollars and influence. To believe otherwise is to buy into a myth that perpetuates our own propensity for destruction.

But where British Columbia is concerned, few buy into any historical myth. Only by our actions do we honour the Victorians' obeisance to unfettered capitalism while dishonouring their paradoxically fervid attachment to family and community. In short, we refuse to learn from them. If we pay attention to them at all, we see benign museum figures, mannequins of snuff and camphor, whose blood, like the delta itself, continues to silt over. But the truth is something else, of course, and fascinatingly common. The first settlers of Ladners Landing, like the first settlers of many towns, came for economic opportunity. The men worked hard, the women persevered valiantly, ditches, roads and dykes were built, a community formed. Time makes heroes and villains, and mostly understudies, of us all. However, in the language of that pioneering ethos, I'm tracking a different prey.

It is not the facts I want, it is the details. Facts are the stuff of history, details are the stuff of life. Shall I explain Ladner's farming and fishing heritage to you by stating the annual numbers of acres harvested and salmon cans packed? Shall I walk you through that museum, which is the museum of the now we all have to endure as we go through our time on earth?

No. What interests me about history, what I find essential about it, is not what's dead, but what remains. And the truth is, growing up along the Fraser River in the late sixties and early seventies, I lived in the remains. My childhood was the sunset of the pioneers' daybreak.

Farming and fishing? All the members of my family stuck their hands into dusty burlap sacks filled with netted gem and warba potatoes. Once those sacks were emptied, we slid salmon into them and out of them, walking from the boat to the dyke to the house. I remember the tight weave of the burlap, and how the sacks, filled with spuds, had little bunny ears at the top you had somehow to knot together. I remember how the salmon, when you slid them out, had potato dust and tiny threads of burlap clinging to their sticky scales. I remember the hard, ungiving weight of the sacks when they held potatoes, the little digs in the back you'd get when you carried them over your shoulder, and I remember the solid yet sliding-in-their-own-slime pounds of the fish-filled sacks, the burlap twisted and scratchy in the hand, a little blood dripping from the sack, like juice drained through cheese cloth.

I remember the dried blood in the weave of the burlap. I hold history's hand. It guides me to the future I want and cannot have except in the resurrection of memory to presence.

IV

A TOWN IN DECLINE is a child's paradise. Within a few blocks of 4853 Georgia Street lay the nightmares of the Chamber of Commerce: six empty, condemned pioneer houses that had been abandoned for years; twice as many vacant lots overgrown with bluejoint grass, blackberry bushes, morning glory vines, and untended Edwardian orchards of plums, pears, apples and cherries; an entire row of gutted condemned shops on the main street; a hulking, abandoned pea cannery filled with derelict machinery and greasy shadows; several collapsing netsheds; a burnt-out Chinese food restaurant with a battered, moon-round, tin Coca-Cola sign; rotting, skeletal gillnetters, even a couple of river sternwheelers; an ash-cold and dark blacksmith's shop humming faintly with the echoes of hissing forges and neighing horses and tapping hammers; and a totem pole so faded that you could hardly tell the raven from the salmon. In addition, most of the inhabited houses in the original townsite belonged to widows with oddly plain and respect-inducing names, such as Mrs. Woods, Mrs. Lord, Mrs. Atkey and Mrs. Hatt.

The latter – thin, tall and spectacled like Benjamin Franklin – always wore a knitted cloth skullcap and hose the colour and seeming weight of wet sand. She appeared to be in continual, fresh mourning for whatever she'd dreamed as a girl back in the English countryside of Kenneth Grahame. It was impossible to see her drifting progress, in painful scratches like a dried October leaf over the cracked sidewalk, without thinking of her husband's tragic death thirty years before.

He'd been struck by a car at the south end of Georgia Street, "only a few doors from home," as my mother put it with a sigh. I wondered, did Mrs. Hatt walk so much in the hopes of encountering his ghost? I didn't know, but I knew well where her steps took her. Under the char-black phone lines looped like my first attempts at cursive and held up by telephone poles so hammered at by woodpeckers and rainstorms that they resembled the salt-eaten spars of square riggers whose decks had long since melted away. Past the vacant houses of jagged window glass and cobwebs of Sistine construction where, no doubt, she and her husband had once attended dinner parties and – God forgive her – she'd tried a sip or two of Madeira out on the verandahs now littered with mouse bones and moonlight. Along the dyke in the shadow of the six massive poplars whose leaves were finer than the lacework of the doilies faintly scented with lemon that protected all her end-tables. To stand, finally, and stare at the river, which she hardly knew except, in summer, as a long drawer filled with sharp, silver cutlery spilling in a soundless clatter across the politer senses.

It won't do. Mrs. Hatt, like all the old women of my childhood, had no reality of that kind for me. She simply inhabited my domain, a bit of controlled black smoke at the edge of my attention. Ah, but I hear my mother say, "Where there's smoke, there's fire." And what is the past except a fire that smoulders but never quite goes out?

Come with me. It's a few days after my first trip to the Prairie Drift. I've still never been to school, nor have I read a newspaper nor paid attention to a newscast; I'm freer than I'll ever be again. My heart beats to the rhythm of my dog's panting as we stand in the May heat and consider the honeybees testing our shadows for pollen. Maple buds helicopter down from my mother's favourite tree. Names I've never heard anyone but her speak, even now (I'm shocked to think), belong to nearby flowers: sweet william, jolly jump-ups, bleeding hearts, lily of the valley, brown-eyed Susie. All along the street, north and south, the sun-dappled, dandelioned and buttercupped lawns slope like whaleback from the chocolate-bar squared and porridge-rough sidewalks. No one is, in my mother's vernacular, "out and about." Only the swallows in their courteous evening coats are discourteous enough to disturb the air, swooping down off the phone lines as if snatching loose gossip. We'll go north, to the river. Why not? A river is as near as we'll ever get to a rent in the universe.

Two minutes and we're up one side and down the other of the dyke, standing on the huge cedar log embedded in the bank above the high-tide line and worn smooth as a seat taken from an abandoned car and turned into a piece of back-porch furniture. Behind us, a sprawling cloud of blackberry bushes just beginning to wear its little Elizabethan collars shelters us from view. We came along one side of the skinny, clutching, semi-circular trail that connects the dyke to the dyke, and will, out of some innate sense of logic, walk out the other side. For now, though, we're well-hidden under the seeming surge of the blackberry storm. No wonder I find so many beer bottles here. At low tide, the muck becomes a saloon-wall tipped horizontally.

But the tide is not low or high. The river's dark as usual, however – the colour of rain that fell into house-side cisterns in the last century. I stare at it, wondering as I often do, but with a new intensity since watching my father pick up his net, what the riverbottom would reveal if all the water disappeared. Anything could be down there, any strange creature I've encountered in books of legends and fairy tales and Norse or Greek mythologies. This is my companion daydream to the one in which the river rises and floods the town, leaving me to row a skiff from one abandoned old house to another, mooring at an eavestrough and scanning the horizon for the spouts of killer whales. Neither extreme, however, appears imminent. My father says the river has never dried up, and the last flood happened many years ago, but he also leaves open the possibility that such events could unfold, just as, decades later, he'll consider the possibility that a man could make a living as a writer of books.

Up at Buckerfields, the forklift scrapes and clanks. I look

at the looming black warehouse. Two dozen gulls, white as starched bedsheets, look back from the peaked roof. At five, I can't tell the several types of coastal gulls apart. But all gulls, as far as fishermen and their wives and children know, are more or less the same. No matter what name you give a voracious appetite and a piercing cry, it's still a voracious appetite and a piercing cry. And it begins again now; the discordant music of hunger descends from the roof. Still a little frightened by the sound, I hesitate.

* * *

The shiver is in the body as the piercing cry is in the egg of the gull. And the one message in the mouth of the drowned bottle is loneliness. Two cents worth. Five years of childhood, five thousand bottles, a hundred dollars. That's what I made off the knowledge I was coming to, and to which I've come. If I had that money back, what could I do? Let me buy you a drink, friend, and tell you about Ladner.

V

IT'S BUILT ON A MARSH. Grass, dirt, clay, water. You can't dig a human grave there. If you want to read a tombstone, you have to drive ten minutes south to the higher ground of Tsawwassen or fifteen minutes east to the higher ground of Surrey. My stillborn brother lies in his unmarked grave in Tsawwassen's Boundary Bay Cemetery, which both proves and disproves Chief Seattle's harsh indictment of whites: "You don't even know where your dead are buried." Well, to be frank, it mostly proves it. The Bowling name isn't found anywhere in that cemetery. As far as I know, my paternal grandparents' graves overlook the Fraser from South Burnaby, though I couldn't find my way to the general area of their resting place if my life depended on it. My maternal grandparents lie in Ontario, unvisited for generations. My father, meanwhile, is ashes kept in twin urns in the house at 4853 Georgia Street; he waits to be sprinkled on the Prairie Drift. When my mother's body is also ash, they'll flow out to the Gulf together.

* * *

Ladner is less than three kilometres from where the Fraser flows into the sea. The first Europeans to lay eyes on it were Spaniards. In 1791. It's hard to imagine how depressing those dry-heat-loving, wealth-seeking Spaniards would have found the mosquito-infested swampy lowlands of the Fraser delta. Captain George Vancouver, who came next, in 1792, would have been more accustomed to the coast's climate and greyness, at least. But even he couldn't muster up much enthusiasm for my home place. The area between Point Grey to the north and Point Roberts to the south, he describes thus in his journal:

> It is very low land, apparently a swampy flat, that retires several miles, before the country rises to meet the rugged snowy mountains... This low flat being very much inundated, and extending behind Point Roberts [Vancouver had just named this point for his friend Henry Roberts], to join the low land in the bay to the eastward of that point; gives its high land, when seen at a distance, the appearance of an island: this, however, is not the case, notwithstanding there are two openings between this point and Point Grey. These can only be navigable for canoes, as the shoal continues along the coast to the distance of seven or eight miles from the shore, on which were lodged, and especially before these openings, logs of wood, stumps of trees innumerable.

Hardly Chamber of Commerce or "Supernatural BC" tourist brochure material. No money in the place at all, not yet. And not in 1808 either, when Simon Fraser journeyed down the river which now bears his name and cursed his rotten luck that the damned thing wasn't navigable enough to be of use to the fur trade. He skirmished with the Salish Indians of the North Arm and skedaddled back the way he came without even seeing the swampy lowlands of the South Arm. The next European to do so showed up in 1824 and again in 1827 on behalf of the Hudson's Bay Company. James McMillan spent nine days searching for a passage through the sandheads at the mouth of the river, and I, for one, commiserate with him – Jason had an easier time getting through that maze with the minotaur than many mariners have had finding a way into Canoe Pass. When McMillan did get upriver, he established a fur-trading fort and called it Fort Langley. The floodgates were open. And when you open the floodgates on the Fraser, look out. Before you know it, four million people producing 10 percent of Canada's gross national product will be crammed into the Fraser Basin.

Speaking of the river, a hundred and thirty years ago when Ladners Landing was only a few years old, the mouth's main deepwater channel churned, boiled and swept past what was just developing into the original townsite. Steam-powered paddlewheelers from Victoria in the Colony of Vancouver Island made regular stops at the Ladners Landing wharf. You could hear them thundering up the river as they entered the mouth at the sandheads, because there was nothing else to hear, except for hooting owls, seal cry and the last sigh of your mother dying young in the slavery of Victorian marriage. Now you can hear unceasing traffic, ambulance and police sirens, ringing cell phones, and the rapid breath of your parents living the slavery of post-millennial clock-watching.

Ladners Landing was so named because the first two whites to pre-empt and purchase acreage in that part of the delta were the brothers William and Thomas Ladner. One was skinny, one ample, and both came from Cornwall, England, briefly to a Wisconsin farm and then onto California as young men, travelling with their father, who abruptly died. The brothers next sailed from San Francisco to Victoria. It was 1858. Gold had been discovered in the Cariboo. The Ladners, like twenty thousand other men, wanted a piece of the action. They hired Indians to paddle them across the Gulf of Georgia and up the Fraser River, past the Anglo-Saxon namelessness to which they'd later give their names, to Fort Langley. The Indians, however, dropped them at Point Roberts several miles south of the rivermouth, fearing the hostilities of upriver tribes. No matter. The local Chewasin (i.e., Tsawwassen) Indians guided them the rest of the way – from Fort Langley upriver to Hope, later to Yale, and eventually onto the Cariboo, doing the work that the place and the time presented – prospecting, mining, running a general store, operating a mule packtrain.

Years passed. The Ladners drifted back to the coast. Together. Imagine setting out in life with your brother.

Where is your brother? When did you see him last? Talk with him? My brothers are in Ladner. One lives on a large lot on the former farmland of Thomas Ladner, the other in a townhouse on the former farmland of William Ladner. A few blocks and a year and a half apart. As children, my mother dressed them the same, so everyone took them for twins, even though they didn't look much alike. Now they're as old as the Ladners were in the 1890s when they could step out of MacNeely's Hotel and stand on the wharf and listen for the thunder of the paddlewheelers entering the rivermouth. In nearly forty years of adulthood, my brothers have never travelled anywhere alone together – once, with our father, they drove to southern Alberta to shoot pheasants. The trip didn't go well, for the pheasants or for them. Yet now they can golf together occasionally on the little nine-holer built at the eastern edge of Thomas Ladner's original property and generally enjoy one another's company, which beats a lot of North American sibling relationships all to hell.

When the Ladners arrived on the coast in 1868, there was no city of Vancouver, just a few settlements scattered along Burrard Inlet – Hastings Townsite, Granville and Coal Harbour on the south shore, Moodyville on the north shore. Thomas Ladner did some logging in what is now Stanley Park. His son, Thomas, records this conversation he had with his father:

Once when father spoke to me of this period, I mentioned that he and his partner had not done a very good job of logging off the area which is now Stanley Park. He replied, "The devil we didn't! What makes you think that?" I pointed out that they had left some very fine trees standing not far from the tide-water. He then explained, "They look fine trees now, but they were not worth much in those days. They were too far apart and it would not have paid to clear the way and build skid roads to them."

Given the opportunity, I might mention that Thomas Sr. and his competitors didn't do a very good job of fishing off the Fraser River, except I have fewer and fewer great salmon runs to point to as evidence. I hear his response anyway. "The devil we didn't. There were so many fish then, we had to toss the pinks, coho and chums back dead. They were worthless." And Thomas Jr., again in *Above the Sandheads,* his memoir of growing up in Ladner in the nineteenth century, records that as a child on still nights he could hear the Indians singing songs to the salmon. Descendants of some of those same Indians currently set illegal nets on the Fraser to circumvent the Department of Fisheries and Oceans' weak conservation efforts. Masked braves in Zodiacs swarm fisheries officers in patrol boats. Nobody sings to the fish anymore.

After a few years of store proprietorship in New Westminster, twenty-two kilometres upriver and on the opposite bank from Ladner-without-a-name, William Ladner pre-empted and purchased 640 acres, and Thomas 500 acres, on the delta, close to the mouth of the river. This was in 1868, the year the colonies of Vancouver Island and British Columbia amalgamated. A century later, the Ladners' place of backbreaking labour would be my paradise of ruins. Doubtless it is some other child's paradise of prosperity now, though, on visits home, I rarely see children playing outdoors.

In 1865, the Ladner brothers married. William's bride was Mary Booth, Thomas's bride was Edney Booth. Sisters.

I knew nothing about the Ladners as a boy. We weren't taught our own history in school, and few children visited the museum unless they dug up an old glass medicine bottle in the backyard vegetable garden and figured it might form part of an exhibit. I visited often, however, as the red brick, Tudor-style building, one of the oldest and most regal in town, sat only a block away and was the halfway point between the comic-book shop and the convenience store, bucolically named the Daisy Dell. My friends and I would write joke names in the guest book and giggle at the ceramic bedpan known as the "gazunda," because it "gazunda" the bed. You couldn't miss the looming photographic portraits of the Ladner brothers just inside the entrance. I took in their gloomy and confident gazes dozens of times just as I took in the unblinking stares of gulls and the blank stares of salmon.

The gloomy one was William. His balding pate was oddly eggshell smooth, given his sixty-plus years of hard living, his eyes small and wounded, and – most strikingly – his wispy, white mutton-chop facial hair was a blast of dragonsmoke that left his small chin completely bare. In his high collar and cravat, with his tweed jacket's one visible button pulled awkwardly, as if the jacket was too small, he looked both imposing and vulnerable.

His brother, ten years younger, is a different kettle of fish or rather, scow of sockeye. Thomas is a pioneer Fraser River Zeus – huge-headed, aquiline-nosed, clear-browed. Indeed, the top half of his head resembles nothing less than a corona of light (his curly brown hair) around a white-hot sun (his prominent brow). While he sports the same mutton-chop design as his brother, Thomas's hair is thicker and darker. And there is no sorrow in his eyes, just the ease of confidence. You'd be happy to have him at the end of your rope if you were captain of one of the farmers' tug-of-war teams whose photographs were also displayed prominently near the museum entrance almost forty years ago.

As a boy, looking at the photographs of the Ladners, I sometimes thought of the fat and skinny farmers in Roald Dahl's *The Fantastic Mr. Fox.* Yet there's nothing so nasty in the appearance of my hometown's founders. Regarding Thomas now, I can almost put my finger on whom he so powerfully resembles. The size of the head, the proud bearing, calmly regal: he's Henry VIII in mid-life! But Thomas only had one wife killed, and he didn't have to send her to the Tower for that. He just introduced her to the pioneer life of the Fraser River delta in 1870. As for keeping his grasp on the crown, rumour has it that one of Thomas's descendants, Peter Ladner, a city councillor, could one day be the mayor of Vancouver, the hub city of a region populated by over two million people, most of whom couldn't tell a sockeye from a coho if their cappuccinos depended on it.

No, I'm not really bitter. Reality, after all, is just one form of reality. Friend, let me get you another drink. A hundred dollars in deposit money goes farther than a pint or two. By the way, this pub we're in, halfway along the old Kirkland Road – did you notice the name of it? The Landing. As in Ladners Landing. So we return history's serve. At some point in the nineteenth century, Ladners Landing became Ladners' Landing, no doubt because possession grew more important as land values increased, or perhaps the apostrophe magically appeared to honour the salmon's leaping progress up the Fraser to home. Eventually, Ladners' Landing evolved to Ladner's Landing, the salmon leaping closer to the canners' monopolistic maw. It's been plain Ladner for generations now, as if the apostrophe hadn't the strength to leap above the past anymore.

* * *

Between the ages of five and ten, I roamed the decayed and empty rooms of the house Thomas Ladner had built in 1894, primarily on the proceeds from his salmon canning concerns. It was a palatial home of its period, considered one of the finest private dwellings in the Lower Mainland. Designed by a highly regarded New Westminster architect, it was a suggestively Tudor mélange of peaks, turrets, tower rooms and many windows, with an oval entranceway at the front verandah and the same oval above for the second storey. There were four thin, red-brick chimneys and a number of delicately carved, very fine railings, pillars and mantelpieces, and so many handsome frames around the almost greenhouse number of thick-glassed windows that I always had the paradoxical sense of constriction and openness once I entered and looked out on the time and town I had just departed.

The approach to the Thomas Ladner house, and to the other abandoned houses of my wanderings, was always through grass above my waist and between gnarled fruit trees crouching troll-like at the edges of the property. A silence even deeper than the usual silence of economically declining Ladner descended on me as I parted the seed-heavy grass, insect larvae sticky on my bare legs and sides, and arrived, wonderingly, at the rain-dark, footworn steps to the sagging verandah. Each time, I expected a different drama to unfold, yet was never disappointed when it didn't, for the thief-like ardour of trespassing on absence possessed a deliciousness I've rarely known since.

How I loved to look out at my hometown through the cracked windows of what it had chosen to forget. The dusty floors, the stained, peeling wallpaper with thick black nail-heads pressing through like the fingertips of the dead, and the narrowness of the hallways, as if I'd boarded a ship bound to seek a passage to the Indies: all this thrilled me to such an extent that I'd spend hours exploring one house after another, until, especially on rainy afternoons, I became a sort of goldfish appearing at different parts of a bowl in which no food had been sprinkled for years. What was I seeing? What was I wanting to see? Time, our one true element, dissolved the window glass and flowed through me. I'd blink at the long-neglected yards and the streets beyond, almost always empty of others, and then turn to the sad detritus of the vanished occupants.

Why, after so many decades, I retain such a vivid memory of the book I found splayed like a wounded bat in a corner of one room must have something to do with my life as a writer – must, in fact, confirm my belief that I wanted to be a writer from a very young age. It was a pocket-sized dictionary with a greasy, blue-black cover unadorned except for the title, which contained the new word "unabridged." The pages were mouldy green at the tops and bottoms, and a dull salmon-belly white otherwise. The type was tiny and fiercely black and there were faint pencil underlines in places. The book had the weight of a dead robin, the texture of a shed garter-snake skin, and the smell of November damp. I must have taken it as a kind of diary of the sadness I felt all around me, if only I could have arranged the underlined words properly. But the underlines appeared patternless. Besides, at my age, though I could sound out new words and definitions, I couldn't understand most of them. I doubt I spoke aloud. I likely mouthed the syllables, my whisper the whisper of some other child vanished long ago. And when I had looked up from the page and seen the weather of life existing in its changes beyond the glass, I must have intuited, in a long shiver, the first intimation of that mysterious division between written language and external reality which is the poet's torment and his joy. It can't have been otherwise.

In any case, I kept the book for years, believing it to be the property of some original resident of the town, some Victorian child who loved reading as much as I did. I'm not sure why, but I needed to believe in the book's long backwards reach, in its close association with the mud-stained nineteenth-century ghosts whose yearnings made the air of the rooms tremble differently from any other air I breathed. I need to believe this even more today. After all, what distinction can be drawn between one's dreams and the past? Both are subtle, subsurface realities whose impact we feel but cannot measure. So we stand in the first moments of dark, the soundless wingbeats of geese passing somewhere over us, the ferocious, silent push of a million salmon in the current below, our pulses quickened by the proximity to mysteries only dimly apprehended. In my barefoot days, at the window of the long train empty but for me and stopping at its six or eight stations to take on a freight of memories destined to be forgotten, I blink out at home, the grasses bending in the salt breeze, the orchards' blossoms like tears in the eyes of a corpse, and language coming alive on my lips as if placed there in a kiss by the maternal dust. Five, six, seven. The utter fullness and intensity of the gaze of those years. No glass in the windows. The world of the living and the dead, without division. The whole world. Unabridged.

* * *

I turn back to the stillness to find a woman there. She is darkly and heavily gowned and sits on a hard-backed rocking chair, staring across the emptiness at me without seeing me. There's a slightly crazed look in her tear-filled expression and a disturbing intensity in the way she keeps turning one wrist in the clasp of her other hand, as if working a lathe of flesh and bone. I have never met her before, but I will spend my life seeking a greater depth of character by plumbing the fatigue and sorrow of her reality. This is a woman who has lost a child. When I see her, I see the history the world does not care about, but which art contains, as the egg of the gull contains the piercing cry and as the school globe pulses with menstrual blood. Life, in its bountiful offerings to the artist, sometimes puts a face to human experience from which our eyes cannot be lowered.

Mine rest on Edney Booth Ladner now. She is alive, her wet eyes are open, but they have no colour. There is no record of the colour of her eyes. I stand motionless, frightened by the silent obsessing of her multiple sorrows. She is not quite forty years old. Her hair, parted severely in the middle and showing a band of scalp like a snowy path through a black forest, is pulled back behind one ear and hangs in a loose braid over one shoulder. Her dress, heavy as a slave's shadow, is braided in an almost military fashion at the shoulders. It disturbs me that I cannot see the colour of her eyes. Tears, but no colour. And around the whole of her still body is a dim white glow, as if a century's long exposure is eating her grief to the bone. For the truth is, Edney Booth Ladner has watched three of her seven children die of disease. Only days ago, her four-year-old daughter, Edith, succumbed at last to cholera. Edney, by this time suffering from the tuberculosis that would kill her in a few years, had listened for hours to her daughter as she pleaded for relief from pain. But there was no relief, not even if the nearest medical assistance, three hours of rowing away in New Westminster, could be consulted. So Edney Booth Ladner held her crying daughter to the last breath.

Now she is sitting on a mahogany rocking chair in her bedroom, chafing the flesh off her wrist. An embroidered, ornately framed imperative hangs on the pink-rose wallpaper just to the side of her drawn face. Prepare To Meet Thy God. She is preparing. In two years, her health rapidly failing, she'll watch her fourth child, also a four-year-old daughter, die, this time from scarlet fever. Finally, in the dead of winter 1883, in a Victoria hospital, she'll meet her God, or not, aged forty-three.

A child can do nothing for her except be a child. And a Victorian child, in the presence of an adult, must be silent. So I stand amongst the solid hardwood furniture, dimly lit with gaslight flickering behind a glass lily cover, and listen to the collision of loss and faith. It's silent, like so many of our most desperate struggles. Outside of it, it's summer, the height of the salmon runs. Can she hear the Indians singing death into their nets? Or a seal pup crying for its mother? In each tear is a photographic cameo of an infant that dissolves to give birth to another in an endless sequence. Edney Booth Ladner's husband, Thomas, stands outside the picture, on the slimy, bloody plank floor of a cannery building, urging his Chinese and Indian workers on to greater feats of butchery.

Between the grieving mother and the venturing patriarch lie acres of ditches, sloughs, furrows, all damp with starlight, looked on by no one but the hunting owl and the sliding muskrat. Between the hiss of the gaslight and the sizzle of the soldering iron sealing tins of salmon lies the history of my place, which is the history of every place on earth – I stand in an abandoned house in a town of abandoned houses, in an absence that, within a few years, will itself disappear. And I grow past the age of childhood illness as I stand there, my bones lengthening and voice deepening, until I'm a young man who turns away, disinterested, and then suddenly I'm a man the same age as the grieving woman in her chair, trying to enter the history that has never been open. Already I'm forgetting even the life I've lived, so that memory too becomes more of an absence than a presence, and writing a kind of Matrushka doll, each new find a diminishment, until the mind is blanked out by a seizure in the stars and the words that cannot comfort us in our extremity will not comfort my own children in theirs.

Edney Booth Ladner is dying again after a hundred and twenty years. As she goes, she points across the room to where a thick, black, leatherbound book rests on an ornately carved walnut side table. I recognize it at once. It is the other permanent book of my childhood, the bible handed down from my mother's mother to my mother – both women who also suffered the loss of children. I walk over to it. It's open, parted in two great creamy waves. My face hovers over the faint, veinous penmanship that records the deaths of ten of my grandmother's children in the first two decades of the last century. I shudder with the sudden realization that I could be reading one of my father's tally books – death is everywhere a statistic and a fact, so rarely a detail.

* * *

I put down my pen. It's August, 2005, in Gibsons. Two a.m. My three children sleep and dream in the next room. I step out on the porch. Silence. Great clusters of stars making no impression on the low dark, which holds within it an old apple orchard and the murmuring edge of the Strait of Georgia. I can smell the salt on the air. Somewhere in those near fathoms the threatened ancestors of what made the pioneer canners on the Fraser so rich elude the counting mechanisms of the Department of Fisheries and Oceans, or else have vanished altogether. These days, either truth is possible.

I decide to leave for Ladner again soon. It's still there, after all, if only in its history of losses. The Fraser still lies like dark flesh flensed off the stars, and the old canneries, sorry as nailheads when the oil paintings have been removed, still tease the currents between their pilings. But now, when I return, and for each time afterward, I carry the final journey of Edney Booth Ladner with me, her diseased body in a coffin on the deck of the dilapidated sidewheeler *Princess Louise* as it churned up the deepwater channel past Ladners Landing, wearing the yoke of its Anglo-Saxon name, past the dimly lit end of Georgia Street where, in ninety years, a boy chucking rocks in the harbour will hear only the indefinable and unceasing echo of the unremembered, unloved past.

Sadness in a child is a form of wonder. I did not drag my shadow through the long grass as if ploughing the Ladners' old acres again, nor did I wear each summer's chestnut tan like a hairshirt. Absence, loss, sadness: this was a legacy of place that I revelled in just as I revelled in the river and the salmon and the wild fruit trees. Nowadays, adults read an unbearable loneliness in the child not busily engaged in some activity that keeps him in the presence of other children – "socialization," as ugly a word as has ever been invented, falls commonly off the lips of modern parents. But what adults always underestimate is the astonishing capacity of the child to inhabit his freedom, a capacity that we set out to discourage, partly out of affection, partly out of fear. More and more, because we are losing the ability to be alone with ourselves, to live without some form of distraction, we project our inadequacies onto our children who, before our influence perverts them, understand in the bone that solitude is not loneliness but rather a gift from the dead.

Did I, aged five, see Edney Booth Ladner grieving the death of another child? Perhaps not. Did I take in the atmosphere of old joys and sorrows from the condemned rooms? Of course. If you stand in summer sunlight, you feel the warmth. If you stand in a place of history, you feel the coldness at the centre of warmth. This is the lesson of our mortality, which no grade in any school system ever teaches because citizenship and commerce do not depend on our attentiveness to emotional experiences lived before our time. Only the richness of our inner life depends on this. I learned early, by walking alone through the fragments and shells of what had once been complete, that death is no friend to us, but the dead are.

VI

WHERE HAS THE BEER parlour gone? The chesterfield and doily, the wooden match? Where is the party line and the old gossip listening in? The giant faces of movie stars kissing above the cornfields – who cut them down? In 1969, my mother said hello in the Five and Dime (oh where is the Five and Dime?) to gracious, elderly men who'd survived the Somme and Vimy Ridge, men to whom I'd later deliver the evening paper (when did the deadlines of the presses change?). Now the veterans of the Great War are gone.

I sit on the steps of Ladner's museum with my eldest son, who is six, my age in 1970, and I remember that at his age I saw a woman walk down the street who as a six year old saw, going past in a horse-drawn coach, Queen Victoria, who reigned at the time William and Thomas Ladner pre-empted the land on which the museum sits. The past means everything and nothing. No one dials a telephone anymore, but the rhythm of that circuit remains in my blood. The first girl I ever asked out, I asked out after dialing her terrifying number. When she said "Yeah, okay," I blurted out "Thanks!" That untarnished capacity for joy is as deep in my psyche as sadness, and language is the plumb I use to sound those depths, a plumb of leadline that once shivered with the desire of the salmon.

Desire? How little we know of other species, yet how much we long to identify with them. A fish, however, makes a difficult emotional companion. As D.H. Lawrence wrote: *I said to my heart, who are these?/ And my heart couldn't own them.*

Nor could mine. When I was a boy, I spent whole days

with stray dogs, hanging my arms around their smelly necks, investing them with complete tragic histories based partly on *Lassie* and *Old Yeller*, but mostly on the dogs' capacity for a human soulfulness in the eyes. Some of the strays, of course, kept a wary distance, but this too was an acknowledgement of my presence. The flock of pigeons near Buckerfields would fly up at my approach, a tomcat would swivel its bruised, assessing skull in my direction, and even a horse or cow appeared to take me into their awareness, if only briefly. No salmon, however, paid the slightest visible attention to me, not even at the height of its mortal peril when it was untangled from my father's net and tossed under the drum. Its look never changed. It did not bark or growl or whimper or cry. I meant nothing to it, so how, over the years, has it come to mean everything to me?

My sister, Nola, visits in Gibsons. She's four years older than me, and so what I remember, she remembers, though with greater or lesser clarity. When I tell her about this book, and about my memory of her teasing me that salmon beg to be put back when caught, she's affronted.

"I never would have done that."

"No?"

"No. I was always sorry for them. Dad used to get frustrated with me. He'd catch a little jack spring, you know, a three pounder, and I'd say, Awww, give him a chance, let him go. And Dad would scowl, in that way he had, not upset just sort of resigned, and explain that another fisherman would just catch him instead. But Dad, I'd plead, at least he'd have a chance. Let him go."

"And did he?"

Nola smiles, probably as much at her idealistic young self as at our father's hesitation. She says, "He couldn't, could he? It was his living."

She then goes on to tell me that her constant harping about cruelty did, in fact, end our father's hunting career. Each fall, during mallard and pheasant season, he and my older brothers would patrol the marshes and farm fields, shotguns cocked, Labs or springer spaniels at their sides, and usually bring home several limp, glossy birds and lie them on the braided mat inside the kitchen door.

"I used to sit there on the mat," Nola says, "with tears in my eyes, and stroke their beautiful feathers. It got to Dad after a while. Plus Mom never liked gutting them either. She was happy to have him quit."

I feel like crying myself, imagining my pretty sister stroking the shiny blues and greens of the mallards' throats in the dim kitchen light of nearly forty years ago, with the leaves changing all around the house and the nights growing longer and colder and my father telling himself that, yes, he could do this much for her, he did not have to hunt anymore. A thought occurs suddenly, and I ask Nola if she remembers eating the meat.

She nods. "I didn't like it much, though. It was slimy, very rich and gamey."

I don't remember that. I don't even remember my father hunting. The dead birds of my memory were shot by my brother Rick. But we didn't eat the meat. Mostly those birds were stuffed and mounted. Our living room was a combination hunting lodge and aviary, for my mother loved songbirds and would walk past the stiff, glassy-eyed pheasants and mallards to open the sliding window and toss sunflowers into a feeder for the chickadees. How well I recall those stuffed game birds! What personalities they had, even in death. Their postures – usually in flight, though the pheasant on top of the TV set stood wings outspread, as if killed at the instant of rising to escape – form a diorama of stasis in my mind. I look away from the TV and there's the flying mallard, I look up from a book and there's the poised-for-flight pheasant, I look up from my supper and there's the most beautiful specimen of all, a huge cock pheasant at once glossy and bright, like the colours in a puddle into which you've dropped an orange peel, its one wing tipping in an aviator's display of skill. But this bird was special for another reason – Rick didn't shoot it. Instead, it smacked into the windshield of the Home Oil delivery truck he was driving.

That the most beautiful bird our home ever knew came to us as a gift of fate rather than as a result of skill probably foretold the death of the culture in which we lived then. Your skill doesn't matter, the incident said, your violence takes an incidental quota without even trying. And now as the fishermen hang nets all winter that they'll rarely use come summer, as my father's 16-gauge Ithaca shotgun rests in the crawlspace, wrapped in an old woollen blanket, we develop and poison and go on living as always, our windshield wipers rapidly washing away the blood of other species and our own until there's no one left even to twist the glass eyes into our corpses.

Home Oil! My father also drove an oil truck. At the end of our street, just to the west, up on the dyke, sat a Home Oil marine station, its long wharf extending into the channel. I remember the bright red trucks with the dull silver tanks and the long coils of hose through which the oil was pumped into similarly dull silver tanks at the sides of houses. I remember oil companies when they seemed harmless (this is before the 1970s Energy Crisis and the lineups at the gas tanks, which we've conveniently forgotten as we sit behind the wheels of our ever-larger vehicles). Esso gave away NHL collector books in which you pasted all these little stamps of the players you received at each fill-up. I still have mine; it's complete except for the Bobby Clarke stamp (one missing stamp for one missing tooth). Once, not very long ago, everything seemed harmless.

But it wasn't. And it isn't. Yesterday's wooden match still strikes, the cornfields blaze, our hugely magnified faces look blankly on over the flames as pheasants fly past in terror and men drag hoses like viscera through the black smoke. And I see the same thing beyond it all, my pretty sister cross-legged on the linoleum, a dead mallard on her lap, her fingers stroking feathers damp with her tears, and a man thinking that, for love, he could change.

* * *

So I return to the salmon, as always. They haven't changed, they still drive forward into the same self-destruction and resurrection, little Christs to which no one prays, little canvases that carry inside them their own oils for their own Last Supper. Do we love our children enough to see the salmon as more than commerce or sport? It's taken me forty years to reach a point at which I can say what my five-year-old self knew instinctively – that these fish are gods and we are heathen before them. And saying this, I am not saying this group or that group is to blame (though they are), or that government policy is at fault (though it is). I'm saying everyone is complicit in the disrespect we show the earth by the manner in which we have structured our lives.

But we can change. There's some wild left in us. The salmon can be our signposts. It won't do. Writers are meant to tell the truth, and poets to "tell it slant." It won't do. The truth is, we're going to wipe out the wild salmon in my lifetime and most of us won't notice. In 2005, the bumbling and budget-fat bureaucracy of the Department of Fisheries and Oceans timidly gathered up the gumption to close the Fraser River commercial fishery completely. The commercial fishermen were outraged, of course (and logically so, since there's nothing commercial about having no product). Many of them, from Steveston and Ladner and other river places, conducted a protest fishery, set their nets for a few hours, took home a few canners and smokers, had their pictures taken by fisheries officers, will pay fines eventually. This is all common fare in the fishery these days.

Ladner's current MP has participated in such a protest, and the fishermen, many of whom froth at the mouth over the Native fishery when they ought to be saving their energetic abuse for bureaucratic mismanagement, environmental destruction and American overfishing, love him for it. Yet he's typical of the problem that brought the fishery to its knees. While he claims to care about the state of the commercial fishery because he was – wait for it – once a fisherman himself (there's nothing like personal experience to justify holding an opinion), he's nonetheless a member of a political party whose primary agenda is unrestricted economic development. Such a party, in government, will do nothing to preserve the wild salmon and will, in fact, rapidly hasten the extinction of the species and the industry founded on it while encouraging the multi-million-dollar plastic salmon-farming industry. It won't matter then whether you're white, black, Native or albino; your job will be gone with the humpback whales and the huge halibut that once thrived just off the mouth of the river.

But in the end, political parties are beside the point, the salmon fishery itself is beside the point. It's comforting to think that overfishing is the major threat to wild salmon stocks. That simply lets us off the hook. The darker truth is that we're not capable of sharing the earth with other species. Every moment of every day, we poison ourselves. How many people do you know who've died of cancer? How many people under the age of fifty? Not fishing for salmon as a way to preserve them is akin to making or not making wooden legs to preserve old-growth forests – some other need is the greater killer. Certainly a complete shutdown of all fishing would improve fish stocks in the short term, but it wouldn't get rid of fish farms, pollution, genetic tinkering, and the human centrist mindset that, in the not-so-long term, will kill us.

Alaska has retained impressive returns of wild salmon to its mostly undammed rivers, you say? What's the population of Alaska? Robert Bly writes, *Wealth is nothing but lack of people.* People feed on the wild just as sea lice feed on juvenile wild salmon. The more people in a place, the more ferocious the feeding. China and India are the world's fastest growing economies. The population of the Lower Mainland is expected to increase by millions over the next two decades. And the remaining fishermen of Ladner complain about the Coast Salish having special rights to the salmon. At least the salmon die with their eyes open.

So what does all this say about my own involvement with the culture of salmon? Only this: what I knew cannot be retrieved except by words and memory. If the wild salmon isn't extinct yet, the culture around it surely is. And if that culture was itself a kind of death, it nonetheless belonged to me and I have every right to confront it and resurrect it and damn it and praise it, for in every death there is something of life. You don't need the cycle of the salmon to prove this, but that cycle drives home the truth we must live with as if the salmon themselves were the beats of the hammer and the vast black between the worlds was doing the hammering. I won't say God, but I will say *Mystery*. For thirty years, I slept beside a great river to which a hundred million wild salmon a year were once magnetically, magically, enigmatically drawn. For thirty years, the salmon's blood was on my hands. It shapes a person.

VII

LAST NIGHT, I STAYED up late reading about the history of aquaculture (fish farms) in British Columbia. Artificially produced Atlantic salmon, reared and fed and injected with growth hormones in aluminum pens from the Sunshine Coast north, are now the largest agricultural export of our province. Governments love fish farms. The Department of Fisheries and Oceans, whose mandate is to protect Canada's wild fish heritage, prefers the fake, plastic product to the genuine article. Aquaculture is a growth industry – actually, a growth-hormone industry, as I've said, but when you live in a society that's awash in poison, what's a few more chemicals in your bouillabaisse? Unrestricted proliferation of aquaculture destroyed Norway's wild salmon culture in the 1970s. And when the Norwegian government finally responded with regulations – too late, but that's SNAFU for governments – the Norwegian investors licked their lips all up and down the relatively unspoiled BC coast. The fortunes of the fish farm business here have risen and fallen over the past three decades, but the world's rapid population growth (over a billion humans rely on a fish protein diet) combined with the eradication of wild fish stocks virtually guarantees the flourishing of an industry that produces an unnatural food source while it destroys a natural one.

In the Broughton Archipelago in 2002, world-renowned whale researcher Alexandra Morton discovered that something was seriously wrong with one of the area's thriving pink salmon runs. The smolts, or juvenile salmon, on their way to the sea, had had to run the gauntlet of the archipelago's fish farms, which means, in simple terms, running the gauntlet of a parasite known as sea lice that attaches itself to well-stocked fish pens of docile salmon the way denial and arrogance attaches itself to politicians, bureaucrats and scientists. Sea lice are normally little cause for concern, parasitically speaking, because they need large concentrations of hosts to be effective – in fish farms, they find just the docilely drugged and crammed-together victims they need. Well, if you take millions of vulnerable wild salmon smolts and run them through herring-sized shoals of sea lice, you get slaughter. Here's what Alexandra Morton saw:

> Everywhere I went near the farms, the fish were covered with sea lice when I took them out of the water. Coho smolts were so frantic to escape the sea lice that they were jumping into boats. I noticed bleeding at their eyeballs and bleeding at the base of the fins, which are classic symptoms of fish disease. I was horrified to see these baby fish being ravaged by these parasites. It was an enormous feeling of helplessness.

Here's what Alexandra Morton's friend, a veteran guide and fishing lodge operator named Chris Bennett, said about the above:

> Anybody who isn't moved by the grotesque image of those baby salmon being eaten alive by these sea lice – their little eyes popping out because the lice have eaten right through their heads . . . well, that person probably can't be moved.

And there's the rub, the rub that most committed, caring environmentalists can't, out of sheer psychological preservation, allow themselves to address – how many humans can be moved in time? It's a nagging and painful question that can't help but throw the whole North American past blackly into our children's faces.

As I read further about fish farms and government complicity in their environmental crimes, then reflected on the pioneer salmon canners' and railroad builders' flagrant abuses of the laws of their day, as I sat staring at the Coast Salish carving of a spring salmon that's hanging on my living room wall beside a partial photograph of the *Rona,* I felt more and more oppressed by the obvious: the same forces that destroyed the buffalo herds of the West are destroying the wild salmon, the killer whales, the Fraser River, and every other natural part of my heritage. There's no sense in ignoring this any longer, or in denying it.

In Alberta, a province no less destructive of nature than British Columbia, I heard little about the crime at the Broughton Archipelago, but I knew from my own experience in the salmon fishery that the wild was vanishing. The following poem comes from my first book, which appeared in 1995, the last year I fished on the Fraser:

STEELHEAD, SPAWNING

What we dreamed of when young, but never found,
comes in with the tide tonight. What we loved,
but lacked the will to pursue, moves swiftly
in the mouth. Beautiful ghost, blushing
in the gills, the saltmarsh sighs to see
your rare body beacon the night. What have
we done to yesterday? The river flexes its
last wild muscle, strong and sure. Casts
its bright hook in our sleep, and pulls.
While we rise to the unbreathable element
of loss again.

The poem, however, is farmed; there's no wilderness there, only the smooth veneer of literature. When I wrote it, I only imagined what the extinction of a wild species meant; I didn't understand it with any real depth. I had to get older, to open my eyes and heart wider, before I could understand the poisoning deaths of bald eagles in Ladner's farm fields and of sturgeon in the Fraser's currents as forms of human suicide. Now when I hear that grizzlies are eating their own cubs or that North Vancouver is littered with the corpses of bald eagles shot for their feathers, I'm no less moved than I am by televised images of human suffering. The animals, after all, are blameless. Most of us in one way or another are complicit at best, actively involved at worst, in their destruction, which is our own destruction. Robinson Jeffers, the California poet, saw all this sixty years ago as he watched his Carmel paradise get overrun with "civilization." In despair, he developed a poetic theory known as "inhumanism," in which he lost all sympathy and compassion for the human species. The critics turned against him, his readers abandoned him, and he died from that most fatal of poisons and wildest of elixirs, the truth.

So is literature, therefore, a dead end if it does not constantly cry out against the crimes perpetrated on the wild of the planet? No. Whatever makes us feel and think outside of the parameters of the mass media and institutionalized society can only be constructive. But we could certainly use more literary concentration on the plight of the earth and its wild creatures. Too much of our intellectual and artistic life can be categorized as Nero fiddling while Rome burns. And that degree of irrelevance can only worsen, given the way things are in our educational system.

While our colleges and universities sign contracts with Pepsi and Coca-Cola for the exclusive right to sell their products on campus, while our elementary and high schools partner up with corporate sponsors in order to buy computers and hold sports tournaments, Alexandra Morton is waking from nightmares in which sea lice are feeding on her daughter's eyeballs. Houston, I think this is a definite problem.

By rights, as a corrective, Morton's essay on the fish farms of the Broughton Archipelago ought to be required reading in English and Science classes at the high school level. She should be given an appropriate readership for her findings: the readership of the future. That might make up for the treatment she received from the Department of Fisheries and Oceans, the so-called stewards of our natural fish heritage. After ignoring her warnings that something was terribly wrong with the wild salmon stocks of the Broughton Archipelago, the DFO threatened to fine her for "taking samples without a permit."

Which tempts a sane man to one conclusion: I'm going to keep my children out of school and read to them from *The Collected Poems of Robinson Jeffers.* To paraphrase Gunnar Ekelöf, *The inhuman is the only thing human/ in the long run.*

We can't accept that, of course. We're all we've got, after all, and we have to make the best of it. What is the best of it? I can't answer for you. For me, I have to archive my affections lest the world turns them to poison. This isn't a literary work you're holding. It's a school of wild words. When the last wild salmon dies, these pages will be dust.

VIII

ON JULY 20, 1969, my parents, along with half the population of the planet, watched the live newscast of the *Apollo 11* landing. I don't remember this, however. Certainly no one made me watch because it was an historic occasion. I was likely still outside at 7:56 Pacific Standard Time when Neil Armstrong finally placed his booted left foot onto the moon, I was likely playing happily in the dirt of the earth. While millions watched Walter Cronkite remove his black-framed glasses and wipe the tears from his eyes, then heard him exclaim, *Armstrong is on the Moon! Neil Armstrong, a thirty-eight-year-old American, standing on the surface of the Moon!*, I perhaps looked up at the familiar, rising splendour and thought nothing at all about mankind, just as the famous astronaut's own seven-year-old son was reportedly outside playing when his father announced, *The Eagle has landed!*

The truth is, memory does not emphasize the universally acknowledged big stage at the expense of the little dramas outside the theatre. For this reason, I remember the salmon's eyes and not Walter Cronkite's tears, just as I remember my father saying that he took a last, considered look at the untouched moon and not Armstrong famously saying, *That's one small step for man, one giant leap for mankind.*

Now, however, I feel a strange affinity between the five-year-old boy I was in the summer of 1969, the forty-one-year-old man I am today, and the thirty-eight-year-old man Armstrong was as he returned to an earthbound life of global celebrity. For the moon is as lost to him as the coast I knew as a child is lost to me; we've both burned out of those orbits of awe and nothing can take us back. Just as I lack photographs of myself on my father's gillnetter, Armstrong, more amazingly, lacks any clear, high-resolution photographs of himself on the moon (Buzz Aldrin, who followed Armstrong down the ladder, mysteriously took none, though Armstrong snapped several of Aldrin). And the ruins – my father's first boat in the marsh, the Eagle crashed into some crater; my messages in pop bottles thrown into the river, Armstrong's college ring left in an envelope in the lunar dust; my memories of an abandoned townsite, and the hundreds of pounds of equipment *Apollo 11* left behind. It's not necessary to leave Earth's orbit and travel a quarter of a million miles away to create a place and a time you can't recover. Ordinary grounded life, especially in North America, makes such loss, such displacement, endemic.

In September 1969 Armstrong, speaking before Congress, commented on the differences between earth-time and space-time. Noting that a whole earth day passed while he was on the moon, but that the sun hardly moved a fraction because of the moon's month-long lunar day, he went on:

There was a peculiar sensation of the duality of time – the swift rush of events that characterizes all our lives – and the ponderous parade which marks the aging of the universe. Both kinds of time were evident – the first by the routine events of the flight, whose planning and execution were detailed to fractions of a second – the latter by rocks around us, unchanged throughout the history of man – whose three-billion-year-old secrets made them the treasure we sought.

He could be speaking of this life, this ordinary extraordinary life on the third planet from the sun. Who hasn't felt this same duality of time? Who hasn't, in the midst of a busy life, caught a glimpse of the risen moon, or of a passing hearse, or of something even quieter, perhaps a bee holding onto a flower in a strong wind, and been shaken with the sheer uncanniness of being and non-being, the past and the present, the moon on the TV set and the moon the salmon were swimming under the night of July 21 when my father, because it was a Monday, the day the fishing usually opened, brought in his net on a high water slack and picked out fifty-seven sockeye.

I was there, but I don't remember that particular tide and catch. I don't remember if I saw my father staring at the moon and frowning. If I did, I would not have understood, just as I would not have understood how a man who had witnessed the vulnerable earth from a quarter of a million miles away could, a decade later and after the Energy Crisis, become the national spokesman for the Chrysler Corporation.

These days, I look at the *Apollo 11* landing with the same chilled admiration I hold for all North American progress, including that of the salmon canners' on the Fraser River. Astonishing, deadly achievements. Buzz Aldrin's first words as he stepped onto the moon, *Magnificent desolation*, have reached us from space, but they're not referring to a distant planet. From far beyond our orbit, looking back, Neil Armstrong saw, as he put it, some greens showing along the western coast of Canada. He wouldn't see so many now. And Michael Collins, the third astronaut on the mission, who particularly loved the salmon salad portion of the stellar diet, would have been eating wild salmon; today, it's almost certain he'd be eating the manufactured variety.

It's easy to cry about what we're doing, as Walter Cronkite cried, removing his glasses and seeing only the partial truth of our astonishing progress. It's much harder to cry without blinding ourselves, to know the full sight of joy and pain and truth that E.E. Cummings referred to when he wrote, *because our tears/ are full of eyes.* Looking ahead or looking back, leaving a place or returning to it, a planet or a town, means looking through a prism altered by the devastating magnificence of our triumphs.

IX

EARLY FALL IN GIBSONS. My children's tans are leaving their bodies and flowing into the trees. Spiderwebs are suddenly everywhere, the tourists have gone. The last blackberries and windfall apples shrivel in the heavy dew. Soon the mists will come that smell like woodsmoke and the woodsmoke will rise that looks like mist.

In some ways, this town is the Ladner of my childhood. There's a sleepy, rural quality to the place even though it is almost a suburb of Vancouver. Gillnetters and seiners draped with vivid red scotchmen rest at moorage along the government wharf. In many yards, untarped aluminum skiffs lie angled between driftwood fences and high grass, ready to fill with the bilge of rainwater. The lots are large, often unkempt and inhabited by wildly bearded old men who limp as if their pasts involved a beachcombing or logging or fishing accident. It's tempting to believe I've escaped into my own youth, if only superficially. But the truth is, Gibsons, like every other small town in North America within an hour or two of a large urban centre, is being rapidly homogenized. Condominiums are replacing the ramshackle homes along the water, an increasing number of residents commute to jobs in Vancouver, and a Wal-Mart – the true death knell of civic uniqueness – is trying to muscle in.

In Gibsons, however, the rural origins of the town remain palpable. It's still commonly called Gibsons Landing, for instance, though decreasingly so each year. And Nature has a more visceral presence. Just the other morning, a black bear ambled down the road in front of our house. Great blue herons and raccoons visit our backyard pond. At night, the stars and silence and woodsmoke almost convince me that my father is alive, somewhere in the neighbourhood, poking an outdoor fire with a stick and looking up to watch the satellites cross the heavens.

Yet the erasure of the coastal culture has begun in earnest here. A few days ago, riding my bike from the village to our house, a ten-minute journey, I was startled by large signs posted on every other telephone pole. They read *This Way to Set*, and a large black arrow on each sign kept pointing me forward. If I pedalled fast enough, would I reach the top of the Prairie Drift? Would I find the *Nola J* and the *Driftwood* there, the *Thunderbird* and the *Queen Bee*? If I pedalled fast enough, would the dead come alive?

I followed the signs, not, as it turned out, "to set," but to "the set." Several huge catering trailers blocked my access to where the American bosses and Canadian crew were filming a remake of *The Fog*. I wasn't surprised, of course. Ladner has appeared several times on the big screen as a town somewhere in Washington or Oregon or even California. And Gibsons, most famous for being the locale for the long-running CBC-TV series *The Beachcombers*, has begun to take its turn as somewhere else. Soon, everywhere will be somewhere else. But not to the salmon. Home is always home to them. They'll bash their heads in to get there. That's why they're signposts. That's why, breathing hard, leaning on my handlebars, feeling the fog of dislocation descend again that first descended a quarter century ago when the Golden Arches and the quarter pounder squatted their bland fat on William and Thomas Ladner's pre-emption, I let the autumn that is still the autumn guide me back to my natal stream.

* * *

I step out of the house on Georgia Street into a dark pregnant with possibility. In the light of the full moon, six pheasants and mallards hang from the clothesline, their shadows on the wet grass. The air's rich with burnt punk, the silence rent every few minutes by the screech of a Roman candle. The fields of Westham Island glow with fat pumpkins; many have been piled into large pyramids in anticipation of the families who will come to choose a good one for carving (we grow our own pumpkins in the yard). When I close my eyes, I can see those pumpkins, packed tight as salmon roe, vibrating already with the strange expressions they will wear so briefly.

A cloud crosses the moon. The dead birds vanish. I breathe deeply, and the riversmell – muddy, leaf-clotted – fills my lungs. I strike an Eddy match and light a punk and quickly print my name against the stars. The red letters blaze briefly in the dark, then disappear to join the dead birds wherever they've gone. Because spelling is new to me, I try my name again and again. It always disappears. When the moonlight floods the yard once more, I'm startled to find the birds in the same position, unchanged. Their stillness, like the stillness of the dead salmon, is actually a constant speed that I watch in anticipation of a crash that never comes. It's as if I know, bone-deep, that life is a matter of continual, silent departure that simply plays at returning. It's as if I carry the knowledge of a time that can't be told with numbers.

So poetry began for me, as a lump in the throat, a homesickness, a lovesickness, to use Robert Frost's terms. Always, from the very beginning, from as far back as memory reaches, I have felt those stirrings, those yearnings for what I know but can't possibly know. And the burning punk – its acrid smell, that flourish of expression and identity and complete erasure by the dark – was the first poem.

My father wrote it too, with the beam of his flashlight, with the line of salmon blood he left behind him as he walked home from the wharf in a living coastal version of *Hansel and Gretel.* That blood is gone just as Hansel's breadcrumbs went. I'm in the middle of the dark forest. And Time, the witch, is at my bones. All I have are my red letters.

GILLNETTING

You're standing on your bedroom floor and suddenly
the walls are gone the floor is spinning
down a black river raging towards the sea.
By starlight, you're staring into the eye
of a dead salmon, which is the eye
of a live salmon, which is the rim
of a dormant volcano.

Geese fly over but you can't see them.
A heron rips its numbed-blue limb
off the bank. You're moving faster
than a seal before the orca's scythe.
There is nothing to do but work. Nothing.
Salmon crash around you like armour.
No sense asking how you came to be here
or where your books and sleep have gone.

Summer blends to fall. You pull
a soaked wool blanket from a world of wool.
Your few feet of sight
are lit up like a crime scene.
You're standing still as you run away.

Winter. The floor's ice.
You can see a great fish
below you, like a foetus
on a screen. Is it rising?

All land is gone. On your hands
is the one task you have left:
to see your blood
as the blood of the salmon
to know your past
as if it lies ahead of you

as if you could die there.

When I write about salmon fishing, I'm not always or purely the "I" of the poem; often it's my father or brothers or some other fisherman who has a greater right to the subject matter. My father, after all, owned boats and licences, his name was in the cannery books, he made the direct link between the salmon's appearance and the food, clothing and shelter for his family. I did none of that. So I write to acknowledge the human genius of survival. "Gillnetting" proceeds from the domestic to the wild, progressing by seasons. It's a fast trip, as befits a poem. But there's colour in the idling of prose too.

* * *

Fall was dog season. Fog and foghorns. A time of mixed catches – a few late sockeye, some coho, pinks, springs, but mostly dogs. A time of huge deadheads rising up with ragged shoulders and rolling out of our net with an awful ripping and a sickening, corpse-like slosh. The river was black and fast; it threatened to spin off the earth, just as the fanbelts on our engine always threatened to snap or come loose. When the fall net came in, a larger-meshed net for the dog species, heavy, as if dripping semen, it made sense that the salmon in it were so fierce and deeply marked. I stood in my gumboots, shivering, and I don't remember ever seeing the sun. A season of mists and mellow fruitfulness, but a season that could kill you too. The deck was always slippery, the water and frost together chain-locked the wrists, and the river wanted to make you pay for the fat luxury of summer's sockeye fishing. The dogs possessed a strength and a sharp-toothed fight that made you believe they hated everything human. The harder the conditions grew, the more they seemed to relish their strength. Give them a thick fog, and clutch your gaff for protection.

Fog. Dog season. Howard Kerr. He was, in the Ladner vernacular, a jungle bum. The fishing industry employed its share of them, old men who mucked about in decaying gillnetters just enough to collect unemployment stamps to finance their winter supplies of Baby Duck. Howard was a regular on the Prairie. His boat was barely floatable. A large, unshaven man with bloodshot eyes who wore mack jackets stained with dried blood and suspenders and scale-flecked gumboots with soles pink as the back of a cat's mouth, he possessed both the comic lunacy and drunken instinct for camaraderie that together formed what could be called a "coastal character." Of course, there's nothing ultimately amusing about alcoholism, and I can't speak lightly of Howard Kerr's life, for fear that I overlook whatever harm his disease did to those closest to him, but he was alive in my childhood, and his presence affords my memory one of its most meaningful and moving sounds.

It's October, a day of damp and scud, dark at midday. A mist thickens to cable-fat coils of fog, then the coils unwind to a mass. Up on the main river, foghorns of the foreign freighters warn the gillnetters of their approach. Then these mournful blasts die out. I'm standing with my father in the rotting-pear light of our stern, listening. Because now the ears have to do the work of the eyes. My father fingers the leadline. He's sensitive as a spider waiting for the tremble of prey on a strand of web. The fog's so thick that I can barely see his expression. It's tense, poised. Around us is the sucking of the current, a cold, inhuman sound. We're drifting but it's impossible to tell how fast because all the usual position marks have vanished; we can't see the cottonwood with the bent branch or the oddly shaped clump of bank or the graveyard deadheads. Just when I can no longer bear the tense near-silence, just when I'm about to ask for Dad's reassurance, I hear it.

A faint sound at first, but it soon grows louder. Clink, splash, a longer clink. Repeated every minute. It orients and comforts me at once. We're nearing the bottom of the Drift, before the slough. Howard Kerr is bailing out his boat! Hallelujah! The wet bells of autumn ring me back to the world, the fanbelt of the river is back on its engine, the drum creaks as my father brings in our net.

The dog salmon are so named for the size of the male's teeth. Greenhorns in the industry were once told that a dog could bite into a log boom and hold on to rest against the tide. While they're not that strong, they are certainly powerful, the second largest species of Pacific salmon. They thrust upriver, the size of a man's thigh. Hook-nosed, averaging between ten and fourteen pounds but reaching up to thirty, the dog is fierce enough in itself, but gains fierceness from the time of year it returns to spawn. No mild summer rains inspire the dog's run to home. Cold drizzle, lashing downpours, heavy frost and fog, dew dripping like blood off the black telephone lines: these conditions partner the dog's death. So why shouldn't it be a yard of coiled muscle prodded with an electric charge?

My father wields his gaff full-time on each drift. Often the dogs hang by a single tooth on a single mesh, and it takes considerable skill and strength to wrest them from their purpose. The river, already churning, churns more. The comforting bells of Howard Kerr's bailing have ceased to ring. My father's arm threatens to yank from the socket. I stare at a big male dog thrashing in its own rich blood in the stern, the colour of death more vivid in the fog, as if we are tearing hearts out of chests. The drum turns slowly, the net's full of sticks and chunks of bark and bullheads. In the pick-up light, the fog's a fine soaked length of gauze that won't staunch any flow. We drift faster, swing into the slough.

The dog has a long, dark purple band along its pewter length. The next dog has it too, and the next. The bands are strips of paint applied carelessly with a roller that drips. I don't know why only this species of salmon wears a purple band to mark its spawning phase, but it seems right, as if they've already scraped through some opening that's bruised them and incited their fury. My father clubs the three fish into stillness so they won't flip up and catch their gills or teeth in the net as it rolls in. Then he returns to his task, a skilled lunge and a wrench of muscle, like an eagle lifting lambs off a mountainside, one by one. Suddenly a foghorn moans up on the main river and the sound could be pouring out of the dead dogs' gaping, canine jaws. It isn't, but wisps of fog are; the fish could be dropped guns, stocks cooling fast, smoke rising from the barrels, so abruptly does their violence end, so chilled is the air in which they've become victims.

Fall fishing didn't add much to a man's living. Dogs weren't highly valued salmon – some fishermen claimed, in fact, that they were called dogs because the canneries sold their flesh for dog food. Certainly the canneries paid much less for them, perhaps a quarter per pound to a sockeye's dollar and a quarter and a red spring's dollar seventy-five. The dog's flesh isn't the lovely dark red of the sockeye's, but it's excellent for smoking. Mostly, my father fished them to earn a stamp, one more credit towards collecting UI in the few winter months he had no income.

Whatever else he was, my father wasn't a berrypicker; a high school dropout, he had no regular professional income to supplement with the rich oils of the sockeye season. Fishing afforded him some independence and some respect for his skills of patience, observation and manual dexterity (he could untangle a complicated fish knot in a minute that would take the average person an hour). But he was working in an industry that was fast squeezing his kind of fisherman out, an industry in which, thanks to the fleet-reducing Davis Plan of 1968, doctors, lawyers, high school teachers and other professionals often went together to purchase enough licences for seine boats so they could take a share of the salmon harvest without ever getting their hands wet, in which "highliners" who were "hungry" roared all up and down the coast with their sonar and fish finders, scanning the tides, their VHFs crackling and their second (illegal) nets heaped on top of their cabins so they wouldn't have to go into harbour to change them. My father couldn't compete with that. He never wanted to. That made him a dinosaur in more than just the increasingly greedy salmon fishery. Neither "hungry" nor a "jungle bum," he eked out a living on the Prairie Drift for thirty years. An excellent fisherman at the level of skill and knowledge, my father was a failure in the eyes of a world that measures success strictly in economic terms. This world. Our world.

He used to quote his own father, a Great War veteran who

nearly died in a foxhole in France in 1915, his boots filling with blood from a shrapnel wound until another soldier found him and carried him to an aid station. My Ontario-born, Alberta-raised grandfather, fed a British schoolboy's philosophy with his porridge, would say as an approach to life, "Play up and play the game." In other words, go by the rules and don't moan about your lot. My father never veered from that Victorian ethic. As a result, anyone who did veer from it earned nothing but his contempt. In the end, my father was lightly ridiculed for his adherence to this code. What did it benefit a man, after all, to live according to a principle that so severely limited his income, especially when so many others had changed with the times?

Perhaps it didn't benefit him at all. His approach to fishing salmon may have been honourable, but we would not have survived as a family if not for his part-time work in the potato fields of Westham Island and, more importantly, if not for my mother's remarkable managerial skills, her deft way with a gutting knife, her plunges into the steam of a thousand cooking mason jars of fish and fruit and vegetables, as well as her part-time income from working at the Five and Dime and then Ottewell's Drugstore. A slinky going down the stone steps of the museum entrance had nothing on my mother's financial stretching ability – her dollar bills were so elasticized that she could have used them to hold up her nylons, though she hadn't worn nylons much since her dance hall days in Toronto during World War II, when she'd met and married my shy father, her cute "sailor boy." And those nylons had been hard to come by. Like many women of that era, Mom became a dab hand at painting straight lines on her bare legs with an eyebrow pencil. But she'd been raised during the Depression in a poor urban family. One of her most vivid childhood memories is of pressing her nose against the window at Christmas time, waiting for the gift box from the T. Eaton's department store to arrive. If she was lucky, there'd be an orange and a pair of socks for her.

With such a foundation, it was no wonder thrift came as second nature to her. Thrift, and a sense of financial responsibility honed to such a fine point that an unpaid bill was like a knife wound (the way people use credit cards these days shocks, even offends, her). Yet government assistance, which she always called "pogey," was acceptable in the form of UI, because you had to earn the stamps; they weren't a handout. Welfare, by contrast, was wrong. Oh, not for others; my mother readily acknowledged that some people, the real "down and outers," needed help. She begrudged the genuinely poor nothing. But we weren't down and out, and wouldn't be as long as she could draw breath.

So Mom became an expert at the coupon clip and the store sale, at the leftover and the rainy day fund (to this day, she still collects "mountie" quarters, has several dozen Black Velvet cardboard cylinders stuffed with them, as well as other containers stuffed with the centennial coins – the seagulls, cougars and rabbits of Alex Colville's masterful hand and eye. My father grew a beard, my mother put coins away. Oh Canada. Oh lost Canada). By the time of my earliest memories, her lot was easier, though she never felt she could relax. Nor could she. Money was tight, always, my father's income varied little from sockeye season to sockeye season, yet I never wanted for anything. In the end, I see now that my father's independence and my idyllic childhood owed everything to my mother's unrelenting vigilance over the family coffers. That my father gave over financial matters to her, a highly uncharacteristic arrangement for a forties marriage, suggested both how little he cared for money and how much he relied on his wife's economizing talent to finance his disinterest. He turned over everything he made to her as soon as he received it, and she, in her own words, "made do." My respect for them both begins with my complete unawareness of any deprivation. I was not privy to their economic or other stresses. Now, as a writer with a shaky, irregular income and three children, I honour the example of my parents. I play up and play the game. I make do. It's the only way I know how to live, as the wild salmon knows only fresh to salt to fresh.

The drum turns. Every few fathoms, there's a thump in the

stern, blood spreads in the mist. Because my father keeps picking branches out of the net (there'd been high winds the night before), because of the thumping and redness, we might be harvesting ripe apples. The smell isn't sweet, however; it isn't the syrup of autumn's Gravensteins and Spartans. It's thicker and heavier, a musk of slime, blood and something indescribable – the salmon's pungent scent, which smells of nothing but itself. It isn't life or death as we know it, it isn't desire or terror, it isn't salt or fresh. It's the past, memory, home. Lovesickness, the beginning of the poem, and the end of language.

The coal oil lantern bobs into view. Gracefully, my father bends over the rollers and sweeps the light aboard. The banks are still lost. Our breath clouds drip. Our knuckles are red as the sockeye's flesh. It's so silent above the idling of the engine that I can believe we've drifted off the river and into the stars. But the only constellations visible lie at our boots. My father steps over the broken dippers and crashed armour and we begin our slow ascent up the fog-choked slough, listening for the mud that tears off the banks, not speaking, the heavy chains of the dog salmons' deaths on our lips.

X

SUMMER'S ALMOST GONE. The nights are cooler, requiring a light sweater. There's dew on the spiderwebs, the blackberries have ceased to swell with the remaining midday heat and their ripeness fades hourly from the air. My mother must hang the bedsheets and other laundry in the morning if they're to dry before dusk quickly dampens them again. I stand in the sideyard, dreaming. If I'm troubled by the fact that my pillowcase swings out on a line where, in a few weeks, dead pheasants and mallards will be all that swings there, the feeling is lost to me now. Still visceral, however, is the steam of the non-stop canning in the kitchen, as my mother puts down more tomatoes and pears and pickles, or grinds them for chili sauce – how close that snapped dillweed is, that little cache of pickling spices, how vivid the flush in my mother's cheeks as she lifts the mason jars from the pot, places them on the counter, and then, over the next hour, listens, head cocked like a robin's, for the pop that signals each jar has sealed.

The peak of the sockeye runs are over. It's been an average season, successful in that no major disasters occurred – no horrific snags destroying half the net, no engine conking out on the morning of an expected good opening, no strikes. And the catch has been enough to carry us through the winter, provided there are enough fall openings to produce the last necessary UI stamps. I don't really know any of this. My parents don't discuss finances in front of me, and while I do detect occasional signs of tension, they're minor, not enough to punctuate my comfortable world – perhaps my father smokes a little more, or he rubs his temples while reclining in his usual manner on the chesterfield, or my mother hesitates almost imperceptibly if I ask for some money to buy candy at Bernie's Confectionery.

Not this year, though. This year, the tension is mine. Next week I'll start school, and my post-summer trips to the Prairie Drift will end. The knowledge of all that I'm destined to lose hasn't sunk in yet, but there's always a sadness about the end of sockeye season anyway; it's a milder kind of Boxing Day, with its own air of deflation and anticlimax. My brother, too, has put away his baseball gear for the season. Rick plays in the popular local men's fast-pitch league for the Ladner Fishermen team, perennial champions, as does my other brother, Bruce, though for the Ladner Hotel (opened in the 1870s by Thomas McNeely) – other teams include the Delta Police and Bill Ball Trucking. The Fishermen, oddly enough, draw much of their talent from the farming community. Pete Guichon, for instance, a descendant of the Guichons who came to the delta in 1883, is the team's home run king. With Herculean biceps built up from tossing hay bales around, he routinely clobbers the ball out beyond the centre-fielders so that it rolls up against the base of the granite cenotaph (a home run fence wouldn't appear until the mid-seventies). Bruce is a big hitter, too, and a skilled second baseman. Rick's forte is hitting for a high average, often switch-hitting and drag-bunting to "get aboard." The Fishermen's catcher, he's earned the nickname of "Pigger," in a nod to the *Peanuts* character Pigpen, who also moves in a permanent cloud of dust.

But the time of the dust is gone too. The rosin bag sits on the abandoned mound, waiting for the next windmill pitch eight months away, and only a few chestnut tree leaves circle the bases. My tan is draining rapidly from my skin, as rapidly as the colour enters the bodies of the salmon. Change is as palpable as my excitement as I follow my father's flashlight beam down Georgia Street, onto Chisholm and up the dyke to the wharf. It's my last chance to go with him for the year, until at least next summer. *Tonight,* I tell myself, *I'm going to make it. I'm going to stay awake the whole night.*

The harbour's crowded. The northern fleet is home, gillnetters are moored four deep, their owners relaxing this opening, tying up to wait for a good tide. We descend the gangway in silence. The river is glassy, sheened like a mallard's throat. The sky is the same black, though not as wet. Flecked with stars, it's the imprint of the river's silkscreen. I look up briefly, then lower my gaze – the last thing I want is to miss the planks between the floats. Already, the air's cooling; wet clothes would be a bad start to the night.

When we reach my father's tie-up spot, and after he starts the engine (it usually catches on the third or fourth try), a strange and graceful dance begins, a matter of slipping the *Nola J* out of her berth while holding onto the two boats moored outside of her. Dad unties the neighbouring boat's stern, side and bow lines after untying us from the inside boat. Slowly he slides the *Nola J* out, then cat-quick leaps to her stern, one hand on her stern line as she's released to the current, the other hand holding the stern line of the outside boat. Deftly he half-hitches the outside boat to the stern and side of the inside boat as he clambers up beside the *Nola J*'s drum gears to grab the outside boat's bow line, then jumps back into our stern, waiting till she's almost clear to hitch the outside boat's bow line to the bow of the inside boat. Finally, still dangling our bow line, he leaps from the bow of the outside boat into our stern and we're away, the current pulling us downriver sideways until Dad disappears into the cabin, slips the engine into gear with the usual small clunk, and turns the bow around. All this is done fluidly and silently, in less than a minute. It's a kind of soft shoe and sleight of hand, erasing us from where we'd been as if we'd never been there at all, as if the *Northern Star* and the *Delta Dawn* had always touched, as if the past belongs only to the motionless and unchanging. We set, as always, on the Prairie.

I lasted three drifts, to just before midnight, and watched my father gaff two huge springs, one of which had three sports fishermen's hooks in its black gumline; one hook had a bright orange hootchie on it plus an inch of heavy test, evidence of the annual Salmon Derby sponsored by the *Vancouver Sun,* the newspaper I'd deliver in a few years to the dying veterans of the Great War. But these fish were veterans too, survivors, at least until now. Like slabs of molten silver dripping sizzling oil, the springs were hauled out of the river and into the stern, where they thrashed in the thick blood gushing out of the gaff-hook wounds in their gills – the sound of puncture was like crunching a film of ice on a puddle.

Eventually, sitting on the main deck against the manifold's faint heat (we couldn't sleep in the cabin because of the fumes from the uncovered engine), I drifted off.

When I woke, it was to pre-dawn's chill and a murmur of voices. Our net was out and we were halfway down the drift, barely moving. A clinging mist hung over the river. The *Nola J* was tied to a larger boat, a packer, the *Maureen G,* captained by a cheerful, round-faced man named Vic Gerard. Vic was about my father's age, even shorter (perhaps five-foot-five to my dad's five-foot-seven), and always wore suspenders and big black gumboots up over his knees. His friendliness and brisk attentiveness to the work of counting and weighing the fish while exchanging pleasantries with my father made him seem like Santa Claus in his workshop a few days before Christmas. His crewman was something else entirely. Twenty years younger, tall, powerfully built, and sporting a huge red beard, Mark, or "Rosie" as he was known (either for his colouring or as an ironic comment on his demeanour, I never learned), hardly spoke or smiled. He was too busy picking fish off the *Maureen G*'s deck and flinging them into the aluminum box of the scale. Together, Vic and Rosie made a good team, and they were still working together in 1995 when I last fished the Fraser.

Back in 1969, I woke to the genial, intermittent banter of the "delivery," and tried to pick out faces through the dripping mist. My father stood on the starboard side of the stern, holding one of the huge springs. This involved putting the index and forefinger of each hand under the gills. He hefted the "smiley" onto the packer's slippery deck.

"That's a beauty, Hector," Vic said. "What do you say? 51?"

"A bit more, maybe. 53."

"Okay, Mark."

Rosie deftly picked the big spring into the box. Vic adjusted the metal bar of the scales, tipped it with one finger, and grinned.

"Right you are, Hector. A tad over 53."

Dad bent at the waist and I lost sight of him. I moved to the starboard side of the main deck. Vic winked at me. "Hi there, young fella. Excited about school?"

He'd ask me and my sister the same question at the end of every summer, with the same mischievous expression, which said, *I know you're not, and I sure as hell wouldn't be either.*

I shook my head, still drowsy, trembling with cold. Over Vancouver, the sky was the blue-black of a coho's back, but the stars had faded. Towards Ladner, it was still dark, and felt colder – I kept my face to the north.

Dad re-emerged from the mist, like an iceman holding a block of ice. He heaved the weight onto the packer's deck, and smiled slightly.

Vic bent to the fish for a closer look.

"About the same, Hector?"

"Close, anyway."

Into the box with a clunk, then the metal bar on the scale shifted a little.

"How bout that?" Vic said. "Just a tad under. Call it the same, 53."

Large springs – those over fifty pounds – weren't rare in 1970, but two of them weighing exactly the same on one delivery was interesting.

A moment later, when Dad had hurled the third smiley across the narrow gap between the roped-together, slightly rocking vessels, even I could sense something unusual was happening. The fish looked the same as the other two, a slab of bloodstained silver with a speckled tail and a speckled tail-fin the size of a geisha's opened fan. The air all around us dripped with the heavy, snapped-mint musk of chinook.

The fish was not the same fish, however. Vic, bending to cut the gumline with his knife, announced white. Still, I could see he was staring intently at the spring.

"Geez, it's close," he said in a low voice. "53?"

Now Rosie squatted for a closer look. He mumbled something I couldn't catch.

Vic said, "Mark says yes."

Dad lit a cigarette. The match sizzled into the dark current. He smiled at me.

After the weighing, Vic shook his head.

"Spot-on 53 this time. How about that? Hiding anything else down there, Hector?"

Dad didn't answer. He just disappeared from the waist again. When he re-emerged, holding another massive spring, I blinked. It was a visual echo. I knew that I couldn't be seeing the same image, because the sky had lightened slightly over the city – the Grouse Mountain ski lights shone faint as scales on blond wood.

Vic said nothing this time until he cut the gums.

"White," he said to Rosie. Then he stepped quickly to the scales.

The spring rose and fell like a sledgehammer. Clunk. Tap tap. Two geese flew swiftly over us and into the marsh. I heard the whoosh of their passage, caught a flash of their white bellies in the dark. Tap.

"Just under," Vic said quietly, as if to himself.

A salmon hit with a muffled splash far off along our corkline. I turned to look. When I turned back, almost frightened now at the hushed behaviour of the men, my father was just reaching under the drum once more. I looked at Vic. His mouth hung slightly open, he had one gumboot up on the edge of the scale. Rosie stood still, a totem pole of bloodsmears.

Nobody spoke when the dead spring was flung through the mist, over the gap between the boats, and slid lifeless across the deck to thump up against Rosie's boots. Dad took his cigarette down from his mouth very slowly, as if weighing it, as if it might be the ounce that made all the difference. He stepped onto the sidelocker for a better look.

For a few seconds, Vic's eyes met mine. I trembled even more, wondering if he was assessing my weight. But it seemed more as if he was worried about my being there.

The pick dangled from Rosie's right hand. He was looking down without bending. Vic nodded to him. I supposed that he'd forgotten about checking for the spring's colour with his knife.

Torn sleeves of nightgowns reached through the air. The current slapped harder at the sides of the boats, pulling blackly. I couldn't stop shaking. Daybreak seeped down the back of my neck.

Vic and Rosie stared at the scales. Dad's cigarette end shrivelled redly in his cupped hand.

Vic murmured something I couldn't catch as he pulled back from the scales and straightened up. He took a pencil from the pocket of his mac jacket, licked the end of it, then jotted something on a little piece of paper. Then, his hand partly over his mouth, he stared above me to where the stars still speckled the dark. Beside him, Rosie, the hose in one hand for cleaning the deck of blood, kept looking at the scales. The red, uncupped, climbed slowly to my father's lips.

"That's all," he said quietly.

The three men looked at each other as the current spun the joined boats downriver in the dissolving mist.

XI

We borrow a friend's old Subaru and cram it with a dozen bursting green garbage bags filled with plastic and aluminum pop and beer and cooler and energy-booster and vodka-spritzer bottles and cans. It's a big day, what we and the kids call an adventure. First, we'll deliver all the recyclables that our eldest child Dashiell has collected off the beaches and out of the woods all summer and stored in our garage (there's plenty of room, since we don't own a car). Delivery requires the use of a car, because the Gibsons recycling depot is in the upper part of town, at the top of a very steep hill, and we have too many items for the bus, whose route doesn't go right past the depot anyway. So the old Subaru suits our purposes today. Second, with part of the proceeds from the recyclables, we'll go for lunch. And third, we'll visit the local hatchery, simply because we've never been before and, now that it's fall, Chapman Creek has spawners in it. This could be a fun experience for the kids, something different. And my wife and I, too, are curious about what exactly goes on in a hatchery.

Well, to be honest, we're suspicious. Even the name of the operation, the Salmonid Enhancement Program, reeks of bureaucratic and institutional fiddling – as Orwell pointed out decades ago, there's a wild English language and a farmed, hatchery version. Our society mostly uses the latter. But that's another story – related, but different. When an officer from the Department of Fisheries and Oceans speaks of the wild fish he and his colleagues are meant to protect as "an aggregate of species," you know he's been attending more seminars than he's been walking creek banks.

We earn just enough money at the depot for our restaurant lunch (as always, and with a sigh, I pass on the salmon dish, suspecting it's farmed). After eating, we follow the twisting Sunshine Coast Highway west and north to Wilson Creek, turn off onto a side road, and a moment later descend a pitted gravel road in the woods until, another moment later, we reach the hatchery compound – a trio of large wooden buildings beyond which lies a chain-link fenced-in area full of circular fish pens covered with plastic green conical covers.

There's no one around. We climb out of the car. The kids, delighted as kids always are to escape from vehicles, run towards the fish pens through an open gate in the chain-link. As it turns out, a few of the covers are off, but there's netting across the surface of the dark water inside, to deter crows and gulls, minks and otters. While we're peering into the pens at the flitting black shapes, a short Native man walks out of one of the wooden buildings and approaches. He's smiling and mahogany-skinned, his eyes crinkly around the edges, his huge, drumskin-tight belly straining against his stained Salmonid Enhancement Program T-shirt. I suppose he's around my age. Immediately, he banters with the kids, holding his hands clasped at the top of his belly (I'm reminded of how, as a boy, I'd put my hands on the school globe in wonder that it was really the earth) and his double chin on his chest. When he speaks to them, he's only mildly condescending, not as bad as most adults. He inquires about the doll our five-year-old Sadie is carrying, asks its name, then segues smoothly to the subject of fish mommas and their babies as he leads us into the dark interior of the incubation building. Obviously, he's used to showing children around the place. As we'll soon learn from him, schoolchildren are regularly involved in hatchery proceedings. As he puts it, city kids need to see where their food comes from.

The interior of the incubation building is cramped and dark, cement-floored. Metal trays in a shelf line one wall. Opposite these are three large, long tubs filled with juvenile trout and coho salmon (separately). The place has a cluttered, shabby feel, like a high school science lab an hour after the last bell of the day – there's a vague chemical or pesticide smell in the close air. Our host scoops some brown pellets out of a sack and waves his arm over one of the still tubs, as if he's scattering grain to chickens. Immediately the dark water erupts with blips and pocks, as the mouths of the ravenous young fish break the surface. Two seconds and the water's still once more. Dashiell asks if he can do some scooping. Yes, he can. Then our host offers the same chance to Sadie and, tentatively, to Levi (at three, he must do everything his older siblings do, of course).

While the kids are feeding the fish, he tells us proudly that the hatchery is expecting a return of 180,000 coho this year. I nod politely, not revealing what I've read about the gross inefficiency of hatcheries, their abysmal rate of return (less than one percent), their response to this by increasing the volume of juveniles released, which leads to greater competition with wild stocks and interbreeding (which weakens the wild stocks' genetic character), and the fact that in most "enhanced" streams wild fish fare worse than before the "enhancement." Then, as Levi feeds the juvenile cutthroat, our host casually explains that they will eventually shock the water, rendering the fish infertile, so they can be introduced into freshwater lakes without harming the wild stocks (anglers can take the hatchery fish and release the wild ones). Later, he'll tell Dashiell that for the salmon, they'll raise the temperature of the water to make them grow faster.

"Imagine," he says, "if someone raised the temperature of the air and you're suddenly graduating from grade seven." Dashiell grins, in that way I know to be politeness masking incomprehension, and our host grins back. I choose not to make a joke about global warming, or to ask if he doesn't think it's disturbing that the hatchery often heats up its juvenile fish in the waste water of the local pulp mill.

Back outside, we enter the chain-link fenced area, where the kids happily scoop more pellets into the tanks.

I ask what's in the fishfood.

Wearily and quickly, as if he's been asked this question before by someone suspicious of the answer, he says, "Herring, anchovies, wheat and vitamins" – the last he pronounces with a short sound on the first vowel. Then, winking at the kids, he adds, "Everybody needs their vitamins, even the fish."

We move on. He shows us the moss-sided concrete tanks half-built into the ground at the back of the property, explains about the salmon's "poop," proudly informs us that schoolkids keep the tanks clean as part of a class project. We're close to the creek now. The water's dark, rippling over large, smooth stones.

"Here's the concrete fish-ladder and containment area where they channel the spawners and scoop them out. Then we slice open the momma fish's belly," he says with a smile, then adds, shrugging at Theresa and me, "She's ready to let her eggs out so we just make things easier for her. Then we take some eggs, some sperm from the daddy," (he doesn't say how they collect this) "and some creek water, mix it all together in a bucket." Hands clasped, eyes crinkling, he concludes, "Just like making a cake, mixing all the ingredients."

"Do the wild fish come in here, too?" I ask.

He shrugs. I think he's beginning to detect I'm not a booster of enhancement. "They're all wild fish now," he says. "How can you tell? The steelhead and the cutthroat, the Americans have been hatching them for a century. They're not wild anymore. But our fish, they're wild. The DFO just likes to categorize them as hatchery fish."

Through the trees' red- and yellow-tinged leaves, the creek is visible, shallow and stone-filled, flowing fast. Dashiell shouts, "I see a fish!"

And he does. The pink salmon are returning. The big humps and hooked jaws of the males can be detected at some distance.

Our host points out a trail we can take along the creek. Then he tells the kids to be sure to stop back at the office because he has a little something for them. Dashiell sprints off into the trees, eager to see more of the spawners. Sadie pulls at my elbow.

"Dad, can we catch a fish?"

She's referring to the fully grown trout in a tank at the entrance to the chain-link fenced area. The hatchery charges $2.50 to catch one with a little rod. And you're allowed to keep it. Theresa has already whispered, I don't want one of those things. I agree. I also don't want to contribute any money to aid the hatchery and the DFO in its cozy partnership. But Sadie – and Dashiell too – would love to try "fishing."

I stand among the covered tanks, watching my six-year-old vanish into the autumn shadows. He could be me, but he isn't. He can't walk half a block from his house to ride out on a gill-netter to a drift on the Fraser River and watch his father catch fifty- and sixty-pound springs. Instead, he'll drop a short line into a hatchery tub and catch a fish who's had its sexual function shocked into dysfunction.

I recoil from the idea, thinking I'll take him and Sadie to the government wharf in Ladner early one morning and let them drop lines into the muddy current for bullhead. Then the thought occurs – what's happened to the bullhead in the last thirty years? For all I know, they're as threatened now as the oolichan and steelhead and sturgeon and rock and ling cod and coho and abalone and . . . I sigh and look towards Chapman Creek.

Where has the wild past gone? It certainly isn't here, unless one of the pink salmon in the creek still has its adipose fin (for identification purposes, the hatchery cuts that fin off its fish). And maybe that past isn't as wild as I've always believed. Maybe it's already gone, subsumed into the domestic, the chemical, the antiseptic – still wild-seeming on the outside, but something else entirely . . . like us. If so, even that kind of wildness is preferable to what many fishermen call the "pus bags" of farmed salmon.

Twenty minutes later, with our bright blue and orange salmon cycle stickers and our Salmonid Enhancement Program pins, we pile into the Subaru and drive home. We've lived in Gibsons long enough to know all the turns and the distances between them. Already we've imprinted on the place. We're

North Americans and adaptable, or so the way we live attempts to show.

But I know I'm not home, not even when the car pulls into the driveway. Home doesn't exist anymore.

XII

Ducks warble in the marsh. A pink light tips the reeds, then reveals the banks, which often collapse from the current's eroding power in dramatic chunks, like piano lids at the end of a concert. A great blue heron perched on a deadhead lifts a wing and shudders dewdrops to the muddy water. We're going in. The tide's dropping and getting faster and there aren't enough fish to risk the snags, at least not this late in the opening. We chug up the harbour channel, cutting the gas at the floats along the way, out of courtesy, so as not to damage the moored boats with our wake, or to disturb the sleepers in the few unpretty float-homes along the mainland bank.

Draw back. 1969 is not so different from 1949. Just past daybreak, most people are still sleeping – there's no hornet snarl of vehicles at the entrance to the Deas Island Tunnel (which wasn't there until 1959 – prior to that, a small car ferry ran between Ladner and Lulu Island on the main river's north bank), no SUVs and tractor trailers moving jerkily along the highway, no lineups at a McDonald's drive-thru or long idles outside a Starbucks at a mall. There's no McDonald's, no mall. The potholed streets are dark with damp, the lawns dew-spangled, the doors unlocked. Unleashed dogs sniff the fresh air as they trot up driveways at the approach of fishermen, who move as figures in a dream, getting back their land legs. The grizzle on their faces could be shards of lead. Their shoulders sag with fish-weight. The phone lines above them sag with dew. The men pass a Douglas fir; its branches are heron's wings raised from the current. A pickup truck glides quietly past with a gillnet heaped on its bed. The truck resembles a giant, sleepy spider searching for a spot to place its web for the day. But it had better hurry. The other spiders have set up shop already; their webs glisten prismatically on the blackberry bushes and between the telephone poles and morning glory vines and the spokes of bikes dropped hastily in yards. The river flows through the air, smelling of blackberries and brine.

Draw back further. Here's the delta, a soggy, fertile, flat expanse of potato and corn fields, sloughs and ditches, an intersection of watery veins through loam as black as the spring's gumline. What's that? A muskrat swimming home to its hole. The ditches and slough banks are flutes of innumerable stops and almost unheard music. The muskrat does not sing. The black dot glides in silence one way, then another. From up here, above the earth, we could be playing a slow game of pinball, without the sound or flashing lights. Watch the ball slide from river to slough to ditch – don't lose concentration or it will slide under out of sight. What's that? A flash of gull wing, a bedsheet flapping on a clothesline at the back of a dark house? Look back. The muskrat's still there, gliding over the dull sheen of water, as if gliding over its own fur, and going home, tasting the current. Like a salmon. There's that flash of white again. What is it? A human face?

Game over. Tilt. The glass is smashed. The ball's a bloody pulp in our hands and we don't have anywhere left to throw it without harm. Let's not be romantic; let's throw the bloody pulp back to the nineteenth century and see where it lands.

* * *

Ladners Landing, late summer, 1890. Here are many of the same ditches and sloughs. Here's the same river, though much wilder, less silted up. And in this water, brackish with a back-up tide, tons of salmon guts, a slosh of loose red – salmon carcasses too, from the fish the canners don't want, the pinks and dogs and springs. And in these ditches and sloughs and channels – typhoid. And on a sternwheeler leaving the Ladners Landing wharf, Thomas Ladner's daughter, May, seriously ill with the disease, needing medical treatment in Victoria, going downriver and passing the fresh memory of her mother's corpse going the other way. Let's drop the muskrat pulp here, in the sternwheeler's wake. And try to wash the blood off as we watch Thomas Ladner pull on his boots and walk to the cannery where the fishguts are dumped straight into his daughter's bloodstream. And try to believe we're any different.

XIII

IT'S RAINY AND COLD, but fortunately I have options for shelter outside of the house. There's the family Ford, a pale-green, hard-topped model from the fifties, complete with fins and whitewall tires. It sits in the driveway and is rarely driven – my mother walks to do the shopping and my father, on the odd occasion when he goes anywhere out of walking distance, such as to a five-pin bowling tournament in Surrey, gets a ride. Nola and I make good use of the car, though. In 1969, its seats are covered with all the comic books our mother has brought home for us from her job as a cashier at Ottewell's drugstore – mostly *Donald Duck* and *Uncle Scrooge* and other Gold Key titles, perhaps a *Rawhide Kid* now and then, though Mom thinks that's a bit old for me. Oh, and lots of *Archie*s and *Archie Digest*s for Nola. We can sit for hours, sprawling on the worn seats, picking a comic like a leaf out of a sloppily raked pile. Sometimes we switch on the radio (it doesn't really come on) and tell each other stories. Sometimes we just stare out the rain-blurred windows, imagining we're speeding down the highway or flying through space or even sinking under sea. When we're not inside it, the car just waits for us, its original use mostly over. It's a sort of spawned-out salmon full of coloured entrails.

Today it seems too confining. I want a shelter, but a more open one, farther from the house. Not a small fort thwacked out of the blackberry bushes and inlaid with cardboard boxes, though that's often cozy. Not the old shed, once a chicken coop, at the end of the street, half-buried in the vacant lot's wild grass – it's too dark and has a faintly lingering smell of poultry droppings. Today there's only one place I want to be.

I cross the street without looking (perhaps two cars pass every hour, perhaps a dozen during the height of the sockeye season). Between an abandoned, two-storey house that drops tarred roof and side panels regularly like calendar pages in a silent film, and Trennant Street, stands my destination – the tallest structure in town.

It's a Douglas fir, a hundred and twenty feet high, hundreds of years old. It stood here, in other words, before Thomas and William Ladner ever set eyes on the delta. There's nothing else like it for miles. Why it survived the townsite's development around it is a mystery, and one to which, as a child, I gave no thought. I didn't even give it a name other than tree. There was no need. "Let's go to the tree" couldn't mean anything else. Three-quarters up its fluted, dragon-hide trunk and you looked down on the steeples of the United and Anglican churches the way an eagle or seagull would. From there, you could see the river and the ocean by just turning your head slightly from northwest to southwest, you could see the tractors in the fields, the cars in the streets, pick out a person walking from his house into town and back again, you could be kin to the birds and friend to the rain, you could be god.

I push through the wet, waist-high grass until I'm standing at the fir's base. Previous generations of children had driven railroad-type spikes into the trunk to create foot and handholds so you could reach the lowest branches. Even so, it's always a struggle for me to make this first part of the ascent. I press my face against the rough bark, embrace the trunk for a brief rest once I've balanced fragilely on the first spike (my arms not reaching halfway around the trunk), and feel my heart hammering like a woodpecker. The sap is rich and thick as melted candle wax – even when I think I've successfully avoided it, I find traces on my wrists and forearms, sometimes on my cheeks. The air is all freshness around me as I rise slowly into the ether of fir, into a world of drooping branches and sharp, green needles and small reddish-brown cones. I'm not a reckless child. I always make certain that my shoelaces are tied when I climb and that I'm not dangling any sleeves or hoods, as one little snag could cost me my balance. And I pause between spikes for almost a minute. Anyone watching would think I was afraid or in difficulty. But it wasn't that. Somehow I understood my relationship to this tree to be special, and I needed a way to honour its grandeur. Haste was not only dangerous but a kind of sacrilege. So up I went, on the craft of generations before me, into pure spirit and a level of consciousness I would never have known otherwise.

In later years, in the 1980s, when protests against the logging of old-growth forests such as in the Clayoquot and the Carmanah were daily news, the derisive term "tree hugger" would be coined for those who valued the forests over material gain. I was caught halfway between in the debate. My family's resource-industry, union background made me sympathetic towards those workers who would purportedly lose jobs due to the protests, but we were also suspicious of big forestry companies who, like the big canneries, didn't put a high premium on workers' rights. And then, too, I knew something about the magnetic power of old trees. I had spent my childhood hugging one, in fact. Only now, with the wisdom built of loss, can I see how any sane person – any salmon fisherman, especially – should have been chaining himself to every tree in every watershed in the province. If more fishermen had fought the power of MacMillan Bloedel and Crown Zellerbach and Weyerhaeuser and a dozen other forestry giants, more streams would have been protected and more salmon would be returning to spawn. But a lot of fishermen worked in sawmills along the Fraser in the off-season and easily bought the short-term economic arguments about job loss.

Fishing, farming, logging: this was as near to a cultural axis as you could get in BC in 1969. Few people saw the harm one industry could do to the other. They should have spoken with the ghost of William Ladner. The one major fight he had with his salmon-canning brother involved the latter's dumping of salmon guts straight into the river. This led to regular outbreaks of typhoid fever and made it impossible for William's cattle to drink from the sloughs. It's not recorded whether, in his anger, William pointed out to his younger brother that typhoid was also killing people. It's certainly no hyperbole to say that William valued his cattle more than the mostly Native and Chinese cannery workers Thomas's cannery employed, but he would have valued his family and the families of his neighbours' more than his cattle. At least I'm prepared to give him that benefit of the doubt.

Once you're up in its branches, the Douglas fir is not especially hard to climb. Yes, it's pitchy, the bark is rough, the needles are pointy sharp – and then there is the matter of its height. But the branches as they connect to the trunk are a good size for gripping – like lead pipe – and spaced regularly and not widely apart. My fir offered ample opportunities for both fort construction and panoramic views, at least in its lower half. Climbing and hammering and viewing became more difficult towards the peak, which was why the final twenty feet were clean of spikeheads and the wood of Japanese orange crates that we used for walls. Instinctively, from our in-the-flesh knowledge of trees and our appreciation for the craft of previous generations, we understood there was good reason not to press our luck. Children are brave in their way, often eager to rise to a challenge, but rarely are they foolish in the hubristic way of adults. We had climbed breathlessly to an incredible height, surpassing any other ascent possible in the town, and that was enough. We had been caught three-quarters of the way up, in our flimsy fort, in violent windstorms, and shuddered to think what would have become of us had we been foolish enough to attempt the summit.

Thirty feet up and I rest on a favourite strong branch with a smaller branch close by for a handhold. The rain is gusting, the tree sighing and pattering overhead, but already I'm sheltered. Below, the weeping willows are flowing like manes, the street is a watermarked page, the black clusters of the ancient fruit trees – cherry, plum, pear and apple – look blacker than ever. The Taylors' old Lab-shepherd cross, Jiggs, limps along the sidewalk on his way to the butcher's for a bone. All the neighbourhood dogs have daily routines involving food, and some of the local shopkeepers are kind even to strays. The social patterns of the animal and human worlds become clearer from the tree. There goes Mrs. Demosten, shawled against the weather, her almost full-term amble down her front porch steps, along Georgia to Trennant and then Laidlaw, neatly and blackly diverging from Jiggs, who limps all the way to the end of Georgia before cutting into town. Eventually, I will see their two black shapes converge for an instant, as Mrs. Demosten pauses and, with difficulty, bends to scratch the old dog behind the ears. Then their merged black will split like a damp atom, and the day will attend to its material purposes once more.

I climb higher, protected in the hush of the rain, a few drops only touching my cheeks and fingers. I climb out of the nineteenth century and the founding of the town into the history I can still touch, though it rests on a fragile branch and I must inch my way along more carefully. I'm high enough to see the mostly empty grid of streets in the townsite, the calm harbour channel flowing into the drifts and sloughs of the rivermouth where my father makes his living, and, back to the south, the park where the cenotaph sits, a smoke-grey, pyramidal structure chiselled with the names of boys who once looked out from this same vantage point, boys killed on the Somme or at Vimy Ridge. Some of their friends who returned will soon be customers of mine, subscribers to the *Vancouver Sun* which I will start delivering at the age of ten. They too will know this tree and this godlike witnessing of dailiness.

A flock of gulls, grubbier and greyer against the overcast, wing silently by. As always, I'm amazed to see them from above. Each time, I can hardly believe it. Is this why they're silent, because I have stunned them out of their usual screeching hunger? Or do their cries only go down?

I'm near the fort now, a hundred feet up. My hands are scratched, my heart is pounding. But I'm in my own time; everything lies below me in damp, street-lit and wharf-lit vistas, all the abandoned pioneer homes, sinking as if in a flood from my searching gaze, the orchards gone wild around them, gleaming like black fists, the whole flow of the Fraser burbling muddily to the sea and leaving all the lights behind, as if the town had never been, as if the tree was young and the only humans who touched it touched it for different, more wide-ranging purposes, touched it because they knew it their whole lives the way I know it as a boy and will struggle to remember it as a man.

Though I can see far to the blurry south, where the local reserve of the Coast Salish lies against the salt tides of the Pacific, though I have climbed through a history that includes them as guides and cannery workers and commercial fishermen and town drunks, I have not touched, nor cannot touch, the twenty feet of fir that once belonged to them, not as a possession but as a fellow life form that, in its richness, provided for others. And here the whole linear nature of my ascent breaks down, for this tree does not belong to our sense of history and place at all. From a hundred feet up, everything becomes clearer and murkier. I might be peering out of the branches into the flow of the Fraser itself, the needles numerous as the salmon once were, and the flesh of the fir and the flesh of the salmon and the flesh of human beings richly woven into something I could access only in the dim, salt-longing apprehensions of childhood.

The wood of the Douglas fir was used to make spear handles, harpoon shafts, spoons, dipnet poles, harpoon barbs, salmon weirs, and halibut and cod hooks. Its pitch was used for sealing the joints of harpoon heads, gaffs and fishhooks, also for caulking canoes. Torches were made from the pitchy heartwood. The Comox people even prepared dogfish by stuffing it with rotten, powdered fir and burying the fish in a pit lined with the same material.

None of these uses killed the tree, or any other species of tree: the cedars, hemlocks and yews. Mostly windfallen trees or limbs supplied enough material. The living giants, like this shimmering anomaly of my boyhood, continued to grow.

How old was it? My culture would have cut it and counted the rings, just as scientists can tell the age of a salmon by counting the rings on its scales. But the exact age of the tree didn't matter to the boy I was. In 1969, a hundred feet from the surface of the earth, the river to the north still rippling with giant spring salmon and sturgeon, the ocean to the west still humming with the secret lives of rock and ling cod and crab and abalone, the town directly below in gentle decline, one muddy boot still in the nineteenth century, the other a shoe being shined for the glossy, modern, fast-food corporate future, I knew, in my body, exactly everything I needed to know to live in an intimate way with the place of my being, and did not know anything about the massing forces of the world that would kill that intimate knowledge in me.

* * *

We avoid death, we refuse to consider it, we say with the utmost confident good sense, "No sense dwelling on the past," we persist in believing our lives are played out in a simple linear fashion. But what companion is more faithful than death, and how can any thinking, feeling person forget, dismiss or otherwise gloss over the absences we carry that are, in fact, shining presences?

Jiggs has been dead for decades, shovelled into the moist delta loam not deep enough for human graves. Pepper, my dog, the same. All the dogs of my boyhood, whose shadows partnered mine, whose necks I hung my arms around, whose laughing, panting faces were expressions of my heart's deepest joy, are gone, yet I still see them, vividly. Mrs. Demosten, who bent in her ninth month to scratch an old, limping dog behind the ears, gave birth to a mongoloid baby (for that was the term used in those days). Only a few years before, only a few years after the birth of my stillborn brother, she lost an infant son to disease. Ten years after I watched her from the Douglas fir, her third son, Archie, the spitting image of the young Elvis, a boy my sister's age, a Golden Gloves champion who taught me how to box and catch a football, drowned up the coast, caught in the bunk of a seiner when a rogue wave hit. Back home, in

Ladner, his young wife was nearly full-term with the boy who'd grow up to look just like him. Am I, growing older, a father of three myself, to unburden my mind of what Mrs. Demosten's pain can teach me of gratitude?

The fir was cut down in 1974 to make way for an "urban renewal" project. I didn't see the event because I was in school at the time. The tree was there, then it wasn't. At least not to be touched and climbed. Its presence lingered for a while, though. I could walk past and see its exact height and width, smell the wet branches and the pitch. Then even that faded. The urban renewal project swallowed up several blocks of surrounding neighbourhood, including the Demostens' property. They moved a mile away, across Chilukthan Slough. Their house, meanwhile, was bought by our next-door neighbour, moved across the street (I didn't see this either, as I was sitting in a row of desks), and attached to his old, crumbling Victorian house to be rented out to his divorced sister-in-law and her two children. A few years later, I'd receive my first kiss from the daughter of that divorcee, in the bedroom where Mrs. Demosten must have cried herself to sleep long night after long night, waking to tend to the needs of a child who would always need her, and trying not to think of the one who never would again.

Our culture, our tree-cutting, death-denying, conformity-loving culture, shrugs and says, *In the past. Move on*, says *The future is farmed salmon, not wild salmon*, says terrorism watches us from behind every veil. I sit in the fort of my forty years of life, seeking shelter from the poisoned rain, and watch Jiggs and Mrs. Demosten exchange across species the briefest of touches and warmth. I carve from the wood of the fir a hook to catch the death that enriches my life, for the only fishing is the night-fishing, the three o'clock in the morning set, with the river dropping fast and the snags reaching up. How to protect the past that trails from me, how to bring it in so I can return to the towhead and set once more, with greater knowledge and sensitivity for the weathers of the task, is the real work of the years to come.

XIV

IT IS NOT SO FAR from Edney Booth Ladner's pointing finger to my childhood. As the great blue heron flies, only a couple of dozen prehistoric wingbeats. In history's textbook measurements, a century of great innovation and violence: electricity, automobiles and airplanes, vaccinations, wars, hydrogen bombs, holocausts. In terms of the human heart, Mrs. Ladner could speak to Mrs. Demosten and my mother and several other women of the town of homesickness and hope and grief, the gesture of her broken spirit could point me to a bible printed in her day and filled with the faded ink record of my ancestors' joys and sorrows.

What was the faith in my home? The family bible – its thin pages gilt-edged, its leather cover scarred like whaleskin, the onionskin over its vibrant illustrations torn in places – held no place of visible honour and was not regularly referred to. Instead, it was kept, swaddled like the baby Jesus, at the bottom of a large cedar chest, my mother's hope chest – this was partly for preservation purposes, but largely due to lapsed religious feeling. My father was not a Christian – as far as the supernatural was concerned, he favoured the Natives' faith in a spirit residing in nature – and my mother deferred to his views without conflict or even personal struggle. Religion caused no rift between them and therefore no turmoil for us. I attended Sunday School at the United Church for a while, was sent home for throwing playdough at the stained glass, and never returned. One summer, I attended a Christian Bible Camp run by the Dutch Reformed Church. From this, I was never sent home, though with another boy, I fell afoul of the camp leader for releasing pocketfuls of grasshoppers in the classroom after the lunch break. Our keenness to experience a biblical plague of locusts was not appreciated. In the end, my mother's commitment to my religious education Petered, Pauled and Johned out, but not before I had been shown the family bible several times, and not before the rhythmic language and the compelling stories had dropped their leadlines into my imagination.

Did Christ not resemble, after all, many of the fishermen hanging around the waterfront? The full beard, the dark eyes, the woundedness and isolation, the nakedness to the elements, and the abiding faith in a force that most others didn't understand. And then Christ was always by the water. Why, he even consorted with fishermen, and they were good to him. "Whoever the fuck that peckerhead is," I could imagine them saying in the Ladner vernacular, "his heart's in the right place and he talks some sense." It was exactly the way Ladner's fishermen felt about Homer Stevens, our town's lone vocal Communist and president of the United Fisherman and Allied Workers Union. Having different views from the masses didn't matter so long as your views were backed up by hard-won experience. Christ was a carpenter kicked around by the boss Romans, and Homer, the grandson of a Greek fisherman and Salish woman, spent a year in jail for defying a government anti-strike order. Two peas in a pod, as far as sticking up for your principles went.

Christ was never a problem for me. In the nineteenth-century painting in the family bible, he looked a lot like my brother Rick, who in 1969 stood on his flimsy plank of plywood, barechested, longhaired and longbearded, hauling in two hundred heavy fathoms by hand as the rapid exodus from fresh to salt threatened to overwhelm him. But then, the only haloes of light associated with Rick were the shining rims the hourglass-shaped beer glasses he brought home from the Ladner Hotel left on all the tabletops and counters in the house. The painted Jesus, by contrast, stood in a roseate glow, his eyes dewy as if his net had just sunk from the weight of the sockeye in it. I felt I knew him, and that meant more than believing in what he said. The Bowlings, as a rule, tended to distrust authority and ideas and put their faith in individuals. As long as you were good to your word and weren't a scab during the almost annual strikes in the fishery, you were, as my father and his generation would put it, "Okay in my books."

And my father's only books were fishbooks, the tallies of his catches each year. My mother's only book, in those days, was her inherited, beaten bible the weight of an Adams River sockeye. Two great bloodsoaked records, of the history I could still experience and of the history I could hear, what Edney Booth Ladner experienced and what she heard, in the same place by the same river, her god a human god, and mine the gods whose blood her husband tramped home on his boots, little crescents shining on the wooden sidewalks until the rain washed them away. It is, perhaps, a greater distance than I thought. She would kiss the hem of Christ's garment. I'd renounce him and every other human god if it would save the salmon. Her finger points to the bible, mine slips under the gill of a spring. In this secular, commercial age, we're both losing.

* * *

A teeming rain, the streets flowing in clear braided ropes, the eyes of the puddles opening everywhere. The grey-black clouds scud and roll, fast as the silts of a run-off tide at freshet. It's dusk at midday. Headlights and streetlamps shine fuzzily. Gulls screech past. Dogs sulk in their wet stink. The telephone poles have darkened, as if flushed with blood. The wind-whipped branches of the cottonwoods and silver birches and maples bend, releasing a leaf every few seconds. Along the river, the tan-coloured reeds arch into croquet hoops, the black cannery pilings shift and creak, rise like Easthope pistons, a few moored skiffs strain at their ropes. On the Prairie Drift, the black-hooded deadheads duck under, then rise up with fierce soundless pleas.

Rain pearls in my brother's beard, drips off the end of his nose. His poncho, heavy as lead, is nailed to him with raindrops. He opens his mouth and shouts, but the words don't reach us. We're climbing slowly to the towhead, he's drifting rapidly to the slough mouth. Is he in trouble? No. He's not rushing about. Probably he's just asking how we made out on that set. Typically, neither he nor my father use shortwave radios to communicate; technology is to be avoided when at all possible. Dad shouts back for him to be careful. He doesn't worry about Rick as much as Mom does, but rough weather makes him cautious, especially when the river's running fast. He's extra attentive to me, for example, looking up from his work more often to check that I'm still there. His black floater jacket is shining wet like a city street. He wears a hunter's cap, with the bright orange part folded out. Ash and smoke stream from his cigarette. He blinks into the rain.

I'm in the open cabin doorway, a foot down on the top step. As my mother would say about my condition, "You're sopping wet." My plastic windbreaker simply soaks up the rain and channels the excess onto my pants. The big orange lungs of the lifejacket are a deep, heavy red. My face is damp. If the storm had started before the opening, I might have had to stay home. So, despite the cold, I'm grateful to be on the river. After all, a storm is dangerous and exciting and there's a genuine thrill in struggling against the elements. And the salmon don't mind; they like a good storm. Especially the Adams River sockeye, the late returns of which we're still catching. The Adams like to mass at the mouth of the river, then rush in when the water level's high enough for them. They take a good rain for encouragement. So how can a fisherman be discouraged by it?

It's hard going against the chop. Our mast chains clink, the bow cleaves the swells and tosses up spray. The river and sky run like molten pewter. Setting is tricky. The wind catches the web of the net and hooks it over the wooden rollers. While Dad unhooks it, the wind and current conspire to turn the bow downriver, so he has to increase the gas when he grabs the wet wheel and yanks the boat around. There's a danger of getting net-in-the-wheel – when the meshes wrap around the propeller – which is a serious problem, what the fishermen call a "jackpot." If you can't unhook it with your long aluminum pike pole or failing that, cut it loose, sometimes by diving under, you'll have to be towed in and put up on the boat ways at Massey's machine shop. So Dad's a blur of motion in the stern, tossing out web and leadline, hitting the gas lever beside the drum, jerking the wheel, and occasionally glancing at me to make sure the wind and swells haven't thrown me overboard. Every ten seconds, a mesh catches on the button of his sleeve and he has to perform a quick wizard-like flourish to free himself. Rarely, he has to step off the drum pedal to do this. Fishermen have been known to go out with their nets, sometimes drowning in the process. Or they've been snagged going the other way and have been wrapped around their own drums and strangled, their eyeballs bursting red from the pressure. Dad is just as careful as he can afford to be.

Once the net is out, we leave the engine running since we'll be picking up again in a few moments. And then, Dad has to keep the boat off the net, hoping that no web is hanging so far ahead of where the corkline lies that he'll run over it. His concentration is as fierce as that of the big salmon clunking into the stern every eight fathoms once we begin picking up again. But for now, I see him, his grizzled profile serious against the violent sky above Ladner, his mouth expending only breath as he has no time for a cigarette. Rain drips off his nose and chin. He watches the net with an intensity that will not admit any other consideration. It's an experience I'll only know years later when writing a poem, moments of time elimination, the world vanishing, or rather, condensing to the one immediate task. My father will die before I ever speak of this analogy to him. I suspect he would not have understood it. While it's possible to watch a gillnet fisherman study his net and to feel the waves of focused energy flowing off him, it's not possible to watch a poet gnawing the bones of his words and feel the same energy. Or, if it is possible, few can access the nature of the energy. Why is that man staring so hard at that page? It's not as though there's a net there in serious danger of being torn to shreds. No, not a real net or a real river. Only shadows on the walls of Plato's cannery, borrowing the smell of salmon and human blood and sweat.

The day darkens further. The dogs and sockeye thrash and die. My father and I stand in a swirl of dusk, fish, cloud scud and current. Around us the changed and changing leaves blow, the *Thunderbird* and the *Queen Bee* and the *Driftwood* drift. To the north, Vancouver's neon blinks on, the traffic lights in their spawning colours flash, the office towers empty. To the south, the commuter houses of Ladner wait for their breadwinners to return (in 1969, most houses don't sit empty all day, most children go home to mothers after school). When I go home, I'll be carrying a jack spring hooked by my forefinger, not a crayoned painting of my family in my hand. And my homework will be to remember everything I don't even know I'm destined to lose.

The tide's too low and snaggy. We tie up alongside the *Thunderbird*, anchored at the towhead. Rod Beveridge offers Dad a cup of tea, which is accepted. The rain's stopped so we stay on deck. Talk flows between the hatches. Mr. Beveridge is an Englishman in his early sixties, a big man with something of Captain Hook or Long John Silver about him. Six-foot-four, broad-shouldered, dark-skinned and broken-nosed, he belongs to an older, more rugged England still clinging to its time-shrouded Saxon roots. He could be Gabriel Oak or Jude or any of the strong, brooding heroes from the novels of Thomas Hardy. Except he's here, anchored on the Prairie Drift, pouring himself red wine as thick as salmon blood out of a great glass jug and grinning in the sheer contentment of the social occasion. For he is an Englishman in some direct ways, including a fondness, even a mania, for "tea." He has given my father a mug of Earl Grey flavoured with evaporated Pacific milk and something from a smaller glass bottle, while I receive a much sweetened and foaming hot chocolate. Now he speaks of the tide and the wind and the likely behaviour of the salmon, calmly, with just a faint trace of a Norfolk accent, and I can't look away. Not only is Mr. Beveridge an imposing size, but he wears a bushy black beard streaked with white and his eyes shine a rare cold grey, as if he's steeping in a coastal fog right up to the level of his expression. Sometimes, he turns his gaze on me, still grinning, and I feel a chill that is not fear, for I know he is not a man to fear. He is, simply put, the king of the river's gentlemen fishermen, which is why he and my father get along so well. Neither is hungry in the classic capitalist sense – there's as big a difference between Thomas Ladner's and Rod Beveridge's kind of Englishman as there is between my father and W.A.C. Bennett, the progress-obsessed Social Credit premier in charge of 1969 British Columbia. Over time, the similarities and differences between Mr. Beveridge and my father will become clearer, as I learn more about their lives, the portraits attaining real clarity only after they're gone.

As a small boy, though, I know enough about the master of the *Thunderbird* to be slack-jawed in his presence. He lives alone in a trailer on the dyke, for instance, and rarely ventures from it, even refers to his property as Shangri-la. He comes by the Hardy legacy honestly enough too, his past touched with tragedy. Grief-stricken at the loss of his beloved wife twenty years earlier, he has chosen never to remarry, which meant raising his two daughters alone, much to the disapproval of a few moral arbiters in town who at least made sure he enrolled them in school. In his darkness and strength and solitude, he seems like one of the old cannery pilings grimly persevering along the riverbanks, except he's not grim; there's a twinkle in the grey eyes, especially when he's telling a story, for he's a great man for talking when he "has a mind for it," as my mother says. He leans towards me now.

"Are you wondering about this face of mine, lad? Why it's so pretty?" His lips glisten red and full against the borders of his beard. I glimpse a broken tooth. "I used to do a spot of boxing in the war. And then I toppled off a motorbike and that put another bend in the road." He lays a fleshy forefinger along his bumpy nose, then raises it to scratch his large brow from which his long dark hair is slicked straight back.

An engine growls downriver. Mr. Beveridge narrows his gaze.

"I'll just put the kettle back on," he says, and stoops into the cabin.

A moment later, another gillnetter ties up alongside and a tall, thin man in a knitted wool toque steps aboard the *Thunderbird.* I recognize him as Jack Brophy, though I don't see him often. He's a policeman in Vancouver when he's not fishing, and there's something edgy in his manner that makes me nervous; perhaps it's just knowing that he owns a revolver, which is somehow dangerous in a way that a shotgun isn't.

Over us, the grey clouds break apart swiftly, like ice floes in a current. The wind increases, blows a smell of damp earth and mulch off the nearby silt island.

Once Mr. Beveridge re-emerges, looking much like the illustrations of Polyphemus bending out of his cave in the book of Greek myths I have at home, the men speak of the weather and the tide.

Suddenly Mr. Brophy's expression darkens. He takes off his toque and wrings it in his hands.

"Same tide, same time of year, I caught that body," he says, looking away. Ten seconds pass, during which the palm of my hand that holds the mug is the only warm part of me.

"Just down off Wilkie's float. I thought it was just a jacket at first."

Mr. Brophy takes a long swallow of milky, mysteriously flavoured tea.

"Till I caught a whiff of it."

My father clears his throat while I try my best to appear not to be listening.

"I damn near upchucked," Mr. Brophy continues quietly. "But I had to keep picking. I just hoped it would slide free. Course, then I got to thinking about the poor bugger's family. So I went easy, pulling by hand, like it was a big spring. But damned if it didn't come loose. So I grabbed the pike-pole – instinct, you see – and tried to hook it before the tide – and it was really boiling – took it away."

He exhales slowly, his bottom lip pursed.

"I wish I hadn't done that."

Again he falls silent, his Adam's apple pumping like a heart in his long neck. In a voice grey as the scud over us, he says, "I pulled the arm right off. Then the body rolls over, a bit of the head pops up, blond the hair was, and under it goes." Mr. Brophy sniffs, wipes his dripping nose with the back of his hand, pulls his toque back on.

I feel Mr. Beveridge's cold eyes on me as Mr. Brophy's question suddenly hangs in the dusk:

"And what in the name of Christ was I going to do with the arm?"

Mr. Beveridge grumbles deep in his throat. "On the subject of the tide," he booms, "she seems to be slowing. I think I'll just percolate out for a set. Time, gentlemen," he ends with a grin.

The interruption works. Once the *Thunderbird* percolates away, my father tries a new subject with Mr. Brophy, duck hunting, and the detached arm is left to my imagination. Years later, when I know the rest of the story – that the arm also slipped free, as if still living and seeking its body, and that the incident kept Mr. Brophy from fishing for a year – I'll not realize with what tact the ending was kept from me. Only recently, after learning more about Rod Beveridge, have I come to appreciate the complexity of character of the king of the gentlemen fishermen.

He served for thirteen years in the military, as RAF ground crew in the desert, in Cairo, Gibraltar, and then in the army in India during the death throes of the Raj, where he witnessed several beheadings. He even kept an illegal photographic record of one of these deaths, which he enjoyed showing to other fishermen, though I never saw it. And yet, despite his long service to the Crown, he was no great patriot. When his twin sons reached sixteen, he brought the family to Canada so the boys wouldn't have to do compulsory military time. Once demobbed, he never again wore leather footwear, for leather was standard military issue and he wanted to put all that restriction of independence behind him. Near Toronto, he worked in the foundries of Alcan, sweating and grunting alongside the Italian immigrants whose swarthiness matched his own. The work suited him and it paid well. Then his wife fell sick, and no matter how much money they spent, including for trips to the Mayo Clinic, the cancer killed her. Numb with grief, unable to bear staying where she died, he bought a new trailer, hitched it to his truck, and, with his eight- and eleven-year-old daughters in tow, drove across the country, aiming to settle on Vancouver Island.

However, on reaching the Pattullo Bridge at New Westminster, and having no money to pay the toll, he looked around, saw some fishboats unloading at a cannery wharf, and decided to become a fisherman. A little farther west, at Ladner, he knew he'd found his home. After all, weren't these marshy lowlands with river and nearby sea just like Norfolk, except without the old country's stifling social structure? Here a man could have room to breathe and be himself. Here he could live simply and put his adventurous, romantic, nomadic youth behind him. He'd done his boxing and motorbike riding, he'd seen the African desert and the hills of India; it was time to settle down, but on nobody else's terms. Military service had given him a distaste for rules and grief had driven him into a vow of solitude; he would not be an employee or a husband again.

So he fished the Prairie Drift, anchored often to have tea, hunted in the marshes, let the game hang outside his trailer until the maggots crawled and he knew the flesh was ripe enough, drank at the Legion, raised his daughters, rolled his own cigarettes, mended his nets with a Clotho-like perfection, and generally inhabited his own flesh with a very un-English sense of ease.

But it was not his Englishness or absence of it that captivated me; it was his fidelity to the memory of his wife. There was something at once deeply moving and yet haunting about his chosen solitude. He lifted marriage out of social convention and tied it to something more basic. Not for him did the funeral baked meats coldly furnish forth the marriage tables, not for him remarriage one year after burial, as in the case of Thomas Ladner. Rod Beveridge was grief carved into a totem of commitment, and he gatekeeped not only the entrance to the Prairie Drift and to Ladner Harbour, but the entrance to a whole way of relating to life and love and money that was rare thirty-five years ago and is even rarer now. Who else named a boat the *Min-Max* – minimum work for maximum production? Who else so proudly, and from such a position of lived strength, resisted the expectations of the society around him?

There were others, but not one was exactly like Mr. Beveridge. And that's the salient point: as late as the 1970s, the coast of British Columbia was inhabited with character, independence, human wildness. The political rhetoric and corporate marketing about democracy, freedom, individuality, had not yet been raised to its current enslaving frenzy; people could still exhibit their right to inhabit uniqueness simply by how they chose to live. Freedom was not simply the right to consume as much as the next person, or to wear a certain brand of clothing, or to drive this or that model of car; it was a matter of principle attached to reflection that grew out of hard-won experience. Rod Beveridge did not relish the restrictions of English society, and once he saw that no amount of money could protect what he most cherished, he turned away from materialism. More than that, as my child self could sense as strongly as the brine on the wind, he fished because he loved fishing, not the money it brought in. Like many men of that time, often war veterans whose faith in abstract phrases and values had been broken on various battlefields, he had earned the right to touch the wild salmon, for he had retained something of wildness himself. The bureaucrats at the Department of Fisheries and Oceans, the managers of hatcheries and salmon farms, the rich American tourist-anglers, even many of today's commercial fishermen who lack the skills to hang and mend their own nets, have less right to touch the wild. Perhaps this is why they are so intent on killing it. It cannot be coincidence that the rise of aquaculture in BC has paralleled the decline of the independent fisherman. A bureaucrat can manage a farmed fish and a farmed man a lot easier than he can ever manage a wild salmon or a Rod Beveridge. The wild is an embarrassment to the un-wild, the truly free offends the caged. How are you going to live your life?

The river gives an arm to you. Hold it. Bear on your shoulders the full weight of the stars. Consider the magnitude of an existence that can change, and will change, despite your careful plans. Then feel the arm pull free and live with its limp pointings back at you as you sleep and work and make love. That's our human wildness. We have a right to it, as the wild salmon has a right to its spawning beds. The arm points back and forward; it's the dead's, the unborn's, it's yours. It points with the urgency of the returning salmon, and you'll follow it, eyes open or eyes glazed, blood pumping or blood slack. As late as 2007, we still have that choice.

XV

THE ARM POINTS BACK, upriver. It points at history, at the several dozen bodies of railroad workers who plunged into the gorges of the Fraser Canyon in 1912 when the Canadian Northern, racing against a deadline to build an unnecessary third rail route to the coast, illegally blasted tons of rock into the river at Hell's Gate, resulting in British Columbia's most dramatic environmental crime. The men hang over the raging waters, then slip off the rocks and cry out. Few hear that echo in British Columbia, even today. But like the bat and the whale, humans are the only mammals who possess sonar capabilities. Unlike the bat and the whale, however, humans can choose to turn off the sonar, which we do with regularity, especially where mere workers are concerned. And when many of those workers are Indians and recent immigrants, well, official history doesn't even look for the on button.

Life was miserable in the railroad camps. Men who couldn't speak English and other men whose great-grandparents had helped Simon Fraser make it through the perilous, steep and rapid-torn Fraser Canyon in 1808 lived on such meagre rations and in such shabby, stinking shacks, that many tried to walk away from what was basically a slave relationship to the railroad labour contractors. This situation is exactly that of the China houses and the Chinese cannery crews. In fact, the Chinese would have been suffering in those railroad camps too, as they had done throughout the nineteenth century, if Richard McBride, BC's premier at the time, hadn't made a secret agreement with the Canadian Northern Railway bosses to ban the

Chinese from the construction work. BC was in a boom phase of development following upon the great wealth built up by a handful of individuals who had expertly exploited the province's natural resources in the previous decade. Chief among these exploiters was the monopolistic and always thriftily plotting cabal of the Fraser River salmon canners.

But that's down at the mouth of the river where the dead bodies of the railroad workers haven't drifted yet. Back up in the canyon, where four thousand workers are living their indentured existence, attempts to escape meet mostly with failure. After all, where is there to go? On one flood tide, a desperate crew of sixty-four men, speaking several languages plus the one universal language of exploited worker misery in the bloodshot eyes and jutting cheekbones, set out on a hastily constructed raft for the coast. They were never seen again, except perhaps by the giant sturgeon lying in their deep channels on the riverbottom. Others died on the job, usually as a result of blasting accidents. Inexperience combined with pressure from the crew chiefs made for a deadly combination. The Indians, whose ancestors had traversed the most dangerous cliffs of the canyon for generations on a series of dangling deer-hide ropes, tree bough scaffolds and bridges made of long poles and tied together with twigs, possessed no inherited skills to protect themselves from exploding dynamite. Their fragmented bodies dropped into the cauldron of seething waters just the same as those of the eastern European races, their disembodied arms pointed the same way to the sea. For the premier and the railroad promoters, men and rocks were alike; for the sake of getting the job done in time for McBride to use the new line as part of an election campaign, everything could be sacrificed to the canyon. And that everything, of course, included the salmon.

1913 was the big year of the four-year salmon cycle, and expectations were high in the canning industry. This meant, as usual, that the canners, with the full support of the provincial and federal governments, got together to figure out ways to keep the price of fish low, to keep the fishermen divided on racial lines, and to block any possible labour organizing. If this sounds a lot like today, that's because little has changed except the companies and governments are even slicker at shaping public opinion in their favour.

But overlook for a moment the indentured and mistreated Chinese and Native cannery workers and the Native men who had been forced out of the fishery once the canners no longer needed their expertise. Focus instead on the fishermen: they, at least, were independent? Oh yes, they were free to sell their fish to the highest bidder, but since the bidders were extremely well-versed in conspiring to maintain a uniform, low price for the product, independence was just another word for employee, which was often just another word for slave labourer.

So, in the summer of 1913, the IWW (or Wobblies) were fomenting strike action amongst the cannery crews and fishermen, the canners were plotting to keep the price for fish low, the police on orders from the provincial government were rounding up the Wobblies, and fifty million sockeye were speeding towards the mouth of the Fraser.

Meanwhile, at Hell's Gate, an already narrow passage upriver through the canyon had been narrowed to just a few yards by the blasted rock. The river thrashed its way through with a force that would throw returning salmon in the air like dynamited Indians. The situation that awaited the salmon and the Interior aboriginal groups whose lives depended on them was as tragic as the situation that awaited western civilization. And the blithe unconcern in the face of it was equally monumental.

The salmon hit the mouth in full force on the last day of July. The shoreworkers and fishermen, who had clearly been listening to the Wobblies, struck. The major canners used scab fishermen and trap-caught Point Roberts fish for a while, but the walkout of the cannery crews completely flummoxed them. Some independent canners offered the striking Japanese fishermen twenty cents per fish, which was five cents more than the scabs were getting, so the Japanese accepted. But some whites and the few Natives still in the fishery stayed off the river. All was confusion, as usual. The Native women returned to work at their old pay scale, while the Japanese women were replaced with "Hindoos." The Wobbly organizers tried to keep the different elements of the workforce unified while they avoided police capture. And the salmon flooded in.

In fact, they returned in such numbers that they overwhelmed the strike. The American traps and the scab fishermen soon caught enough to feed the gaping maw of the cannery monster, which forced the strikers to capitulate and return to work. The price of fish dropped to fifteen cents. Scows were overloaded and dumped when their contents began to rot. Overnight, the carnage and the canners' profits set new records.

And at Hell's Gate, on August 5, just as the strike was ending at the mouth of the river, BC's fishery commissioner J.P. Babcock was gaping down from the rocky cataract at an astonishing sight. A school of salmon sixteen kilometres long was massed in the foaming waters downstream of the Gate. In a panic, Babcock headed upstream. The news was even worse than he feared. Only a few salmon had been caught by the Indians, only a few had returned to his beloved hatchery project at Seton Lake.

Yet a full month passed before Babcock accepted that the canyon was blocked. Only once the pinks had joined the sockeye in the mass below the Gate did he contact the federal fisheries minister with the news of the disastrous situation:

> Through rock and gravel slides consequent on railway construction, Fraser Canyon above Yale practically impassable to salmon with the result that ninety percent of sockeye cut off from four-fifths of river during entire season.

Babcock urged the feds to send an engineer to blast a passage for the fish. Ottawa, as Ottawa is wont to do, moved glacially. When an engineer did arrive, he blasted a few channels and left quickly. A few fish made it upstream, but dropping water levels soon left the channels dry. The salmon kept being flung back, like cards in a gold-rush poker game that ends in a brawl. The river was black with live, dead and dying fish for miles. Hundreds of thousands of fish, then millions. As Babcock described the scene:

> the air was foul with the stench arising from the dead fish that covered the exposed parts of the river. The shelving bars and banks were covered with great numbers of seagulls and crows feeding on the eyes of the dead sockeye . . . which were so numerous that the appetite of the birds was satisfied without turning over the bodies to obtain the other eye.

In one of the most painful sentences ever connected to British Columbia, Babcock concluded, with an unblinking conciseness worthy of any poet, *the living were not spawning and the dead were unspawned.*

Death and rot at the mouth, death and rot at the Gate of Hell, and terrific profit for the canners. So terrific that the federal fisheries inspector at work on the river, a man named Cunningham whose real job was serving the interests of the canners, brazenly ignored an order from Ottawa to put a halt to the harvest. Indeed, he and other officials ridiculed the idea that the salmon were having trouble reaching their spawning grounds. Right into October, it was business as usual at the mouth.

At Hell's Gate, in desperation, Babcock and several Native helpers blasted a few channels for the fish, allowing perhaps a million to escape. No doubt, those Native workers, as they set explosives and cleared rock and clambered along the steep cliffs, thought of relatives and friends who'd been dynamited and swept downriver just the year before, their bodies somewhere far out at sea, drifting with the last of the returning salmon.

Meanwhile, in the festering sunlight on the salmon-gut clotted tides off Ladner and Steveston, weary workers raised and lowered their fish picks as they heaped more bodies on the planks, the heavy tramping of exhausted humans echoed along the stinking moonlit boardwalks, two dozen races saw a river of blood in their dreams, and a few dozen men narrowed their eyes in the cigar smoke and tried to make out the little black figures of their profits on the unrolled maps of commerce as they already plotted the next year's assault.

1913 was a tragic year in British Columbia, but, growing up, I never heard anything about it, just as I never heard anything about the history of my place. The world was always more important, and still is – the world that goes to war in Europe or the Middle East, the world where men count weapons and human bodies instead of salmon. But when a person gets older, the world gets clearer, and what is seen is seen with the same pair of eyes.

In 1915, my grandfather was hit with a shell fragment and thrown into the bottom of a trench. His boots quickly filled up with blood. He would have died, just another casualty of the Great War, if another soldier hadn't happened to see him, then carry him on his shoulders to an aid station. Because my grandfather lived, my father lived, and because my father lived, I live now, and can write down that the war wound in my grandfather's back was the size of a salmon's eye and the darkness of both is a mystery shrouded with the tragic imperatives of industry, science and greed. I can stand before the cenotaph in Ladner and read the names and wonder why there are no names etched into the totem pole outside the museum. I can remember my boyhood in the place of genteel decay and see with an almost blind rage the European tour of 1910 and 1911 that Thomas Ladner and his worker-hating son, Leon, enjoyed together before the son returned to take up a law career and eventually reap the benefits of all the growth stimulated by war production. I can hear the same powers now dismissing me as a Communist because I have my eyes open at last and my tongue working in conjunction with them.

The torn arm of the rivermouth points forward and back. The corpses, all the useless, innocent corpses of the world, cram the banks from the Gate of Hell down, but they are not there, not in the Fraser River, there is no history there, no myth, no poetry. Who do you think you are, boy of the sloughs and marshes, sucking on the end of your pen, writing poems in what one critic referred to as an "unlikely Lake District."

I've known the answer all my life. I knew it when the first big spring tumbled over the rollers, I knew it when the ghost of Edney Booth Ladner moaned her grief out of the cheese-clothed walls, when my mother sang the story of Bloor and Ossington and my father waited at the corner of Alive and Dead and I walked up to him and touched his eyes closed with these fingertips. I knew it on the deck of the *Nola J* when the creatures of the silt revealed their ancient mysteries to the air and I knew it when the great blue herons cracked open their fine parchments of flight above the flowing passageways and the cracked pavements and I knew it when the pages of the books fell away like flensed meat and words gave me the beginning I would need to understand the diminishment of everything and the triumph of the diminished. I've known this answer all my life, but speaking whatever truth we come to, whatever truth is given us, takes time, and, in the end, has little to do with us alone.

The Hell's Gate crime devastated the salmon runs for three generations, but the slaughtering mentality had taken hold in our world long before then. Who did the canners on the Fraser sell their packs to? Mostly to the English. Why? Because in England, home of the Industrial Revolution, the salmon rivers had been dammed, filthied, and emptied of salmon decades before. How much of a staple of the British diet was BC's canned salmon? It even formed a part of the soldier's ration, those soldiers marching away in the millions to defend the property rights of the few, those soldiers who once laboured along the railroad tracks or in skiffs bobbing at the mouth of the Fraser. Like it or not, Ladners Landing is part of the world, part of history, part of the present and the future. It isn't even a likely district of lakes; it's a wet corner of farm fields and pavement beside a silty, polluted river once filled with salmon.

People live and die here. Children are raised to adults. I like to think that some of those children, at least, will bypass their culture and come to these words.

* * *

There's one body I still haven't mentioned, one anonymous corpse drifting through the Fraser Canyon out to sea. It's the body of a Native who, in 1914, while the European earth was being shelled into a wasteland, drowned trying to save the future of his people. All through 1914, in fact, an engineer from the federal Department of Marine and Fisheries, John McHugh, used Native labour in a struggle to preserve the salmon runs for the future. Working in torrential autumn downpours, McHugh and his workers battled the chilling waters to blast rocks out of the river even as the Canadian Northern Railway crews continued to blast at the rockbed above them. Many of the Natives were injured by falling rock, and one was killed, his body borne rapidly downstream as if in pursuit of the dead railroad workers of 1912. Meanwhile, the heavy rains caused landslides throughout December as the CPR got into the act too, double-tracking and dumping rock straight into the river near Yale. Finally, in February, Canadian Northern blasting sent half a mountainside into the river, again blocking it.

The next summer, as McHugh's workers dangled from ropes to drill and hammer a fragile wooden flume into place and give the salmon a passage over the blockade, other Natives dipnetted and carried salmon, one by one, over the slippery, jagged rocks, often losing their footing, the fish sliding out of their grips. One man, one sleek, silver life in his arms, running to save the future of his people. Another man, a corpse, already food for the crabs. It is hard not to see them as the same man, and that man as representative of the native populations of North America. It is hard, seeing that image, to accept the racism in what remains of the fishing community still preyed upon by opportunistic politicians. Who, after all, paid the biggest human price for Hell's Gate? The Interior

Natives who, deprived of their food supply, starved to death by the hundreds in the winter of 1913? Or all the Natives of BC who had their fishing rights immediately withdrawn under the guise of conservation by governments who made a priority of the cannery cabal's ongoing profit margins? Once you know this history, it becomes much harder to complain about today's Native fishermen receiving privileges. Then again, where salmon fishing is concerned, all the workers are losers to some degree. Even my father, who made a living without having to bow to a boss, ultimately lost to the canneries and the government. If you consider what he earned from what he caught, what the canners earned from what he delivered, and what successive governments allowed to happen to the salmon and what they're continuing to allow, he and every other worker has lost a great deal.

But awareness of that loss is the first step to victory. A small and only personal victory, perhaps, but it's a triumphant feeling to know your eyes are open and nobody's conning you. "Supernatural BC" is a lie of power. The pioneers as patriarchal builders of community with golden hearts is a lie of power. We need to look those drowned Indians of 1912 to 1914 straight in the eyes, then pick the disregarded past up in our arms and start making our way past the blockading deceptions, for the future's sake.

XVI

I GREW UP IN a Russian village without Russians. Earth smell, starlight, barking dogs, men and women whose hands were intimate with guts and hides, a general peasant sense of fun and flesh-entrenched resignation, faces lonely and scarred as the moon's face, and an unkillable belief in the future. The river and streets of that village remain, several buildings, even the smell of fish, but humans don't inhabit that place in the way they once did. It's spawned out, and the proteins of its decaying feed no one. The harbour's quiet all year, children aren't visible except as faces pressed against minivan glass, and the pioneer orchards and houses were levelled decades ago. Ladner's centre has shifted east. Two large malls border Trunk Road on the eastern side of Chilukthan Slough, itself tame and sluggish now, and these malls form the western edge of the new town centre, which sprawls east past the McDonald's, over the highway, and onto several expensive subdivisions built on once-protected agricultural land.

Many who call Ladner home rarely come into the old townsite; there's little reason to. Vancouver, Richmond, Burnaby: all have more shopping and entertainment choices. But there's a popular seafood restaurant next to the original wharf site at the mouth of the slough, and a popular pub next to that, and a kayak rental service further along, so there is activity. The old downtown, too, is attractive and lively enough. It's quaint, there's a big mural of gulls and whales and fishboats, the municipality recently widened and improved the main street and sidewalks, and there's a sort of faux-heritage style to the new houses built in the surrounding blocks (heritage on acid, as a former childhood neighbour of mine describes it). Hell, I even like the old town. It's a damned sight nicer than the usual North American conglomeration of strip malls, fast food franchises, and imminent pedestrian death. My last time home, just after Thanksgiving, I walked out of my mother's house at the foot of Georgia Street to a refreshing familiarity and a weight of absence that made it feel as if my hands were bearing the ghosts of big salmon.

It was quiet. The stars shone faintly. I could smell the mud of the river and the damp earth below the grass. A strong odour of fish wafted down from the Seven Seas cannery, and I momentarily put out of my mind the fact that these fish had been trucked south from Alaska. The streetlamp at the corner of Georgia and Chisholm hummed dully as it cast its faint yellow, and seemed like an old friend. Much remained intact from 1969. Though the property immediately next door to my mother's house was sand-covered in preparation for the building of four faux heritage houses, the old Buckerfields warehouse, grey as ever, still grandfathered the riverbank, and the other Buckerfields buildings opposite, now occupied by a cycle and kayak shop, hadn't been razed.

Up on the dyke, past the cannery, a large aluminum-sided complex built in the late seventies, there was the same stretch of blackberry bushes leading to where the main netshed and upper wharf once stood. They were gone but nothing had replaced them. I climbed up past the *No Trespassing* sign and looked down at the linked sequence of old floats, mossier and more decrepit and sunken than ever. Only grass grew on them. No boats were moored there. Still, that my father's tie-up spot existed at all! I tried to see myself as a boy walking along in my orange lifejacket to the *Nola J*, with my father just behind, whistling "Santa Lucia" (he never whistled on the boat out of superstition). I could almost do it. This was as close as I was liable to get to a plank of the *Rona*. However, knowing what I did about the collapse of the commercial salmon fishery and about the deaths from cancer and old age of so many fishermen who didn't rely solely on technology to do their jobs, and whose skills had died with them, made complete retrieval impossible. The quiet wasn't of the off-season, but of no-season. Despite the presence of gillnetters and seiners moored on the far bank of the harbour channel, the thriving, active salmon culture of the seventies was extinct. The czar's army had been through.

More and more, my retrieval pulled in ghosts, dew-damp, fog-ponchoed, bloodshot-eyed. And like anyone who passes the age of forty, I couldn't believe so many ghosts belonged to me. I walked on, slowly, stricken with the generosity of the constellations; they at least had not abandoned us. Nor had the river, though we'd weakened it over the decades, changed its flow, caused it to silt over places at a faster rate. Nor had the darkness; we hadn't managed to dispel it entirely with our inventiveness. I was still attached by a thinning piece of flesh to that ancient human world.

Gratitude, however, soon merged into sadness. I walked up the main street towards the totem pole outside the museum, my ghost soldiers marching on gravel behind me, and stopped where the Delta Freight Lines once parked its trucks. A slogan they had on their sides returned to me, as if my burning Halloween punk from decades before had magically scrawled the words on the damp air: *The fish we offer for sale today/ Slept last night in Boundary Bay.*

I looked back expectantly, as if I could see my boyhood self crouched on the ditchbank behind the Demostens' house, a damp face among the overhang of blackberry bushes, my ears picking up the gurgling of the murky water, my eyes widening at the muskrat's approach, its nose lifted and sniffing like a dog's. But the long, broad ditch had been filled in decades before, and muskrats no longer penetrated into the townsite itself. I saw a different scene, an older scene, one that belonged to me every bit as much as what I'd lived.

* * *

The night is killer-whale black, its sides glistening with heavy rain. Thousands of twenty-six-foot-long wooden boats, uncabined, powered by sail and oar, drift in the rivermouth. Fishermen huddle under little canvas tents, their legs sticking out and covered with oilskins. On the cannery-owned boats, they are the second shift, having taken over at 6 pm from the earlier crew. If they are contract, "free" fishermen, they work to the limits of their endurance, for shares. The fleet's a mix, with some Indians still on day wages, because they might want to leave to go hop-picking and because it's cheaper for the canneries. Most fishermen, though, receive a price for each fish.

Here and there, firelight flickers from the cut-off five gallon oilcans the fishermen use for stoves to heat their strong coffee. Otherwise, with the moon and stars clouded over, there's no relief from the blackness. The river's a heavier, faster, more dangerous version of it. From the stern of each boat or flat-bottomed skiff, a gillnet of flax twine, hemp corkline, lathed cedar floats or tin cans, and chunks of lead extends a hundred and fifty fathoms into the almost soundless void. Faintly, cattle low in the distance. Nearer, a seal cries. Out in the gulf, where some of the fleet have ventured to escape the crowded conditions of the rivermouth, a blackfish surfaces and blows vapour, its slick bulk sliding neatly under a bobbing boat where a fisherman sits up, startled, gaping. It's so dark he can't be sure his eyes are open. He wonders again if perhaps he should have fought for space nearer to the canneries.

Back there, between the Gulf and the towns of Steveston and Ladner, another crew stirs to the quick thrashes, then the softer, muffled splashes of struggling salmon. Soon it's like a rainstorm of impacts under the rainstorm. The fisherman speaks excitedly to the puller, the man who handles the oars – sometimes, as in Indian boats, the puller's a woman. The language spoken could be one of dozens in dozens of dialects and accents – Halkomelem, Kwakiutl, Japanese, American Negro, Finnish, Norwegian, Scots, Gaelic, Greek, Austrian, the English of the King James Bible, modified for the Fraser's blunt commerce of bloodspill. But words are few. The puller backs the boat towards the net as the fisherman hauls it in by hand, over wooden rollers if he's lucky enough to have them, stopping constantly to club the struggling fish and pick them out. His muscles strain to breaking. He stands precariously above the flowing black. He could be pulling the gut from a whale. Within minutes, he's drenched with rain, sweat and slime. He shouts to the puller, "She's sunk," and his voice is both frightened and excited. No longer does he carefully pile the corkline to one side, the leadline to the other; he knows his shift is done.

The puller knows it too. When the last fish-swollen fathom is finally humped over the gunwales, he hoists the patchy canvas sail. But the wind's not strong enough, so he heaves into the oars, his back cracking, cheeks puffed out with exertion, raising himself inches from his seat. Hurry, hurry, the fisherman encourages, crouched in a squirming mass of silver, his fingers raw from chafing along the corkline and pulling the top, exposed salmon free. Rain and sweat run in equal currents down both men's faces. "Hurry, hurry," he whispers in a feverish mantra, for he knows that, in the event of a glut, the canners will impose their two-hundred-fish-per-boat limit. But if he and his partner can get their catch delivered to a pot scow or to a wharf before the other fishermen, their earnings will be considerably higher. At eight cents per sockeye, an extra two hundred fish means sixteen extra dollars, a huge sum for a day's work in 1897. *Pull! Pull!*

The river's a frenzy of activity now. The darkness moves like the inside of a burlap sack filled with drowning kittens. Shouts of urgency erupt in myriad tongues. Everyone's hauling in, pulling at oars as if tearing the blackness before them in half, again and again. In its sinews, the Fraser feels the madness of human ambition, the same mad hunger of the gold-rush days of forty years earlier. Some of these sweating, drenched men, grinding splinters out of the ten-foot oars, hunched over the salmon as if each was a sifting pan, are themselves veterans of mining, logging and railroading labours; all understand the avarice of the salmon canners and the riskiness of the fishing trade. If the fish are too few, there's little money; if the fish are too many, the canneries can't keep up, the bottom drops out of the market, and the bonanza of red flesh dissolves into worthless silver scales.

The rain doesn't relent. It seems to have increased with the number of salmon in the silty river. The large pot scows of the canneries fill up, boats crowd around them, jostling, vague figures toss slabs of silver onto other slabs with a dull smack, a cannery tallyman makes pencil marks in a book, coal-oil lanterns burn, grotesque shadows reach over the current as if the reflections of men are hungry to wrest the reflections of salmon from the depths. *Pull! Pull!*

The only hope now is to reach the cannery wharf before the steam-powered tenders tug the scows in. The night's still black, but human voices flay its thickness to strips. The wild gives way to commerce, cold-eyed and edgy, each man for himself, hearts pounding, salmon slippery and subtle as muscles wrapped in their genes. There's nothing gentle or forgiving in nineteenth-century competition; it's survival, life and death. In an economic decline, people can actually starve, die of diseases related to malnutrition. Each dollar is a portion of health. *Pull! Pull!*

Deft fingers peel back the gills, slide the fish free of the meshes. This is the big year of the mysterious four-year sockeye cycle. No one knows why, but the sockeye always return in larger numbers every fourth year, with the following year also strong, the next two weak. No one knows much about the salmon in 1897, except for the Indians, and even their expertise for catching the salmon is becoming less important. In a few years, the Japanese, with the support of the canners, will squeeze them out. The canners like the Japs; they're excellent fishermen, very dependable, and well-behaved. For now, though, the canners still need the Indian women as slimers, and if you take one Indian, you take the lot – kids, mangy dogs and all.

Our puller checks his oars at last. He breathes out, slumps over. The boat drifts. The bank's a clamour of voices and shadows, clunks of wood and slaps of fish flesh. Beyond the wharf, the black maw of the cannery waits in the mud and salmon-close dark.

It won't wait long. The glut is on. The China Boss shouts his crew awake. Dozens of Chinese men stir in the tiny cubicles of China House, a barn-like two-storey building of cheap wood off to one side of the cannery with a red dragon flag flapping from a pole attached to the roof. The interior's a sodden cloud of strong odours: opium smoke, stale cabbage, rice, and the grease, steamed fish and sweat pouring off the workers' drenched blue blouses. A coal-oil lamp hanging from a ceiling beam emits weak yellowish rays. Various masks, prayers and charms float in the half-light. The coolies – for so they are commonly called – roll out of their three-tiered, plywood-plank mattressed bunks and drift into the long, narrow hallway like smoked-out wasps. Mostly peasant bachelors far from the hope of any family, they wear the sallow, haunted expressions of men for whom a woman's or a child's tenderness is a fading memory. As they move, their long queues swing in the smoke like the chains of censers. Many will take their identification number, written on a shipping tag, and, after wrapping their queues around their shaved heads, stick their tag under the braid. Others will stick it in the band of their soft felt hats. The number must be visible, as the white bookkeeper notes each entry and departure of each numbered man on large, ruled timesheets tacked to a salmon box lid. Tallying dead fish and live Chinamen keeps the cannery's ten or so white employees busy all summer. That, and keeping the soldering machines and steam-gauged steel retorts, the guts of the canning process, in working order.

The dark's slowly lifting. Rain drips off the corners of buildings and pearls in the thick blackberry bushes. A soft pocking sounds off the river surface. Voices murmur; it's hard to tell if the attached bodies are close by or far away. The coolies walk along the slick, black planks until they disappear into a dark building where a white man's lips move, heavy with numbers. Wood thunks against wood. Strange pipings and whistles rise out of the sloughs. Fish picks pierce the gills and the tossed fish slap the mounting heap.

Now the Native women – known as *klootchmen* – emerge from the "rancherie," the sloppy conglomeration of makeshift houses along the riverbank where the cannery lets the Indians live. The houses are mere shells with walls of split cedar and roofs of split cedar, rush matting or perhaps scrap tin. There are no foundations or windows, and only a narrow gap in the planks for a door. When food or heat is required, the Indians tend open fires inside their houses; smoke escapes through a hole in the roof. Huge, overturned canoes draped with rush matting lie like mangy animals near the houses. A few smoke-houses – two poles with a rush matting windbreak on one side – stand on their heron's legs in the lifting dark. From behind the row of misshapen houses wafts the stench of urine and excrement.

One by one, the *klootchmen*, some with babies on their backs in slings, emerge from their dwellings, leaving behind a litter of blankets, cooking tins, tribal masks, and several sleeping children and dogs. On the one rickety table sits a five-gallon oilcan filled with tea-coloured oolichan oil going slowly rancid; the Indians use it for butter. Broad-faced, mahogany-skinned, in the flensing dark the women could be taken for the wives of the coolies. But these women have come to the cannery from much nearer – from Vancouver Island, the Queen Charlottes, Washington State, the upper reaches of the Skeena and Nass Rivers to the north. Most arrived with their husbands, children, dogs and chickens in flotillas of twelve or more fifty-foot cedar canoes after weeks of paddling, living on the open water, drifting in the star-perforated dark.

The great maw opens and swallows them too. The coolies change into slitters, fillers and butchers, the *klootchmen* mostly into slimers. Dawn breaks, as if the sky's been slit to reveal the pink flesh inside. Eighteen hours a day without a shift change that slitter works and no one records his number, though he comes and goes and stinks of fish and blood and steam just the same.

Like the river's current, breaking apart and rejoining around sandbars and silt islands, the delta's human flow builds its strands into a slimy, clotted rope. The Indians, Japanese and European fishermen cluster in their laden skiffs and boats at the cannery wharf, the coolies and *klootchmen* take up their positions in the damp butchery, hunch over, wait for the raw fish. Now the boilers devour their cedar chunks and the dragon roars. Now the flywheels whir and the belts whine and the tins clank, now the knives swish and streams of cold water rush down from ceiling pipes in an endless drizzle. Now the steam hisses and rises in a ghostly embrace, wooden wheelbarrows dump endless loads of sockeye until the planked floor's covered with a slippery heap forty feet long and ten feet wide. Now fingers vanish in blurs of motion even as faces harden and eyes fix and mouths close. The roustabout, often a Native boy, spikes a fish through the gills and slides it to the slitters' long U-shaped table. A slitter grabs the fish by the back of the neck and gills and cuts off the head. He slits the belly, scrapes out the satiny guts, cuts off the fins and tail. In a few seconds. His knife slides the waste into a trough in the tabletop that runs into a hopper under the wharf (later, when the tide's right, the hoppers will be emptied into a pot scow and the scow will be towed out to the Gulf and dumped). The remaining fish slab is slid through a small opening in the wooden screen that prevents one slitter from splashing another, where it drops into the sliming tanks of running salted water. A slimer grabs it. With her knife, she scrapes off any loose scales, more thoroughly scrapes the inside, and then, with a stiff, pointed scrub brush, scrubs the inside clean. Next she dips the fish in the salted water and drops it into a hopper for draining. From there, it's on to the hand-operated gang knives where the fish is roughly sectioned. Then, the butchering, so expert and rapid that each of a thirty-man crew could accurately split two thousand fish into the appropriate section size in a ten-hour shift. The knives move invisibly, whirled down by arms that once drove down the spikes for the railroads whose waste would almost destroy the Fraser's great salmon runs just over a decade after this summer night.

Chop, chop – the sixteen-inch knives fling blood to the steaming air, the sections of flesh drop into wooden tubs that are carried – *hurry! hurry!* – to the two, parallel filling tables facing each other. The sections go into a V-groove down the centre of each table. The fillers can put up to three pieces into each salted can, dark skin against the sides. A tight fit is best, but don't overdo it. Enough to satisfy the English buyer, that's all. Ah, but Allee Chinee loves his Chinese puzzle. If he ever smiled while he worked, he'd smile now, in this demonic version of Santa's workshop, where the dolls are cut into chunks and the elves reek of opium and blood.

The filled cans go to the wipers, who use old pieces of gillnet to wipe off any guts or blood attached to the cans. After the wipers, the cappers, who put the tops into position, then the crimpers, who crimp the tops to the bodies of the cans, then on to the soldering machine. Hiss. Drip. Sizzle. Whoosh. The cans clunk down the track from the soldering machine. Expressionless celestials hold a bar of solder and a small acid brush in one hand, a hot copper soldering iron in the other. Muriatic acid in a nearby tin keeps the brushes wet. Fire pots with charcoal fireboxes blaze nearby to heat the soldering irons. Quickly the vent hole in each can is stopped.

On it goes, everything in constant motion, and no speech. What are the workers thinking? Is there time for a coolie to calculate the amount remaining to pay off his indenture to the China Boss? To think he might never get home except in a wooden box, if he's lucky? History keeps no record. When a *klootchman* slimer takes her baby off her back to nurse it, does she think of the child's future? Does she long for home, or is she happy in her work? Her thoughts don't come into the history books. Few history books even mention these Chinese and Natives; they are cogs in a terrifying, impressive machine that remains as just a few blackened pilings now. And as the wild salmon die out, the past obsessed with them dies out too. For now, though, their faint images still wear sheets of flesh, as the nipple's unsuckled and the wrists ache and the fish keep coming, more and more, thousand upon thousand, million upon million.

The cans must be cooked. The bathroom crews take the stopped cans (heaped on coolers – woven strips or iron – themselves placed on trucks) to the hot water testing kettles. Chains, pulleys, overhead tracks, double block and tackles. Immersion. Any bubbles from leaks, out goes the can for the leak to be soldered. Next, back onto the trucks for the cans, into tanks of water boiled by steam pipes strung in the tank bottoms. One hour of cooking. The cans come out, the tops are perforated by means of a small mallet with a pointed nail in one head. Once all the steam's escaped, more soldering's done to stop up the holes. A further immersion and testing for leaks (it's bad business to kill off your English customers), then onto the final cooking via low-wheeled, steel-framed cars running on steel tracks. Here the coolies must – they must – sometimes think of the railroads and the high mountain passes and the cries of their comrades who slip into the frothing waters of the gorges, their bodies slung like dead salmon to the sea. One Chinaman for every mile of track, so history records somewhere. How many salmon streams per mile of track, how many millions of salmon?

Get on with it! There's no time and this is dangerous work if you don't pay close attention. The cars are slid into large steel retorts, the doors are lowered and screwed tight, and live steam is released into it by the retort man. Once the thermometer shows 240 degrees, he shuts down the steam sufficiently to maintain the temperature for a full hour, after which the steam pours out through a waste pipe in the floor and the cars are wheeled out with a hooked steel bar. All the livelong day. After cooling, it's into the packing room. Here's a delicate task, the testing, a kind of sorcery, the Chinaman tapping a small metal instrument with a ball-shaped head onto each can. Just by the sound, out go the underweight cans (no stiffing the English buyers, if you please) and the cans with leaks. The good cans get piled fourteen or fifteen high, then the tester taps them again, playing a xylophone of commerce with one hand as the steam pours behind him and the hoppers below spill over with guts and the white foreman casts a wary eye over the workers to catch any sloppiness and the China Boss hovers around to do the same, for the coolies do not take kindly to reprimands from whites.

This is the way you make a pack, day after day, and well into each night, because this is the big run of 1897, one of the last big runs the Fraser will know, after thousands of years.

Outside, day has broken fully. The rain has stopped. The loaded scows from the floating fish camps are in, their sides sloshing silver. Gull cry pierces the sky's thin flesh, snotty-nosed Indian kids scramble around under the cannery wharf, looking for knives and whetstones that have slipped through the planks. Dogs bark. The dayshift for the cannery boats takes over for the nightshift. Fish picks rise and fall like soldier's rifles. The sockeye leap one last time through the damp grey, the flag on the China House hangs limp, as if a salmon entrail has been hung off the pole. Orders are shouted in Chinook, the old trade language, because it's the only way to communicate with this mud and blood-walled Tower of Babel.

Up on the dyke a broad silhouette hoves into view. It's Tom Ladner himself, in the flesh, and there's a lot of it. 250 pounds but only five-foot-seven, he cuts a familiar figure under his usual saucer-shaped hat. Does he rub his hands together with glee as he sees the almost-sunken scows and skiffs, the heaped flesh on the wharf, the steam clouds? No. He's not the type of man to be satisfied, and this salmon game is unpredictable. That's why it's so important to keep control of the industry, so others can't buy in, so the chancy profits remain divvied up by the few rather than the many. A large pack, as he well knows, can drive the price down. But this is a good sign. The season's been quiet, and a good week of catches will mean a healthy season. He sighs. His second family is larger than the first and needs more financing. Remarried in 1864, a year after the death of his first wife, he has not reined in his appetites or his expectations. Canning is a chancy business. Now there are almost forty canneries crammed in the rivermouth. It can't go on. Something has to give, and Thomas Ladner is not foolish enough to be generous where his living's concerned. If Ewen can be canny, and Todd can be tight, why then, that's how the game will be played. Amalgamation's in the wind, not just the stench of dead fish. He breathes deeply. It's a pleasing smell, the smell of banknotes. His figure disappears below the level of the dyke.

The catches aren't just good for a week, they're astonishing for nearly a month. The great steaming, fiery dragon's maw is insatiable, crews work overtime and extra shifts, the two-hundred-fish-per-boat limit is strictly imposed after the first day, the price per fish soon plummets, and many fishermen stop going out. The canneries back up. Whole scow-loads of fish spoil and are dumped to make way for the day's fresher fish. Carcasses sink into the silty depths, then rise up bloated and putrid, become perches for the eye-pecking gulls. On every backup tide, tons of dumped salmon guts drift into the river and wash up on the banks. A pulpy, stinking, red and silvery froth lines the riverbanks for miles. Two feet deep, in some places two hundred feet wide, the waste lipsticks the brown mouth and fouls the air. There's not a fresh breath to be had from Ladner to New Westminster. Hundreds of thousands of rotting carcasses, millions of pounds of looping, festering offal, and low tides combine to keep matters pestilential into autumn.

And the fishermen and the cannery crews? The former throw nets off the end of wharves to catch their daily limit, which they might sell for a quarter penny a fish, if they're lucky. Most aren't. The latter sleep in stink, when they sleep, hear clanks and clinks and hissings in their brief dreams, lose fingers, get scalded, or otherwise maimed or burnt as a result of fatigue. Their numbers blur as they trudge to and from the dark dampness, their hands raw and ankles swollen. The live dragon has flown down off the China House and is merciless. Sunlight is a soldering iron that seals nothing. Disease spreads. Indian kids die. Their corpses are put into cedar boxes and placed in the branches of trees. At the season's end, they'll be paddled home. Dead Chinamen, if they're lucky, will have their bones sent back to China. Fishermen drown, as they drown every season. The crabs get their corpses. Opium helps, as does alcohol. Why bother to sleep? Might as well stay awake and gamble. The streets of Ladner are lively. Missionaries sniff around for converts. Gulls screech. Dogs bark. Proper women hold cloth to their noses. The air is red with salmon rot. It's material. Don't swallow outside, as the little bones of the future you're building might stick in your throat.

Can't fight it, so we might as well go up on the dyke, take a look at the slaughter. It's really something, isn't it? Death everywhere you look, not even a gull today on that drifting pulp of guts. Wait. Did you see that? Something black just dropped out of the sky, only there's nothing up there. Where the hell did that come from? Christ, it's a torn-up muskrat. See it. Why the . . . would an eagle take a muskrat? I've heard tell that a grizzly will eat its own cubs if it's hungry enough. But how can an eagle be hungry with all these fish around?

No eagle. Just the future that is the past. Tilt. Game over. The earth's a machine of lights and motion that we've been booting hard for well over a century. The old lines of the nations split wide open and menstrual blood gushes out with the roe and salt to flood the classroom floor and seep into the hallways. What shall we do? Shall we manage it? Shall we put our business suits on and sit in the Hotel Vancouver with the minister of fisheries and the president of the Salmon Farmers Association and the CEO of Dow Chemical, and manage?

Go on. Earn your paycheque. Invest the money for your retirement. Maybe you can catch your daily limit of plastic Atlantic salmon with their sawdust grey flesh (chemically dyed red, of course) when you're an old man.

Me? I'm just a coolie with a bloodsoaked number on my queue who's never going to see his home again, I'm just the son of a fisherman who never had any hunger, I'm just bones in a box of flesh, part of the great pack of humanity being sold overseas. A wild salmon digs a redd in the left side of my chest every night and keeps me awake. It might be the last wild salmon. Tom Ladner, stout old ghost, sing me to sleep. I was a boy in your streets, I ran there and laughed there. Tom? What am I going to do? I'm from your place. I know what a fathom is. Six feet. Grave depth. But it's something else. I looked it up. It's from the Old English, older than you, Tom. A fathom is the length of the outstretched arms. Your wife's for her dead babies. These outstretched arms.

XVII

WASPS CRAWL INTO the fat windfall pears beside the house where my father sits in shadow, hanging a fall net. In one hand, he holds a wooden gauge for measuring mesh size, in the other hand he holds a plastic needle of twine. He straddles a wooden bench, one end of which holds a piece of net between two vertical sticks. His hands flutter quickly at the task, weaving, measuring, snapping off the twine. From a thick bottom branch of a pear tree the loose web hangs, a smooth waterfall of green. A pile of multicoloured corks enlivens the shadows. The air's thick with fermenting fruit. Pepper, our springer spaniel, holds a fat pear between his front paws. He looks like the Sphinx with the gold of the desert before him. A juice-dazed wasp flies out of the pear. Pepper snaps at it, swallows it. Every fall, his muzzle puffs out with stings. Springers aren't the world's smartest dogs, but they're good at retrieving ducks and pheasants.

It's still warm in the full sun, but cool in the shade. I don't notice Rick until I'm closer. He's grinning and nodding at something Dad's saying. They're both relaxed because the tension of the sockeye season is past. Both wear white T-shirts that aren't stained with fishblood. Rick holds a stubby brown bottle of beer with a tartan label on it.

"It's all Hollywood," my father is saying in his quiet voice. "Cameras, actors, sets. You can't spend all that money and then not have something to show for it. Besides, they need to take people's minds off that war somehow."

Rick doffs his ball cap and shakes his long black hair before responding. "I guess so, but how would they keep it quiet? Somebody would blab."

Pepper chomps at another wasp, then goes back to gnawing at his pear.

"Ah, it wouldn't take many to do it. And they'd be well paid."

Dad notices me standing at the shadow's edge and winks. "Hi Monk. Want a pear? There's some good ones lying around."

I scan the grass. Most of the pears are split and squishy, but I see one that's green-red and firm. I bend and pick it up.

Rick takes a long swig of his beer. "You don't really believe that?"

Dad shrugs. "There's no real proof they were up there. We're just supposed to look at the TV set and believe what we're told?"

"It could be true, though." Rick's statement comes out sounding like a question. I can tell he's not sure how serious Dad is.

"Moon's a long way away," he says flatly, his right hand a blur. "And I'll bet you a dollar to a doughnut those astronauts were walking on styrofoam."

Mom opens the side door and says that tea is ready. "Shall I bring it out?"

But Dad's already getting up. He musses my hair as he passes, leaving a wake of cigarette smoke and sweat to flow faintly over me. In seconds, the ripe fruit reclaims the air as I bite down on the sweet, running taste of autumn, of another century. For the pear is a Clapp's Favourite, an old stock, part of a diminishing diversity, like a Horsefly or Quesnel sockeye, something whose flavour is made melancholy by the imminence of its extinction. I don't know this then, of course; I just let the juice run down my chin and look up at my brother.

His dark hair almost reaches his shoulders. His beard's full but not bushy, and he sports straight sideburns. He's wearing a canvas hunting vest that reveals his leanly muscular arms and chest and a pair of dark blue jeans. The slots in the vest for carrying cartridges are empty. There's a fox-like handsomeness to his face, but of a fox at rest not at prowl; his blue eyes are small but bright, his lips are red, his teeth small and white, the incisors showing when he smiles. And he likes to smile. Why not? He's twenty-four and single, he's just bought a 1969 Mustang fastback with a 354-horsepower engine, and when he drives it around Ladner, he can't go a half-block without being waved or honked at.

He drives it to baseball and hockey games, the interior funky with the wet leather of his goalie pads and the residue of beer and the skins of muskrats he's placed between the front bucket seats. Not even the wicker spice ball or mint Christmas tree air freshener hanging from the rearview mirror can defeat the smell of Rick's bachelor pursuits. He drives the car to the farm fields to hunt, so sometimes there are dead pheasants and dog hairs on the floor mat of the passenger side. He drives the Mustang to beer parlours and house parties and parties on the dyke, so beer bottles and beer caps and perhaps even a piece of a date's clothing mix in with the gaunt, gaping white goalie's mask, eyes black and big as a harbour seal's, and the wooden bats and the duffel bags of rosin and liniment and jock-strap and sweaty uniforms. He drives it to the ice rink on the eastern outskirts of town, a converted airplane hangar from World War II, where he whips around in a bright red attendant's jacket, breaking up fights with his sense of humour, sending sprays of snow up against groups of giggling girls. He drives it to family parties, where he is solicitous of the older relatives, as befits a first-born.

In a famous photo of a Bowling Christmas party, it is Rick who balances on the plastic Twister mat with our eighty-year-old grandmother, it is Rick who holds her lightly by the elbow, it is Rick who knows how to touch the past. He lives in pioneer Ladner the way the salmon live at sea; the town's all his, he knows it through all his senses, he can travel the streets and the fields blindfolded, he knows everyone and everyone likes him, from the old Chinese farmworker with no English to the Mayor and the town council. He touches the present and the past, his dashboard quivering with the latest hits yet his back strong from pulling nets by hand. He dates widely, even – believe it or not – twins named Candy and Honey, yet has a conservative, almost worshipful attitude towards the institution of marriage. Long-haired, a flashy dresser, licentious, he nonetheless attends Remembrance Day ceremonies and scorns the users of marijuana and stronger drugs as "hippies." Outwardly rebellious, but inwardly conservative, he's a hinge between generations, he stands in the dappled early autumn light like a doorway of flesh and muscle and says, "Want to go for a ride, Bud?"

Do I? Of course I do. Ah, but it's too late. From the street comes a clop of hooves. A large black horse emerges from the direction of the dyke and stands at the end of our driveway, whinnying at the bumper of Rick's car as if the namesake was real. I like horses all right, though they frighten me a bit. This one's called Danny and I've fed him a carrot before. No, Danny's not the problem; it's the young barefoot woman on his back with the long braids and splash of freckles and the wide smile who's the problem. I know the horse's name but I don't know hers, or at least I never remember it. Rick knows a lot of girls. He's always talking with them at the ballpark, the ice rink, around town. Just as he's talking with the girl on the horse, looking up at her, his hand almost touching a bare thigh, both their faces bathed in light the colour of ripe pear skin.

I stay where I am, sulking, knowing that my sulk won't be noticed. That's all right. There's a lot else I can do before supper. I can chuck rocks in the river or climb trees or play in one of the abandoned houses. I'm never bored. Sometimes I just lie on my back in the tall grass of the field behind our house and watch the sky and listen to the mud wasps. Maybe I'll throw a chunk of bark into the river and pretend it's a ship and try to sink it. Or I'll build a raft out of driftwood and spare lumber and go sailing on the big ditch behind the Demostens' house. If all else fails, I can find my sister and her friends; maybe they'll let me play a board game with them or kick-the-can or hide-and-go-seek. I like to play with them sometimes, until they start to tease me or until they want to play something

I'm not interested in. Often I just wander alone through the neighbourhood.

I cross the street to the Douglas fir, shading my eyes to look back once at Rick and the girl on the horse. Still talking. So much for my ride. But Rick will make it up to me later; he always does. I stand very still in the tall grass, feeling the season's changes in my body. The ivy on the sides of the abandoned house has turned a violent red, and one vine trickles from a dark glassless upper window until it's a huge salmon eye crying blood. Out on the river, the alders and birches of the silt islands cast coloured leaves over the dark, ropey current and the big dogs below the surface push their hooked snouts against the flow. Soon there'll be another opening. That's why my father was mending his net.

I look down at the sound of panting. Pepper has emerged from the grass, burrs stuck in his brown-white coat. His pink tongue hangs out, drenched with slobber. I rest my hand on the top of his head, which is warm and soft. From somewhere I hear a shriek of laughter; Nola and her friends must be coming outside. But then the silence resumes, as if I'd heard only a ghost girl's laugh. For ten minutes the only traffic on the grey, potholed street has been the horse. Pepper pants, a breeze plays in the fir boughs. Rick and the girl on the horse are slowly swallowed by a giant shadow. The ivy darkens too. I don't expect or want anything to happen, but a million things do, at once, always. And I'll never be so close to them again. The shadows extend along the whole length of Georgia Street as if cast by a silent, invisible army whose passing leaves only a cold tremble on the earth. I watch the quick, orderly progression until a lilting whistle from my mother's lips, the call of the red-winged blackbird, signals my lucky, light-laved zero hour and I rise out of the field, a boy who plays guns but will never be a soldier as my father and grandfather and likely my great-grandfather were, and leave behind my town of ruins, shelled only by years and changing economies, the harness shop giving way to the garage, the old gone at last into nursing homes, to enter a kitchen pungent with ripe tomatoes and pears, their sloppy remains spread all over the formica countertops as the aproned woman with the hazel eyes the size of half dollars, her molasses-thick black hair tucked under a nylon headkerchief's perfect *V*, hovers over a steaming ceramic pot, the birdsong of spring still playing on her lips.

She smiles at me. A damp strand of hair swings over one eye. "Now wouldn't that just frost your navel," she says. "I lost count. Pook, go in and ask your father if he heard a pop."

I take off my rubber boots and walk the few feet across the worn linoleum into the living room. Dad's reclining on the chesterfield, his feet up, the afternoon newspaper broken-winged in his hands. I ask him if he heard a pop. He glances at me out of the corner of one bright blue eye and lightly shakes his head.

"Pop heard no pop," he smiles, then snaps the paper back into place.

I repeat his answer to Mom, and she sighs. "Well, then we'll all just have to risk getting botulism this winter." More strands of hair have slipped loose, but she starts humming and singing now, something about being as restless as a willow in a windstorm. With a dishcloth in each hand she reaches into the big pot and pulls out a steel rack that holds several glass mason jars of pears. These she quickly swings over to a clear spot on the counter next to the fridge. Other jars – of pears, tomatoes, chili sauce, cherries, dill pickles – are lined three deep and ten wide along the counter. They've been labelled on top – Pears 1969, Cherries 1969, etc. On the pull-out wooden cutting board lie chunks of pear and tomato – it looks like a pulpy mulch of fallen leaves. My mother's arms are bare to the elbows, damp and red, smeared here and there with bits of mushy fruit. From June, when she starts canning the Stuart run of sockeye, which she prefers because they're just the right size for the jars and the flesh is so red and firm, to well into the fall, she's a one-woman cannery: slimer, wiper, butcher, filler, retort crew, tester and labeller. The kitchen's always filled with steam and rich aromas, the sink with blood and guts and heads and fins, the floor with scales and feathers. Often there are shotguns and oilskins heaped on the braided mat, salmon or mallards laid out on newspaper on the floor, gumboots, hipwaders, black metal lunchboxes scattered between the door and the table, on which always sits a clay, volcano-shaped vase Rick or Bruce made at school two decades before. Now it's overflowing with the pale blue and dark purple heads snipped off the hydrangea alongside our driveway.

"Set up the TV tables," she says lightly, "but not one for your brother. He's gone out already."

I nod, unsurprised, for I had seen that his car was gone. How was it that I didn't see or hear the horse leave?

Pop.

"Oh for the love of Pete, how many's that now?" She chews her bottom lip. "Seven, I think. Or eight."

I leave her in her numerical quandary and start snapping together the TV tables. For some reason, we always eat in the living room, often with the news on, or the hockey game if it's Saturday. This never stops us from talking, however. The presence of the outside world somehow deepens our feeling of intimacy. Certainly meals at our house are more casual and relaxed than I will find them to be at friends' houses in later years. But then, when the father is away at work all day, mealtime provides the one reliable opportunity for everyone to be together and talk. Not so for the Bowlings. We stay up later and rise later than most people, even during the school year. As a boy, my father regularly ran afoul of the truant officer, and when my own time of social servitude begins, I will do my share of banging out chalkboard brushes after the three o'clock bell.

It hasn't begun yet. I'm sitting before a TV table on which a pattern of ringnecked pheasants is frozen against an autumn sky. Across from me, on the wall above the mantelpiece, the ruddy-coloured bodies of three stuffed pheasants reflect the pattern. Their feathers are slightly darker than the hardwood floor stretching below. On top of the TV set, positioned between the rabbit ears, stands the angry, poised-for-flight pheasant. As always, I wonder whether it will rise up with a wild flapping once someone pulls the button of the TV set on.

Nola pulls it, but nothing happens right away. Then a tiny white dot appears in the middle of the screen and slowly widens as a faint humming begins. Finally, with a short sizzle, the dot flickers and a black and white image of a serious male face fills the screen. The pheasant does not even flinch. Disappointed, I return to my bowl of steaming scotch broth. From the kitchen comes another popping sound, an exclamation of "Lord love a duck and double-jointed sausages!" and more humming. My father smiles, the newsman's voice drones on, the mounted birds hang in their perpetual final flight, while outside a harvest moon swells with blood and my brother races his roaring horse below dykes hand-built by the pioneers to a bonfire party by the sea.

Night deepens. The river slows, the salt tide pushes in, the moon sets. My brother is drunk by fire and won't come home until the wee hours, as my mother calls them. She'll not sleep well until he's safely back. It's in her nature to worry, but it's not in mine, not yet. I won't even wake when he stumbles into the room we share and empties his pockets of keys, coins, packs of matches, bottle opener in a gentle unleafing that turns our little bedside table into the underside of a Christmas tree. I will never learn why Rick empties his pockets this way; it's a mysterious ritual that I've come to acquaint with those rites of adulthood inaccessible to a child. That the mystery remains, that I have no desire to solve it by simply asking him, suggests the unwillingness to sacrifice myth to mundanity that continues to inform everything I write. But myths must be torn down to make way for truth to become its own new myth. For no one can say what is myth and what is truth. The ancestors of Ladner's pioneers, and, by extension, of every Canadian town's pioneers, believe their great-grandparents to be giants to whom we owe an ongoing debt of gratitude. Look at all they've given us! Look at the soft lives we have, the luxuries, the conveniences!

I'm looking, but what I see is a Native man standing in a compound beside three men in business suits instructing him to mix ingredients into a bucket: the roe of a pink salmon, PCBs, menstrual flow, dioxins, sea lice, the tears of children in residential schools, antibiotics, the milt of a dog salmon, typhoid virus, and polybrominated diphenyl ethers normally used as flame retardants in foams. Schoolchildren wearing Canadian flags run around the compound, munching on farmed salmon burgers laced with toxins, several of which are known to cause memory and learning difficulties. Untreated raw sewage is pumped into the ocean – BC's eighty fish farms release sewage equivalent to that of a city of 500,000 people. I'm looking again, and the romance of the railway, the Last Spike, the National Dream, which I was taught in school, is destroying my heritage, wiping out my birthright, killing Chinese and starving Indians, scattering millions of carcasses along the clear-cut banks. A Vietnamese fisherman blows up his van in front of Vancouver City Hall as a desperate protest against forces which keep him from earning a living. Inside, the great-grandson of Thomas Ladner looks up briefly, then returns to the council minutes on his desk. In his library at home, there's likely a copy of his grandfather's book *The Ladners of Ladner*, which portrays Thomas Ladner as a saint who, travelling the western US in the 1850s, thrilled at the herds, sixty million strong, of buffalo rippling across the grasslands. *How sad*, Leon J. Ladner concludes, *that those great herds dwindled to nothing because of the slaughter born of greed.*

I'm looking at these pages and the stink of rotting salmon rises off them and forms a steam around me through which I can just make out Thomas Ladner standing on a scow surrounded by seventy-five thousand sockeye. He's grinning. Someone hands him a telegram: *Family increased this morning all doing well.* But the twin boys are soon dead, which was, as Leon J. Ladner puts it, "a source of much grief to my mother." Thomas Ladner's expression fades and the faces of nameless Chinese hover in the steam, numbers in their pigtails, as they flail away at the silver just as anonymous as they are. A steady stream of minivans packed to the rooftops with disposable diapers and frozen farmed salmon and greenhouse vegetables crashes through the steam, scattering the Chinese, and disappears into the tunnel under the Fraser River, heading for Vancouver and the denuded mountainsides of the North Shore whose empty creeks once trembled with salmon and trout, while farther up the coast, past the ghost fishing camps and the government-killed fishing towns, into clouds of sea lice, three men assess the contents of a bucket, discuss profit margins, plan meetings in Victoria and Ottawa and Washington, DC, beside a Native man whose own band operates a gravel quarry that can be seen from space and a McDonald's whose grand opening was the largest ever held in North America. I'm looking and I'm trying my best to see something else, but what I want to see is gone, except for a few faint strands from thirty-five years ago, which I'm remembering, which I'll remember, until the chemicals of profit and progress scorch my skull of memory.

How can we love the past which has brought us to this? Can we honour and admire it even as we condemn what it has led us to? Yes. As F. Scott Fitzgerald wrote – and he knew something about the rise and fall of fortune within an historical context – the ability to hold two contradictory ideas in the mind at the same time and still function is the sign of intelligence. But one idea always wins out. So I remember the vanished coast of my affections and I name the criminal activity. It's 2007. In the full steam of progress. Look.

Admiration, disgust. Hope, despair. The tide falls, the tide rises. The rivermouth is the tanned chest of Gulliver strapped down by sloughs, ditches, silt. The salmon is the blood, and we? I know what Jonathan Swift would write if he was alive and behind this pen. We are the sea lice on the eyeball. And we're more voracious and deadly wherever we mass together. Yet I love many people and I love the world, and you probably do as well. So why are we killing ourselves and believing that it's all right? Is it as much in our nature to destroy as it is in the salmon's nature to reach the spawning grounds and die? If it is, I will take the stand of Frost's farm woman against grief when she says, *I will not have it so.* I will sit by fire beneath the constellations and listen and marvel and be the older soul my culture does not honour. Look.

The sideyard between our bungalow and the neighbours'

decrepit Victorian house is a narrow fifteen feet wide and cluttered – with garbage cans and bicycles and hockey sticks, chunks of fishnet, coils of leadline and corkline, a hockey net made of 2x4s and thick black seine webbing, an outboard engine under canvas, a staved wooden rain barrel slopping darkness and dead leaves, scattered bits of driftwood, machine parts and unwanted or broken furniture. Halfway between the kitchen door and the backyard, right up against the house, Pepper's straw-filled doghouse never closes its round black eye – somehow that arched darkness remains dark, day and night, as if transformed by the elusive magic of another species. Near the back of the house, outside Nola's bedroom window, an ancient Gravenstein apple tree scratches its branches against the stars. Beyond this reaching black shimmers a reddish glow, comes the crackle of wood, the richness of smoke – this last flows towards me as, with great care, I carry a steaming mug of tea to my father. The air is damp and earthy, then sweetened with the sharp, sad tang of windfall apples, then flavoured with smoke. I've passed a dozen spiderwebs, and those are only the ones I've noticed – vast, intricate, swaying slightly: the lungs of autumn. For it is the season of spiders. They turn up everywhere – in the bathtub, on the sink, on your pillow. Unbeknownst to me, it is their mating season and the males have no choice but to pack up their instincts and wander until they find the sticky thread of a mate and follow it to reproduction and likely death. So I pass the empty webs and the orange light from my sister's room where she's bent over her homework, reading about the building of the railroads or the Family Compact or the midnight ride of Paul Revere, and stand on the brink of a deeper darkness lit with the first fire.

The grass is wet, but there's a hard, beaten trail between the sprawling vegetable garden, all but harvested now except for the pumpkins and squash, and the gnarled Bartlett pear tree, a leftover from a pioneer orchard. My father sits in front of a brick-enclosed pit, poking at the fire with a branch fallen from the towering Queen Anne cherry tree just beyond him, where the yard ends abruptly in a row of hazelnut trees groaning with abundance. A small, dark shed with a sloping roof of uneven cedar shakes marks the final human achievement for a half-mile, as a field of waist-high grass and blackberry bushes runs along the dyke and eventually dissolves into the ramshackle remains of the Chinatown that built up around the China houses back in the boom days of the canneries and was mostly destroyed by fire in 1928, smoking out the mysterious residents and scattering them into the dark, pungent alleys of Vancouver. I stand halfway between the shrunken dot of the TV screen and an acre of the wild delta. How can what my father tells me here of this world be anything less than an oracle?

Bats flit between us and the Great Bear and the Twins. We watch for them, the bats and the stars, as the smoke climbs palely and the fire cracks its knuckles. Many nights, my father tells me about the river and the salmon. I can sense them, just outside of the light to the north, moving as they've moved since the glaciers retreated ten thousand years before, except I don't know this scientific fact. My father's not that sort of learned man. He hated school and quit in grade nine to box groceries and labour in the farm fields (his father insisted he get a job), but mostly to hunt and play cards and shoot pool. He knows that the salmon die once they spawn, but he does not know that they are anadromous (fish born in fresh water who migrate to sea to mature, then return to freshwater to spawn) and semelparous (a fish that dies after spawning once). What he knows of the salmon's life cycle he's picked up through his senses and through the passed-along wisdom of the waterfront vernacular.

The same goes for his knowledge of the river's character. From my father, I'll learn to watch for a big spring in the net if we've just caught a little jack spring – they always seem to travel together. And I'll learn to expect a good catch if there's a haze around the moon. As for tides, he teaches me not to rely on books. She goes out and she comes in is about the extent of useful human knowledge. Certain tides – high water slack, for example – appeal to the fish, but each run behaves differently; the Adams River sockeye, for example, like to hang around the mouth of the river for weeks before beginning their final run to the spawning grounds, while coho and pinks prefer to migrate by day. There's a lot of mystery involved, and the main thing I'll learn from my father and other gentlemen-fishermen of the Prairie is that you can stand in awe of life even as you're energetically immersed in its dying. The weak efforts of generations of government biologists to count salmon and anticipate their behaviour would bring a bemused smile to my father's face and the comment that you can't beat Mother Nature.

Yet I am a learned man, having handled many more books than salmon, and I've discovered things about the salmon and the river that, while unearned in the sweat and blood manner of the past, nonetheless deepen, rather than penetrate, the mystery. By the pit fires in my childhood, my father would have enjoyed hearing these things, for he did not have a closed mind. After all, he never dismissed my ambition to be a writer, and that was a rare generosity in North America, then and now.

So I decide to tell him what I've learned. In the fireglow, with the river at our backs, the stars thick over us, and only the breathing of the spiderwebs to accompany my words, I tell him what I never told him while he lived.

Salmon are among the most primitive groups of bony fish. When the first primate humans showed up, around four million years ago, the family known as *Salmonidae* had already been around for eons, at least 180 million years. They've even found a fossil, what they call a dawn salmon, from the Eocene Period, fifty million years ago, but it was a freshwater fish.

You mean like the kokanee sockeye, the ones that never leave the lake.

Yes, but that comes a lot later. The Pacific salmon, the salmon we fish for, are pretty recent, about two million years old. About then, the Pacific and Atlantic Oceans were connected across what we now call the Arctic. This connection was lost due to land and sea-level changes, so two different genera of salmon developed. Actually, the Pacific genus – *Oncorhynchus* – developed from a far-flung stock of the much older Atlantic genus known as *Salmo*. *Salmo*, by the way, is Roman for "leaper." Apparently Caesar's legions named the fish as they tramped all over Europe, crossing rivers, and kept seeing these beautiful fish leaping against the sky.

One giant leap for fishkind, eh?

I smile, making a note to ask him later about the time he looked at the moon. But for now, I'm on a roll. Anyway, I continue, *Oncorhyncus* broke off from *Salmo* in the Pleistocene Period. There were lots of changes in the land and sea then, lots of ice moving around, and this created many isolated bodies of water that lasted for between fifty thousand and a hundred thousand years, plenty of time for *Oncorhyncus* to firmly establish itself as a separate genus with the half-dozen species we know today.

Half-dozen? You're counting the steelhead, then? I thought they figured that for a trout.

No, I'm not counting the steelhead, though they say it's a Pacific salmon now. For a while, they figured it was more like an Atlantic salmon, or a seagoing trout. Now it's a Pacific salmon – *Oncorhyncus mykiss* – but there are so few of them left that there's no sense counting them. Besides, it doesn't die after spawning once, which is a funny thing, because neither do some Atlantic salmon. For some mysterious reason, the sockeye, springs, dogs, pinks and coho all became semelparous, probably because they had to migrate so far to sea in order to survive. Not a lot of nutrients in that glacial freshwater, so they had to go and find them.

They agree it's a fish, though? He exhales, then asks me what the sixth species is.

There's a Pacific salmon that returns only to Japan, and it's the oldest species. It's called the masu, which means cherry trout, because the fish return when the cherry blossoms fall.

Ah, that's nice, one for your poetry books.

I smile again, more than a little pleased by his effort to understand me, and return to my lecture. The amazing thing, I go on, is the range of these fish, from California and Japan down south up to Arctic Russia and Alaska. And some runs go all the way to the headwaters of the Fraser, up in the Rockies, near the Alberta border. Springs, mainly. They're the big travellers. Them and sockeye. The pinks, dogs and coho don't spawn so far inland.

Right into Alberta? No kidding.

At one time. I'm not sure about now. A friend tells me they get a few really beat-up salmon in the stretch of river on her parents' property in Tête Jaune, but I'm sure those runs are almost extinct. But they figure some salmon travel up to sixteen thousand kilometres before they make it home to spawn. And no matter where they are, when the time comes to go home, they just start going at the same time. Weeks before they're scheduled to return, some might be as much as two thousand kilometres away. But a huge percentage of them, and we're talking millions of fish, at least historically, enter their home rivers within a two-week period at exactly the same time each year.

Where's this again?

Actually, in this particular example, it's Bristol Bay, up in Alaska. But the same thing applies to the great Fraser River travellers.

My father drags on his cigarette, points up at the sky with a burning branch and asks if I can see the satellite creeping across between the multiple, fixed points of light. I realize I'm beginning to tell him the obvious. He's been fishing long enough to know that when the fish move, they move. He doesn't need to hear about the different life cycles of the species, how the pink salmon spends only one year at sea before returning to spawn, how the juvenile sockeye spend one or more winters in nursery lakes before migrating to the sea, how some chinook runs have a seven-year cycle. The point is, and he knows it well, the salmon of the Fraser River are born inland, anywhere from the mouth to the interior of the province, they mature at sea for a period of one to five years, then return to their exact birthplace to spawn and die. The details, which science works so hard to uncover, don't mean as much to him as the mystery of the whole process. But I persevere anyway. It's pleasant out here in the backyard, just like I remember it. And when Mom steps out of the darkness, bringing more tea, it's even more pleasant. She gives us our cups, then settles into her chair. In the faint fireglow, I can't tell how old she is.

That's another dozen pears put down, she says, then raises her eyes to the stars.

Even today, I continue, not sure what the year is, no one truly understands the homing instinct of the salmon. It's innate, we know that, because they only return once; it's not like they're going on experience. So it's built right into their genes, which is why hatchery fish are such a pale reflection – taken from the natural process, over time they lose the sharpness of instinct that defines the wild species. Anyway, how do the salmon get back home with such precision? There are only theories. But the best ones focus on the salmon's sense of smell, which is a thousand times more acute than that of dogs.

You hear that, Pepper? You might just as well have a head cold.

I read somewhere that, in martini equivalents, a salmon could detect one drop of vermouth in 500,000 barrels of gin.

Just like your Uncle Stan.

Yes, yes, very funny.

Is that what they mean by drinking like a fish?

Go on, Mom urges, and I can tell by the way he's not poking the fire that Dad's interested. He simply can't resist a joke, especially now that his favourite audience is here.

Well, the idea is that when the salmon get near the river and when they're in it, they use a combination of *rheotaxis* – which is the detection of the direction of flow – and their ability to sense temperature and salinity changes in the water and to pick up different smells from distinct watersheds. But what's really mysterious is how they navigate at sea. There are a lot of theories, having to do with following the stars and the sun, for example.

We all look up, as though imagining ourselves as salmon thousands of kilometres from home, relying on that tangled lacework of distant light to get us safely back. The Milky Way is spread like milt against the black, and the smoke from the fire has the same life-creating flow. I'm suddenly tired of speaking, tired of science and analysis, but my parents enjoy hearing me talk. I figure I might as well finish what I've begun.

One recent theory holds that the salmon use the earth's magnetic field to navigate. This field produces an infinitely divided, arcing grid of very low-voltage currents which a salmon would be sensitive enough to track back to its starting point on the coast. From there, it's a matter of current, water temperature, smell. Apparently, they can detect, at very high dilutions, pheromones secreted by smolts. And every river has a unique mix of chemical elements. But really, exactly how they manage to return to the same spot where they were born after thousands of kilometres and several years is still a mystery. There's actually not much that we know about it. Which isn't surprising. David Suzuki estimates that we've only identified 15 percent of the species on earth and that we truly understand the lives of maybe 1 or 2 percent.

I like him, my mother says. *That's a good program he has on the TV.*

Dad tosses a dry chunk of bark on the fire. He picked it out of his net in the summer, now it helps to warm us in the fall. I think of the beauty of the salmon cycle all up and down this coast, how the ocean proteins in the spawned-out carcasses flow into the soil of the forests and the bloodstreams of other creatures, enriching the entire world in which the salmon live. All the greenery in the Yukon, so it's believed, comes from the salmon deaths in its rivers. No wonder the Salish and other First Nations honoured the salmon with rituals. No wonder they saw them as supernatural. How else could they die on the spawning grounds yet return the next year? The Salish and the Kwakiutl and the Nisga'a weren't catching spawners and squeezing their eggs and sperm into buckets, then watching in darkened incubation rooms as the alevins hatched and started to feed off their bulbous yolk sacs; they weren't plotting to understand in the name of enhancement so that the resource could be better understood and therefore better managed. They weren't dissecting the cellular construction of the egg or testing the chemical content of streams or even making percentage guesses of how many species there are on the Earth. They were singing and putting the bones of the first salmon back into the water so it could reassemble and tell its family to come back again.

Tim, don't let your tea get cold.

The wind has shifted and I blink into the thick smoke. Above, the bats have stopped feeding. With the stillness comes a deeper chill. Somewhere along the dyke, a dog barks four times, each sound quieter than the one preceding it, as if someone in heavy boots is walking away.

Rivers, glaciers, ice, oceans. Ten thousand years. Millions of tiny eyes clustered under gravel, great clouds of darting silver hovering and feeding in the delta marshes, then, after a mysterious migration at sea, rippling tonnages cleaving the silt. Almost silent to us now.

I rise from the burnt-down fire and take my mother's arm. It's late, and getting later fast. Then I remember.

Hey, Dad, do you remember telling me about the time just before *Apollo 11* landed when you took a real close look at the moon?

My father doesn't answer. He isn't even there. Someone in heavy boots has walked away.

XVIII

It's the summer of the moonwalk and I'm carrying a little jack spring home from the wharf. Men have built a great rocket and flown it into space to stand on the moon and look back at our blue-green planet with awe and humility. Americans planting a little American flag, they realize their country is embroiled in an unpopular war and a period of rising domestic turbulence. So they make a plea for all the nations of the world to get along. From space, the earth looks so vulnerable. If only we could all stand on the moon, they say, perhaps we wouldn't try to kill each other.

I look up. The moon's small as a salmon head and scarfed with cloud. Who could stand there? My father doesn't believe anyone could. And even if it is true, he says, so what? Isn't this world good enough for them? What the hell do they want to go traipsing around on the moon for?

Early evening. The air's blood-warm and cut-grass rich as I descend the dyke and turn the corner onto Georgia, the three pounds of silver blooming an ache in my fingers and wrist. I'm not going to drop it, though. This is an important job. I feel as if someone on the moon might be watching to make sure I succeed. The whole night is eyed, like the gravel beds of thousands of streams and creeks in the fall. Eyed, but not threatening. What watches me watches with curiosity and almost tenderness. I'm a boy carrying a salmon that my father has caught and my mother will clean. It could be the year before the moonwalk, it could be the year before the Ladner brothers ever saw the Fraser River, it could be seven thousand years before the birth of Christ.

I reach home, and stand grinning in the kitchen light. My mother lays down a page of old newspaper on which there might just be a headline about the moonwalk. Carefully, I place the fish onto the paper, and the connection to the past immediately begins to deepen. For when the jack spring is cleaned, when my mother has cut off the head and tail, slit the belly, heaped the still-gaping head, tail, and guts onto another page of old newspaper, where they are bound for the backyard garden as prime fertilizer, I will carry it in a plastic shopping bag up the street and give it into the arms of an old woman.

There I go, and there she is. She's short, her thin, curled white hair like a head of dandelion seed, and she bends to me with the intensity of connection between the very old and very young that renders moonwalks and flags and annual canning packs ridiculous. Grandma Atkey, we all call her, though she is not our grandmother. Who is she? She's a woman who, widowed young, raised her three sons by taking in boarders – in this house, just up the street, many decades before I was born. All the years of my childhood and well into my adulthood, I will take a little jack spring to Grandma Atkey. On the river, bringing in his net, my father will stop the drum and say, "Here's one for Grandma Atkey," and I will learn to assess the salmon by their potential as gifts. And the gift will be returned, as it is the next night, and many nights.

Images flicker on the clapboard of the Atkeys' house. Grandma's son, Ken, has set up a projector on the front lawn and is showing silent movies to the neighbourhood children. The hour's windless and yet the hat keeps blowing off Buster Keaton's head. He's running, a thousand women in wedding dresses are chasing him, we're all laughing, the white stream flows, moonlight, milt, the Milky Way, everything's in motion, the perfume of the grass rising to the stars, the blood pumping through our bodies, the celluloid whirring on the reel. The comedian's charcoaled eyes flare wide, the moon slides out, the film breaks, there's a long sigh. Underneath it, all around it, the sound of salmon splashing in a net is a mild cheer for all the millennia we've killed.

Nothing is separate. In the 1920s, on one of the Prairie Drift's silt islands, the lumber baron H.R. MacMillan hosted a pheasant-shooting party for Douglas Fairbanks and Mary Pickford, "America's Sweetheart." They ate salmon from the stocks MacMillan's company hadn't yet destroyed by clear-cutting in watersheds. Thirty years later, Buster Keaton, his fame long over, made a promotional film for the Canadian National Railroad. Charcoal-eyed, he madly pumped a handcart over a line whose laying down almost destroyed the Fraser River salmon forever. And from the moon in 1969, beside the little American flag, did Neil Armstrong and Buzz Aldrin look down on Ladner and see their young countryman, Carl Enders, crawl stoned into the granite clock-tower in front of the museum? For that was where he chose to dodge the Vietnam Draft – inside the William Ladner family's 1922 gift to the town in the name of their pioneering father. Did the astronauts see Carl Enders from the moon? Under a clock that never worked, he slept and dreamed while the present slowly evolved into history. If he had climbed out one night and dangled from the clock's hands like Harold Lloyd over Times Square on the front of the Atkeys' house, who would have seen the substance that cast the shadow, who could even tell the substance from the shadow?

Connections everywhere, cycles completing themselves and starting up again, the beautiful and the sinister, simply as our bike wheels revolved when we turned our bikes upside-down and pedalled with our hands to turn blades of grass into popcorn. If you had a Georgia Street in your past, it's a shadow falling off a corpse today, but even that shadow must mean something.

I phone my mother. She tells me they're making a movie all along Chisholm, the roads are blocked off, that whole end of the old town, the waterfront end, is all lit up. She tells me it's a murder mystery.

I don't tell her I know who's been murdered and who the killers are. She doesn't need to hear such things from her child who is also the father of three of her precious grandchildren, she doesn't need me to blacken the future. But it's blackening all the same.

Cut, the director says, and the canneries rot on the banks. *Cut*, and the boats disappear. *Cut*, and the ten thousand different stocks of wild salmon dwindle to the hundreds. My childhood realm lit up like a crime scene. Is this meaningless? The catering trailers hum as the actors, between shots, eat farmed salmon while condo-dwellers leave their wall-sized television screens to perhaps catch a glimpse of the flesh and blood substance of some of those flickering shadows.

Can the schools of Fraser River salmon be seen from the moon? The flag and the human footprints will still be there when the wild salmon are gone.

Roll the credits.

* * *

No one's filming this. No one takes over the streets of my childhood to film a "birth mystery." It's the fourth day of November, 2005, and I'm walking with my wife and three children through the rainforest. The heavy rains stopped an hour before. The trail's flooded in the low places and the creek's flow is raging somewhere ahead of us, or beside us, the sound's hard to pinpoint, for there's still a rain murmur in the giant cedars and firs, their runnelled trunks are black from the recent drenching, except where the thick shag of green moss covers over them and glistens. Large sword ferns drip the water that has been dripped on them from the boughs above, but silently, for the creek owns the forest now.

We bend under a large deadfall and emerge on the other side to a stunning, controlled violence. Two feet deep, twenty wide, and rushing as if some chute's being repeatedly drawn back, the creek is a shout of now in the timelessness. Glass-clear, rip-torn into white bursts, and shining black along both banks, the water changes as you look at it. For just as your eyes fill with the broken jade and hoarded Spanish coin of the creekbed, colours so fluid they could be molten, a shadow darts into your vision. Or perhaps you simply blinked.

We step closer to the bank, but not to the very edge. After a heavy rain, erosion can weaken the overhangs; any extra weight and the bank is likely to give way. Besides, what we have come to see can feel vibrations in the ground.

My wife points to a shadow. "That's a fin," she says.

I try to focus on the stillness below the rapid motion, but it's like watching the dead prey in an eagle's clutch without noticing how the eagle soars. The creek still owns my senses.

Dashiell runs ahead twenty yards to another good viewing spot, and Theresa, with Levi on her back, follows. I can't resist hurrying either. With the creek flowing so hard and fast, eager to touch all its sharp angles, it's difficult to remain still. I take Sadie's hand and lead her away. In a few seconds, the tree-sweetened air dissipates and we plunge fully into the salmon's world. The smell's thick but not unpleasant. For me, it's the smell of the past, I'm holding my own five-year-old hand and taking the child I was back home.

Underfoot, the gold, ochre, pale yellow leaf-fall is slippery, and the surrounding maples, alders and birches ripple their remaining foliage like fins. But still the great conifers dominate. I look up and see a tangle of arm-thick branches covered in the green moss; it's as if all shadows turn to moss here, as if even what's cast from the material is so fertile that it seeds growth.

"I see one," Dashiell cries, "I see a fish!"

"Shh."

Theresa touches me on the shoulder as I come up beside her. "Look," she whispers.

There's a deeper pool with a sandy bottom at the near bank. Between this pool and a downed cedar in the middle of the creek, its Medusa head of roots black as a cave mouth, flows a narrow tunnel of clear water over shining glass shards of stone. The fish – a female dog salmon, judging by her smaller size and paler colouring – wriggles her tail to hold herself against the terrific force of the creek. Suddenly a darker, larger fish thrusts in with a quick tail-splash, his dorsal fin rippling the surface, and rubs his flank against the female. But he lies there only a few seconds before another male erupts onto the scene and bites at the first male with his hooked jaw of large teeth. The two of them whirl away as the female, still wriggling, maintains her position. Near us, slightly below the pool and where the creek's raging, a third male glides into view and hovers, still as a naked arm held out in a storm of wind and rain. His jaw too is hooked, his dark back slightly arched, his dark body splotched with white and streaked with purple, like parchment, a piece of stained treasure map. He doesn't appear to move, yet he holds perfectly still and straight for over a minute before he's flung back and disappears, his dozen pounds of fierce desire suddenly lighter than a leaf.

Farther out, there's a splash, a circle of salmon bodies, a rippling knife-cut along the surface – then nothing. Amazingly, the female holds her position, conserving her diminishing energy (salmon stop eating once they leave salt water to return to fresh) so she can make another plunge forward, seeking out the exact place to dig her redd (or nest). The males, meanwhile, also weakening, will follow, brandishing their fins to attract a mate, fighting each other off with their canine-like teeth, sometimes tearing a chunk out of a competitor's back. There's nothing genteel about the spawning process. Time is pressing, every minute their tissues are softening and absorbing water as the roe and the milt in their bodies ripen further and all their internal organs begin to shut down.

While we stand on the bank, in a silence dramatically unlike the civilizations we've built, and, at our ease, feel the cheapness of our culture sliding off us, the salmon fight desperately to complete their journey. While our children excitedly rush for the next break in the creekside foliage, and I wonder briefly if theirs might be the last generation to see wild salmon spawn, coho fry race invisibly seaward in these shallows, their inches-long bodies miraculously adjusting for a life in salt water instead of fresh. Out of over nineteen thousand species of fish identified on the earth, the salmon is one of the few that can live in both salt and fresh water. The metabolic adjustment is a mystery. While we whisper and point and marvel at the strength it must take to swim against the creek's flow while fighting off the competition, the salmon simply go about their ancient business. There's no human romance in the process for them. They must unburden their bodies of thousands of eggs and quarts of milt, then die. Before that, there's work and violence.

* * *

I'm alone now, watching the wild salmon spawn for the first time in my forty-one years. No one films me. No one watches from the moon. But somehow I feel I've never been more exposed. The air is eyed, as are the trees and the creek. Even the November sun, dropped below the last bank of inky cloud on the horizon and bathing the flowing waters and my open hands in gold, blazes with witness. What am I meant to do? Only what my culture discourages in a million ways every minute of every day: to stay still and attend to a sequence of moments outside of my ego and control. I look the day back. A tail splashes. Two flanks rub together. Two jaws gape in unison. A few hundred of the velvety orange, pearl-sized eggs are released in perfect simultaneity with the male's sperm. The timing must be precise, the eggs being fertilized as they sink through the sperm cloud, for once they descend to the redd, they immediately harden in order to be protected from the gravel and silt the female swishes over them. Even in the most pristine circumstances, only 50 percent of the eggs are successfully fertilized. However, 99 percent of those that are fertilized will hatch, a necessarily high rate, for the likelihood of each egg to complete its cycle – from winter under the gravel, to hatching, to life as an alevin feeding on a yolk sac, to the fry stage, the smolt stage, followed by years of long travel at sea, ending finally with the return to the birthplace to spawn – is less than one percent. Each female will lay close to four thousand eggs in three or four nests, usually selecting different mates for the fertilizing. Afterwards, her supply of energy almost spent, she'll stay alive a period of roughly ten days to protect her eggs from the frantic nest-building of other females before she becomes a carcass of rich protein feeding the forest that shelters her and provides the creek with the oxygen necessary for the growth of her young, which she will never see.

None of this is visible to me as I peer at the shadows under the rapid flow, but I know that clusters of protected eggs are holding firm on the creekbed. After only a week, an embryo can be seen in each egg. The first thing that can be easily recognized is the black dot of the rudimentary eye. Is this what watches me? I think of the five-year-old I was, on the banks of another estuary, staring into the hunger-haunted eyes of the dying and dead salmon. I felt witnessed then just as I do now. But I know it's my own gaze that's haunted.

My children call to me and I walk out of the trees into the full sunlight flooding the vivid green grasses of the estuary. A variety of ducks – canvasback, mallards, pintails – feed at the edge of the twinkling bay. Far across the water a float plane engine starts up, its crescendoing buzz a surprising reminder of how close we are to civilization. Downtown Sechelt is just over a mile away. On the crest of a slope to the southeast I can see the grey contours of the gravel pit. But here, where the fresh and salt water meet, I'm alone with my family and the ancient processes that continue to defy our culture's ongoing efforts to destroy them.

Theresa and the children have found a dead male dog salmon under a shrub about ten metres from the creek. It's freshly dead, for the visible eye has not been picked out by a gull or crow, and the flesh is still firm. Dashiell does not want me to touch it. Levi says quietly, "I feel sorry for that fish." And Sadie, with whom I have watched spiders capture and wrap their prey, asks me to turn the fish over so we can see what the other eye looks like. I agree to do so, but promise to slide the fish back into place afterwards.

It's not a large male, only about seven pounds, but its jaw is hooked and sports four prominent doglike teeth. I point these out, as well as the purple bands along its dull silver-black flesh. Surprisingly, the other eye-socket is completely reddened, as though hardened over with blood. I don't know what this means, so just stand there, holding the fish by its tail, wondering.

Dashiell, who has moved away, shouts out another find. I gently slide the fish along the slick grass to its original resting place. Rising, it occurs to me that some predator must have dragged the fish from the creek and under the bush – quite recently too. A bear, perhaps. Possibly something more than my past and the salmon eggs' future is watching us.

We stand around the bleach-white skulls of three salmon, their eye-sockets black and gaping, their jaws open in a soundless howl. Rough flakes off the moon. Shelvings in the dead letter office. Arrowheads rotted off their shafts. Suddenly we've all had enough of seeing. The kids are hungry. Theresa and I are looking forward to a good cup of coffee. I snap a quick picture of my family as they stand in the golden light almost devoured by so much beauty and silence, and then we follow the urgent pointing of the still-spawning salmon back the way we came, this time against the flow of the moments we've already lived, our eyes softly touching again the place of their widening.

XIX

IN THE LAST YEAR and a half of my complete freedom, that precious period before starting school, fate gave me a wonderful gift. One sunny April afternoon, I was standing on the sidewalk at the head of our driveway, trying to whistle on a blade of grass between my thumbs, when a beat-up station wagon coughed around the Buckerfields corner and rolled to a stop in front of the collapsing Victorian house immediately next door to us. Vacant for a few weeks, ever since old Mrs. Taylor – who had taught my brothers piano way back in the misty past – had moved out, the skinny, listing, moss-eaten, two-storey remnant of the nineteenth century seemed destined to join the ranks of the original townsite's permanent black holes. Already I had begun to wonder if there was some natural force that ate away at buildings in our neighbourhood, perhaps from underground. Would our cozy bungalow be next? The decay was literally too close to home, and so I had done no more than peer through the thick windows of 4857 Georgia Street, for fear that, should I find a way in, I might hasten the process of abandonment destined for the remaining houses of the neighbourhood, including our own.

But I needn't have worried. The creaking station wagon with the plastic imitation wood panelling and the inch-off-the-pavement chassis bore an exuberance into my childhood I could never have anticipated. At five, my playmates were my sister and her friends, and sometimes her friends' younger sisters. When I was born, my mother was thirty-eight and my father was forty-one, and few of their acquaintances had small children. And even if they had had them, this was not the era of playdates and playground get-togethers and widely read parents concerned with socialization. I had "the whole of the great outdoors" for a companion, to borrow my mother's phrase. And if I got tired of being alone or of trailing around after my sister, I had Pepper. Certainly I felt no lack of congenial company. That didn't mean, however, that I wasn't greatly intrigued by what spilled out of the station wagon, which was itself a spectacle, stuffed as it was to the gills with cardboard boxes and chairs and loose clothing; there was even a mattress strapped to the roof with – I did a double take – corkline.

The boy was smaller than me, but not much, so probably near my age. He wore a pair of frayed cut-off jeans and black gumboots a couple of sizes too big for him. His hair was long, uncombed, and the colour of salmon roe. So many freckles were scattered across the bridge of his nose and cheeks that it seemed a butterfly was resting there. Once on the sidewalk, he paused only long enough to spit – twice – before disappearing at a flopping run through the gap in the cedar hedge at the top of the Taylors' property.

The rest of the Bemis followed. The father, Don, was a blocky fisherman with a quick temper whose most striking physical characteristic proved to be the deep bum-crack which showed every time he bent to some task, and he was always bending to some task. It wasn't long before Rick – who else? – had dubbed this sight "the crack of Don." Mrs. Bemi, Jane, was in her late twenties, like her husband. A short, cheerfully rounded but not fat woman with a Wife of Bath gap between her front teeth and chestnut-coloured hair tied back in a bun, she carried a year-old baby in her arms as casually as she'd hold a paintbrush or cigarette between her fingers in all the years I was to know her.

"Jeffy, you little bugger, wait for us!" she yelled, then immediately laughed, deeply and warmly.

The father slammed his door and, at a half-run, whipped down the tailgate, grabbed a box, and plunged through the hedge as if he was disposing of a bomb. A few seconds later, the front door of the house slammed. Meanwhile, a noble-looking black Lab had leaped out of the back of the station wagon and was peeing against the black iron lamppost between the hedge and the sidewalk. At my side, Pepper growled, and before I even thought to hold him, he burst off, teeth bared. The Lab rose to the challenge. Soon the April calm was torn apart by a maelstrom of ripping snarls and hackled fur.

"Shamus!" The woman kicked at the circling, snapping dogs with her sandalled feet. "Get out of there!" Under her arm, the blanketed baby whirled but slept on. At least I couldn't hear any crying over the vicious sounds of the dogfight, the first of dozens Pepper and Shamus would engage in, each one undoubtedly to the death, unless someone intervened.

"Bee!" The woman was shouting louder now, her face panicky, perhaps because she'd seen the tears streaming down my face as I cried desperately to Pepper to come back. He was losing. The younger Lab's strong teeth had sunk into the white fur at Pepper's throat and blood splattered on the sidewalk. But Pepper turned his head and kept snapping, which made Shamus turn too, so they became a locked combination of fierceness, a blur and a continual jarring burst of deeper and deeper growls.

"For Chrissakes, Bee!"

It was my father who came, however, dragging the garden hose, the nozzle of which he turned on full-blast, the spray hitting the dogs' joined heads. Behind him, in a floral print apron, stood my mother. Her hands were over her mouth and, above them, her hazel eyes were even larger than usual. "Oh Heck, stop them, stop them!"

The roe-haired boy was suddenly beside me, his own cheeks wet. Then, as soon as his dog let go of Pepper's throat, he jumped in and yanked the Lab away by the fur on its neck. A second later, Mr. Bemi lumbered up and booted the dog in the hindquarters. It yelped and tore free of Jeff's grip. At the same time, my father grabbed Pepper, firmly but carefully, and, backing up several feet, proceeded to assess the damage. Amazingly, the wound was not serious, just a surface tear, more blood spilled than harm done, as my father said, while Mrs. Bemi repeated, "Jesus, I'm sorry about that," and my mother clucked, "Oh no no, it was both dogs fighting, it takes two to tango," and I snuffled and wiped the last tears away and looked at the roe-haired boy who was looking at me as he stood in the thin April sunshine in his black rubber boots, stamping them in the puddle of hose-water, and all around us the lilac and honeysuckle and dogwood and the bee-weighted flowers of the scarlet azalea eased the lingering violence from the air.

So it was that the Bemis came to Georgia Street, with a bang and two dogs whimpering.

* * *

Much more than me, Jeff Bemi – followed by his baby brother, the cloud-blond Mike, and eventually another roe-haired boy, named Robin – was a true wharf rat, a once common coastal type almost non-existent nowadays. Most of his childhood was spent barefoot and half-naked with a hook and snarled line in one hand and a garter snake or bullhead or some other creature in the other. You knew just by looking at him that he was destined for a life in the wild, or whatever would be left of it for him to find. It wasn't his ineffable creaturely shyness, or his expansive vocabulary of swear words and his permanent state of readiness for getting into trouble, that marked him as a breed born of place and therefore destined to suffer in the coming decades of corporate-spawned consumer conformity. It wasn't his flaming bright and always uncombed hair or his scratched and bleeding or bruised and grass-stained skin, and it wasn't his impermeability to all weather conditions and his Hollywood Indian stealth. It wasn't even his hatred for school and team sports and church and Cubs and all other forms of social organization. It was something much simpler and much deeper and I recognized it right away: he lived in his environment without fear of it, as if the idea that a river or an animal or the top of a tree could hurt him had never crossed his mind.

Perhaps he inherited this fearlessness from his parents, for they certainly expended little energy worrying over Jeff's safety. His outdoors was so vast and so much a part of him that it was always something of a shock to see him indoors. If the average child today spends three hours a day watching television and playing computer games, Jeff spent easily twice that much time lying on a wharf in the rain or creeping along a ditch to check a muskrat trap or just wandering around town with Shamus. When I think of the wild salmon and the culture that's dying with it, I can't help but think of the rainforest beyond the Skeena River far to the north, where a now forty-year-old man tries to live out the promise the earth made him in his childhood and which the earth has not broken. How can I not see a shadow on a trapline and two green eyes blinking through the snowfall at a fishless river when every level of government, with our complicity, sets out to destroy our birthright?

Yet the human world that's killing the past and the future with ever-accelerating speed is the same world that gave me friendship and the capacity to honour it. When I think of British Columbia, that pioneer boot on the gills, that opium smoke reeking of blood and loneliness, that somewhere-else, some-other-time name stamped on the here and now, I think of a boy I knew whose baptismal waters were those that the salmon smelled far out at sea, those that fed the roots of the four-hundred-foot forest. A Salish boy in a white skin. Chinook on his tongue, trading his own pelt for joy.

* * *

We were inseparable. The abandoned houses and shops and all the other interstices between the centuries knew the exchange of conversation again, and our laughter lightened some of the heaviest shadows. Jeff was almost always barefoot and he rarely wore a jacket; when he did, on the coldest winter days, he never zippered it. There was no time for such niceties as tying laces and buttoning buttons and zippering zippers. There was time only for exploration, which meant that, inevitably, breakfast left strawberry jam and peanut butter smears on your face or maybe you wore your pyjama top outside all day, if you'd bothered to wear one to bed the night before, that is.

Jeff's arrival quickly expanded my territory. At his lead, we ventured farther along the riverbanks, east and west, squelching in the low tide muck to collect beer and pop bottles, which we carted home in a Red Flyer wagon and washed down with a hose before turning in at Magees' recycling depot on the banks of Chilukthan Slough. With the proceeds, we bought supplies for the next day's adventure: I remember once paying the princely sum of two dollars for a huge slab of bologna, which we cut off in chunks with a jackknife (Jeff owned several of these). Bologna on white Wonder Bread slathered with ketchup, a brown paper bag of mojos and candy bananas and strawberries and "nigger babies" from Bernie's Confectionery and a pint carton of chocolate milk: sometimes we bundled these things in a large handkerchief and dangled them, hobo style, off the end of one of Rick's broken goalie sticks – this was before the day of backpacks – or else we borrowed one of my father's old black metal lunchboxes. Then we set off. To do what, to go where, and to speak of it how?

Speech wasn't important; mostly it took the form of Jeff saying, "Come on, let's go and chuck rocks off the dyke," or, "Come on, let's build a fort," or, "I bet I can hit that deadhead." We handled more rocks than an army of Davids – rocks, fallen fruit, and clay and dirt bombs. We hucked, chucked, lobbed, chunked, skimmed, winged, and whizzed our preferred weapons at every available target, specializing in tree trunks, driftwood, and – it must be admitted – certain people and houses.

At the end of Georgia Street, over the dyke behind the high mass of blackberry bushes, a couple of the local jungle bums liked to kill a bottle or three of cheap wine on a sultry evening. Or else a trio of teenagers would take a case of the tartan-labelled Uncle Ben's beer down and sit on the huge cedar log embedded in the dyke and talk about whatever teenagers talked about. We'd spy, of course, creeping up to listen. The old men sang songs found only at the bottom of wooden radios and slurred the lyrics, the teenagers said *fuck* a lot and talked mostly about how drunk and stoned they were and about how drunk and stoned they were going to get. None of this interested us much, and so, eventually, we returned to the dyke, let out a couple of war whoops, and started hucking and lobbing rocks over the blackberries. The old men never even stopped singing, and the teenagers, on those occasions when they were sober enough to notice, cursed loudly or tossed an empty bottle back; either tactic chased us home, hearts hammering, where we lay under the blazing azalea bush in the dusk, poised to jump up and escape into one of our houses should a host of bodies plunge down off the dyke.

As for houses, we targeted one in particular. It was the 1970s. Just as a candy store could sell "nigger babies," people could refer to Chinamen without risk of censure or, if truth be told, without any real awareness of the prejudice. Those few, mostly elderly Chinese still haunting the remains of Chinatown were natural attractions for children who interpreted difference and privacy as twin elements of a mystery equal to those submarine mysteries our fathers engaged in. As far as we could see, it was no coincidence that the carp Jeff sometimes caught with little chunks of gillnet hung between the floats could be sold to the Chinaman who ran Kin's grocery store on the edge of Chung Chuck's property – the link between the sole remaining fragment of Chinatown and the murky depths of the Fraser River seemed natural, and neither of us knew anything then of the history of the Chinese in the delta's salmon canning industry. What we knew, what we somehow picked up from the culture around us – comic books, TV shows, the non-assimilative tendencies of the elderly Chinese themselves, and the occasional open expression of adult prejudice – was that a Chinaman was dangerous and secretive, prone to flashes of machete-wielding temper and bursts of a language that sounded as if each word had been dredged up out of mud and had begun to stretch the instant it hit the air.

Chung Chuck, more than anyone, contributed to this stereotype. Rumours swirled around him: that he had murdered a wife back in China, that he had attempted to sell his three daughters into slavery, and that he possessed an entire library of law books which he consulted every time he ran afoul of the local authorities, usually for diverting water from the town's pipes to his haphazard collection of float homes. The truth, however, was more prosaic. He had come to Ladner in the nineteen-teens and had built, over decades, a small empire of land and property holdings, the centre of which was his potato farm, several dozen acres of rich loam on the western edge of the original townsite, near the charred planks and pottery shards of the once-crowded Chinatown. On this farm, in 1970, as an old man, he still prepared for planting with a horse and plough, his flopping straw hat loosely tied under his chin, his three daughters, thick, squat, mannish in their men's denim overalls and dusty coke-bottle glasses, always nearby to take their turn at the plough or to heft stones out of the way, while he barked orders and criticisms at them. The rumours hovered around Chung Chuck like so many flies to be swatted away by his pure indifference to public opinion, an artistic masterpiece of temperament that overwhelmed the facts of his life, even if you could uncover what these were. One incident, though, had secured his legend in Ladner, regardless of whether you admired or loathed Chung's part in it.

During the Great Depression, the Chinese of the Lower Mainland were proving to be more than the slave labourers they had been for the railroad and canning companies in the nineteenth century. By 1936, in fact, the Chinese had become highly successful in the market gardening business and held an increasing portion of both the wholesale and retail fresh produce market. This did not sit well with the white majority, or at least with those whites involved in the same industry. After some heavy lobbying by an inflammatory MLA (who, oddly enough, held his seat in Peace River, 1,200 kilometres away from the Lower Mainland), the BC Coast Vegetable Marketing Board established the price for potatoes and set a quota for each grower. Every sack of potatoes to enter Vancouver was to be tagged to prove its legality.

Chung was not impressed. Early on a misty morning in March of 1937, he drove his heaped-over-the wooden-slat-sided truckload of spuds onto the Fraser Avenue Bridge, on his way, as usual, to one of the wholesale headquarters in Vancouver. Within a minute, however, he had encountered a large timber blocking the way, behind which stood five burly, white potato farmers and an inspector for the marketing board. When ordered to unload his potatoes, Chung instead burst from the cab of his truck, wielding a crowbar, which he immediately swung against the inspector's leg. In the ensuing skirmish, the inspector and one of the farmers also received knife cuts. Chung, meanwhile, fled the scene, leaving his truck and his harvest behind. The whole incident ended – and this was to be a familiar pattern over the decades – with Chung bringing charges against the six men, a case which he did not win, but which effectively kept him from being found guilty of any crime himself.

In short, no one, least of all a pair of boys, knew what to make of the man. Was he a heroic guardian of freedom, or a thug and a criminal? My father, at any rate, admired him, perhaps because my grandfather, the wounded Great War veteran and town plumber, was a good friend of Chung's and regularly played poker in the basement of one of Chung's seedier properties. Ah yes, but then, didn't Chung deliberately set fire to one of his slum rental buildings in order to evict a family of East Indians who refused to leave? Didn't he get into a fistfight with one of them and gouge out one of the man's eyes? Didn't he swoop in after the internment of the town's one Japanese family during World War II and buy up their valuable property and boats for a pittance? Certainly his daughters did not fare well under his authority. One year, Grandma Atkey insisted that they attend school, but the girls were so exhausted that they kept falling asleep in class, so Grandma had to give up. And then there were those rumours about murdering a wife back in China. And what could you make of a Chinaman who named his two sons Napoleon and Winchester? No doubt, as my grandfather had insisted, Chung had read every one of the thousands of books crammed into his library, legal and otherwise, and only spoke pidgin English and played the ignorant "Chinee" to gain an advantage by turning the white system's prejudice against itself.

Whatever the truth and whatever the legend, Jeff and I inevitably gravitated towards the blackberry-bush-shrouded and morning-glory-entwined shacks at the bottom end of one of Chung's rental properties. To get there, we walked a few minutes west of Georgia Street, along the dyke, to the open field behind our houses. The grass tickled our bare legs and stomachs as the three giant poplars on the western edge of the field, which bordered a broad, muddy slough, threw long shadows across our cautious advance. For now we were entering a world of sinister silences and exotic pungent aromas, where carp and bullhead and, as rumour had it, dogs were eaten and where a violent old patriarch hunched over thick tomes of tiny print, one potato-dusty finger tracing the cramped legalese, to save himself from the gallows. Even to trespass here was a risk. To throw a rock at the house just beyond the overgrown, almost subterranean sequence of shacks was to puncture the impermeable bubble of protection our white birthright had given us.

Instinctively, we crouched, found the narrow path through the blackberry prickles, and descended into the musty, sawdusted ruins. Only now, thirty-five years later, do I realize that those ruins were likely a rare stretch of a long-forgotten China house, that I was going down into a heritage that transcended ethnicity, where the Chinese and the Indian and the English founders of my hometown sweated and shouted over the silver bodies heaped into their senses by Finns and Japanese and Austrians and Greeks and a dozen other races, until the eyes and the hands, moving so quickly at their myriad tasks, become only human and, finally, not even that, but simply alive, as if gaining speed and fluency from all the death around them. Of course, these shacks had long been used for other purposes – there was no physical evidence of the cannery operations, just a torn mattress with broken springs stuffed into one corner and a general smell of mould and woodbugs crawling on the angled doorframes. But the darkness, because it was daylight outside (we lacked the courage to do this at night); belonged always to the distant past. And the distant past, like the distant future of space travel that the moon landing promised, was always exotic. Where else, Jeff and I asked ourselves wordlessly, with that subtle exchange of quickened pulses unique to fast friends of early childhood, could you find lychee nuts growing?

So we emerged from the oriental grave into the whispering poplar light, the alien gift in our hands, and, dazed by our successful trespasses and an inchoate sense of having violated something more mysterious than our few years could fathom, something belonging to an "us" that might never be born, we responded as humans do, with a desperate reclamation of the boundaries we understood. We picked up rocks from out of the tall grass and, careful not to break a window, we chucked them at the side of the Chinaman's house, a large, shambling structure every bit as old as the one in which Jeff lived. No one ever ran outside in anger, or even appeared. The echoing silence that rolled over us was complete and final and more frightening than a cry of outrage would have been, because inside the silence lay our knowledge that we were insignificant and our awareness that even a shatter of glass would soon have dissolved into the unnervingly steady whir of the dragonfly's wings. We turned away, not speaking for several seconds, as the riversmell rose up over the dyke to meet us and Jeff finally cried out, his barefooted stride flattening the horsetails as a giant's tramples church steeples, "Come on, let's get some cherries," and we were back in the idyllic time whose throat life had just closed its hands around, the time that gasps at the end of memory now.

* * *

The days as we live them are mountains, and after thirty-five years they become grains on a beach of dark sand. I pick up a handful of 1969–74. I can catch a glimpse of mountain valley, a whiff of forest, even a taste of pure headwater, but there's no definition, none of the categorical ordering that science and history demand from human existence. I wrote that Jeff Bemi and I were inseparable. That is a lie of memory conflating the past into one long, drawn-out experience of bliss. For in truth, my solitude, while diminished, never disappeared. By the age of five, I had a taste, almost a hunger, for it. Many hours through my childhood, I was still that moonwalker of the first years, staring through windows that belonged to the dead, or lying on my back in the tall grass and hearing my pulse thread in and out of the clouds and the sun. And as my ability to read developed, I also needed to be alone with books, to touch those pages just as I touched a cherry ripe on the bough or Jeff's wrist after our jackknives had made their little nicks and we had bonded solemnly as blood brothers. An intensity of friendship of a kind I'd never know again, and a falling away, a natural ebb, as if I needed to recover myself in the familiar channels of solitude.

Then, as well, Jeff had the same need. Often, he woke hours before me and set off for the river and sloughs and marshes, the deep jade of his eyes burning the mist off the heron's wings and the muskrat's blink, as he checked and rebaited his bullhead lines and carp nets and, eventually, his muskrat traps, going deeper into his wilderness even as I retreated from it. After those first, unschooled years, I was inexorably pulled towards the solitude of a book-reading rather than river-reading devoutness and, like most children, had to snatch the first, primal pleasures when I could. For Jeff, it was otherwise. The nick in his wrist never stopped bleeding for he never stopped testing the blade. Mine, meanwhile, spent much more time folded in my pocket than open in my hand.

Ah, but the first year of friendship and the stolen hours afterward – what a mountain range they made, and how small my adult shadow appears on the sand.

* * *

We came down from the backfield, into the vacant lot, and stopped at the ancient Bing cherry tree growing alone exactly in the middle. It was a mast from the top of which we could see the few gillnetters of the gentlemen's fleet on the Prairie Drift. The boats were only blurs, but on a clear day, if we had binoculars, we could tell the *Nola J* from the *Thunderbird* and the *Queen Bee* from the *I'll Be Damned* (the *Driftwood* was almost impossible to find, for it resembled nothing more than a floating log). If we were lucky, we managed to time our crow's nest vigilance to the moment of my father's decision to come in for supper, something he didn't always do; it depended so much on the tide and the catch. In any case, there was no exact time for coming in. At the height of summer, with the sockeye returning, he never missed the dark set. No fisherman did. Prior to the late sixties, in fact, before the federal government put restrictions on licensing, anyone in town who could find a craft navigable and seaworthy enough headed out for the dark set, that one particular drift when, the darkness and the silt combining to render the meshes of the net invisible, the canny sockeye could not stop and swim around the obstruction. Even in 1970, there were still those oldtimers who made a point of catching the dark set. Often, Jeff and I watched the broken, puttering, part-time fleet leave the harbour in a kind of drizzling aftermath to the day's greater violence, their varied sizes and manner of progress swallowed by the spilling of the red sun and, finally, the dusk fine as the silt in the river beneath them. Yet rarely did we see the coughing and clanking return to harbour after dark had fallen, for we were small boys, active all day, and the sun's setting was the mesh that wrapped us round in sleep.

This particular day, the sun had not begun its final descent, and we did not have binoculars to bring the boats into focus, so we climbed down the rough and ash-grey trunk and walked past the still fronds of the massive weeping willow, a golden tree which, during a rainstorm, opened and closed like a jellyfish in a frenzy of mating with the sudden wash of tide. Beyond its now-motionless presence, we cut through Jeff's cluttered backyard and went through the back door of his house into the large kitchen, which was really two rooms together without a wall. Here, we found Jeff's mother, cigarette in one hand, paintbrush in the other, putting the finishing touches to a portrait of some incredibly wrinkled elder from the Tsawwassen reserve.

"Old geezers and animals," she had told my mother with a throaty chuckle, "that's what I like to paint."

And it was true. On several easels placed around the coffee-mug- and-ashtray-laden kitchen stared back the elderly and the wild, crinkled men and women from fishing families and dying tribes, black Labs and golden retrievers, chickadees and sparrows and red-winged blackbirds and a dozen other species of songbird, the light falling on all of them through windows of thick glass fitted in another century. And the eyes in most of the portraits were the same – soulful, dark, but vibrant, as if in the act of committing their sight to canvas, Jeff's mother used the blood from the most guarded and cherished corner of her own heart. Many of the canvases, however, contained boats, either spiderwebby pencil constructions or freshly gleaming finished jobs drying in the swirls of cigarette smoke and waiting for the owner's wife, who had commissioned the work, to drop by and pick it up and take it away forever, but not before sitting for an hour or two to gossip (or, spread the bullshit around, as Mrs. Bemi put it) at the formica-topped table on which an orange-striped tabby without a name (my family called it BOC, for Bemis' orange cat) slept. Dozens of vessels – gillnetters, trollers and seiners – from the Ladner fleet were moored for months in that smoky harbour of paint fumes and wet dog fur as some forest on the way to the Nass River darkened around them and an old Nisga'a looked on sorrowfully at all the ingenuity and greed that had destroyed his culture and baby Mike crawled around happily on the sloping, cracked, and ash-covered linoleum.

The Bemis were representative of a common family structure now gone from the coast, a strucure in which husbands spent months away from home to earn a living in the salmon fishery. Ever since the Mifflin Plan brought in by the federal government in 1996, which restructured licensing so that an independent fisherman could no longer with a single licence chase fish all up and down the wet edge of the province, the summer-long absences of husbands, along with a comfortable income, have ceased to be a noteworthy social statistic. Since only the big canning companies can afford to hold licences in several areas (each licence costing more than fifty thousand dollars), and since conservation efforts have severely restricted fishing time in any one area, marriages like the Bemis', which were more standard in the fishing industry than that of my parents', no longer exist. I don't point this out to be nostalgic for them. The 1970s, as I've written, were a boom time for the ambitious fisherman, and the salmon and herring stocks paid a heavy price. I wish to record only how much has changed in so short a time, a whole social structure collapsing to parallel the diminishment of the wild salmon.

Let's take a peek at what's on the kitchen table, for example, in the early 1970s. Here's a stamped envelope padded an inch thick with hundred dollar bills sent, through the mail, from up the coast or on Vancouver Island where Jeff's father was currently fishing. Mr. Bemi always mailed cash home, thousands of dollars at a time. And what did Mrs. Bemi do with the money? Perhaps it sat on the kitchen table for a week as she pulled out a few bills as needed for groceries. Eventually, however, she put it in the big freezer in the room off the kitchen, where it froze beside the previous year's sockeye and venison and moose meat that her husband had harvested on his travels. Tens of thousands of dollars, iced stiff, after having migrated hundreds of kilometres to Ladner, just like the Fraser River salmon. All this wealth from the wild salmon, swimming down in envelopes, the bills stuffed like entrails into the white flesh – and Mrs. Bemi was almost indifferent to it.

Her husband, however, would use it, as most other fishermen did, to increase his catching capacity, to invest in better technology and gear and boats, an investment encouraged and supported by the society around him screaming more, more, more, which now tut-tuts naughty, naughty, naughty, even as the government okays licences for clear-cutting in old-growth forests and financially supports fish farms and the big multinational canning companies who, together, are more complicit in the destruction of the wild salmon than any motley collection of fishermen – aboriginal, white, or otherwise – could ever be, even as we vote these governments in, or don't vote at all out of laziness and complacency, as we sit in rush hour in our oversized vehicles waiting to maneouvre, like spawning female salmon, for an open space in which to carry forward our urgent lives.

Jeff slathers peanut butter onto two slices of Wonder Bread. His mother paints flesh onto the coast's dying people, his mother who herself will be dead of cancer by the age of fifty. And I listen to the open letters whispering the strange poem of my time and place. Ucluelet. Barkley Sound. Bamfield. Rivers Inlet. Nitinat. Namu. Port Hardy. Alert Bay. Ocean Falls. I smell the salmon, I hear the rain falling on the sea. In the darkness, a tenderman pitches each drop and together they strike and run down this window in a café in Gibsons Landing three decades later where I stare out at all the murmuring, sighing absences in the harbour. Bella Bella. Bella Coola. Klemtu. Alert Bay. Horsefly, Chilko, Quesnel. Coho, chinook, oolichan. A Douglas fir, a veiled Greek woman, a fleet, a town, a father, and a myth. When I rise and walk away, my heart quivers slightly in the black redd I drag behind.

XX

One morning in Gibsons, I woke to foghorns. Looking through the bedroom window, I saw the heavy, dripping white of memory's November shrouding the street and the neighbours' apple orchard, and experienced a delicious feeling of vertigo. The fog, the first of the damp, ghostly circulating variety I had known in over a decade, immediately backed the earth around the sun thirty-five times, lifted me from the quiet breathing of my two eldest children, and placed me down, a boy again, in the tall grass of the vacant lot across from the house on Georgia Street.

* * *

Jeff is with me. We're both wearing the Davy Crockett caps my mother had brought us home from the Five and Dime where she works. My father has had a good sockeye season, or perhaps he's worked more hours than usual this fall driving a tractor on Roland Savage's potato farm on Westham Island, or else my mother has received more than her usual employee discount from her boss. Whatever the case, we wear these gifts with pride as we pass under the boughs of the Douglas fir, itself only a shadow in the fog, a remote stillness, a tree we dreamed about and were slowly losing to wakefulness. But there's no true waking in such weather. The chill and the blurriness of all defined edges, the added hush to the quiet, as if we had stepped from our beds straight into the reality of our imaginations, keeps us blinking and rubbing at the damp on our flushed faces. We can't even hear Shamus panting beside us. All movement, including our own, takes on this same silent violence of objects flowing from the soundless cracking of the fine white shell around them.

The silvery grass seems to part before we reach it. Every spiderweb we pass has been turned into an attic cobweb, the bare apple and plum branches into the shawled and reaching arms of crones. When, from somewhere distant or near we cannot tell, a high, harsh peal of gullcry sounds, we stop in unison, breath streaming over our cheeks as if we are swimming, before flowing forward again.

We cross Trennant Street, its pavement brittle and slick, and stand before a vague, high wall of dark. This is the Eustaces' great cedar hedge, which we had already used for the walls of a medieval castle and which now suits perfectly for the walls of a fort in the American West (to our knowledge, Canada had never had such forts, let alone a Davy Crockett). With a glance and a nod of encouragement, we creep through the narrow gap. The iron gate creaks like a faint echo of the gullcry, then slides away behind us as, so excited now that we give up all play-acting, we walk quickly towards the orange blur and the grating buzz of Mr. Eustace's garage.

Jeff and I step into the orange light, which, because the door of the garage is open, mixes with the fog to make a strangely vivid swirl around Mr. Eustace's short, bare-armed figure. With his white sleeves rolled up and his body hunched over the table-saw in the dimness, he could be a baker sliding bread into an oven. Instead, he is a man near eighty, a recently retired barber who has never touched either of our heads, but has touched the heads of generations, the heads of my father and my uncles and my brothers, the heads of my grandfather and other Great War veterans, the heads of boys who'd gone to fight the Second World War and never returned, the heads of boys and men who'd drowned or had drank themselves to death or committed suicide or been killed in car accidents, the heads of atheists and communists and ministers and bankers, touched them with skill and not ungentleness as he listened to the life of a town and a time that was dying as clearly as if he could read the future in its shorned skulls.

His name is Sam, but we call him Mr. Eustace. He wears suspenders and very small-lensed, round glasses. His nose is large, his lips full, and red as his suspenders in the curious broth of light and fog. At his feet, shavings almost the pink of salmon flesh pile up as he expertly guides the wood towards the saw. A rich aroma of cedar wraps around us. We carry it with us to the edge of his presence, our heads almost bowed. So eager are we for the gift that he has promised that we have become shy as foals. For a long moment, he does not notice us, but goes on angling the wood, looking down through his lenses which are like knotholes of white in his face.

Finally, wood in hand, he lifts up from his work and looks straight at us. At first, it is as though he doesn't see us, or can't believe we're real. In the sudden silence, we can almost hear him blinking.

"Hello boys," he says at last, "you have very good timing. I have just finished."

And he reaches down, grabs another piece of wood, then steps forward and gives one to each of us. We simply stare at them, two perfect rifles, heavily redolent of the forest from which they came, the stocks grainy but smooth, the barrels pointing ahead with what we know to be immaculate precision.

"It's a good day for sneaking up on the Indians," he says. "Plenty of cover."

We still can't speak, and Mr. Eustace smiles. "Go on then, before your cover lifts."

At the garage door, I look back, and he's just standing there, staring, but it doesn't seem to be at us. Remembering my manners, I murmur a thank you, but he doesn't seem to hear. It's the last time I'll ever see him, or the last time I'll remember, which amounts to the same thing and which causes, more than all else, the feeling of vertigo when one reflects on the past.

If anything, the fog is thicker as we pass Chung Chuck's abandoned restaurant, a two-storey building whose round metallic Coca-Cola sign we often use for a rock-throwing target. The upper storey is charred from the fire that made the building unuseable two years before, and sometimes I can hear the ghostly cries of the last poor renters who eked out a living there, selling that bizarre blend of bird's nest soup and greasy hamburgers that defines the immigrant Chinese diner of an earlier era. Jeff lifts his rifle and fires at a blackened window almost invisible in the fog. "Got one," he says, and blows smoke off the barrel's end.

On the main street, we stop as always at Wellburn's Meat Market. The place has an irresistible appeal because of its sawdust floor and the huge moose head hanging over the counter. When we step inside, I immediately shrink back, for somehow the moose head seems to move towards the fog at our backs, as if the fog was the magic he'd been waiting for that would break the spell of death and give him his life in the forest again. Bloody-aproned and smiling out of his thick black handlebar moustache, Mr. Wellburn gives us each a raw weiner, whistles appreciatively at our rifles, then goes back to chopping with his cleaver.

We stand outside his shop. Across the street the six empty shops with their smashed windows beckon, but we are distracted by the sight of a man walking out of the Ladner Hotel and straight into the granite clock tower outside the museum. This is something new. I won't know who the man is or why he disappears into the clock tower until I'm forty years old. He is completely forgotten, then dredged up by my brother, Rick, and this brief sighting comes up too. Just as quickly, though, it sinks back, for the man does not emerge. Jeff and I wait, rifles poised, for a long time, or for what feels like a long time. The clock's hands never move, and in any case, we can't interpret them if they did. One car goes past, very slowly, like a hearse bearing the body of the sun away, and we shoulder our rifles out of respect. Far out on the river, a foghorn's long, two-noted lament deepens our pleasure. The eagle and the killer whale on the totem pole keep sliding away and coming back to position. We decide to make our way to the waterfront.

On the journey, we pass the tiny building sandwiched between the Legion and Oeuvray's garage where Mr. Eustace had his barbershop. I press my face against the cold glass, which is so thin it seems the fog must break through it at any second. I can see nothing but a dark which is darker even than the charred storey of the abandoned restaurant. Jeff keeps moving. After a few seconds, Shamus, perhaps missing me, barks. I run to catch up, and the fog swallows the three of us, as if we've never existed at all.

The fog remains heavy as we walk towards the river, conducted on our way by the mournful rise and fall of a freighter's foghorn. Finally, we reach that emptiness along the street's last half-block where, only a few years before, a row of shops and houses, including my grandparents' combination home and plumbing business, had stood. The fog swirls over the crushed grass and split boards and rusted nails of the vacancy and feels colder here, enters deeper into the skin. I shiver and pull my coat together at my neck. From across the street comes the disorienting nautical clang of the garage's bell hose for the gas pumps, as a pickup truck with buttery headlights glides to a stop. Where are we? It is easy to lose perspective in the fog, even with the most familiar distances. I look up to the blank feet of air where my grandparents and my father and his five siblings once lived, where my brothers and older cousins played and where, in that lost year of my emergence from the womb, I was held by my grandmother, the only widow of all the widows of my childhood who ever held me. No one looks back. The fog drifts through the parlour and the bedrooms and the kitchen with the massive cast-iron stove, flows down the long narrow staircase and up the brick chimney, pushes open the front door, soundlessly breaks the windows, and settles on the skin at my wrists.

I don't linger. Jeff and Shamus have vanished up the dyke, and besides, I'm chilled right through, I need to keep my blood flowing. My fingers have gone numb on the stock of the carved rifle, as if I have become my grandfather in the trenches, poised, waiting for the rush of sound that will end all sound. When it comes, it's not a rush or an ending, but disturbing nonetheless.

As I step off the curb to cross Chisholm Street to the dyke, I hear whistling and the sound of wheels turning. The whistling is patterned but almost tuneless, like a killdeer's cry of distress, and the slight swish and creak of the wheels maintains the tempo. Abruptly the whistling stops, but the sound of the wheels increases until, at last, an old man on a bicycle emerges, his skullcap pulled down to just above his eyes which, amazingly, are shut against the cold. He wears a wildly snagged Cowichan sweater and gleaming black hipwaders and rides in a precarious looping fashion, as if still following the tuneless pattern that no longer falls from his lips. In the few seconds between his appearance and disappearance, I do not recognize him, nor does he appear to take any note of my presence. And yet, once he has gone, the piping whistle starts up again. I can't help but think that it must have stopped because of me. But why? For weeks, I will try to see this old man in the faces of the old fishermen at the waterfront, only to come away disappointed. He remained what he was in that one meeting, a genie of November stillness, Jack Fog, whistling as he pedalled his chilled vapour through the streets.

On the dyke, we walk into the now faster-flowing fog and soon stand on the slick planks of the upper wharf. An orange light shines fuzzily above, the river's either as black as I've ever seen it or else I'm seeing darkness instead of water. Jeff peels a strip of wood off the net-rack and begins to chew it. Then he bends down, picks up an empty beer bottle glistening with damp and hurls it into the harbour. The splash seems to come from miles away, from another river, and there's no echo because, immediately, a great blue heron rises with a terrific *skronk skronk* from a nearby piling and vanishes into the air across the channel, holding my heartbeats sloppily in its bill. Shamus doesn't even bark. He's too busy lifting his leg against the metal lamppost. A sizzling steam rises around him as if he's set fire to his fur.

The clink of mast chains surrounds us. The darkness now

moves like the riverbottom, shifting its silts. Then silence falls for several seconds. I can hear Shamus panting, Jeff sniffling, but nothing else. I'm surprised it's so late, that it's become even harder to see. The mast chains break the silence again. Clink clank. It's as if some ghostly plumber is working on the pipes that keep everything alive.

I turn around. The fog's burned off. It's a summer night. Men in T-shirts crusted with old fish stains stand shoulder to shoulder on the wharf, their faces tight and drawn and shrouded with cigarette smoke, the word *fuck* thunking like lead to the planks. Most of them hold a thin sheet of white paper in their hands, and when they hold these up to squint at them, I think they are going to open their mouths and sing, they look so much like a choir. But *bastards* and *goddamn peckerheads* and *fuck* are lyrics to a song no one but the singers ever hear. I keep to the shadows, not wanting to be seen and sent home by my father or brother. They stand together, off to the side near the top of the gangway. My father is looking at the paper, but Rick has already made an airplane of his and floated it towards the lone man who stands, elevated on an overturned fish box, on the far side of the net-racks. His back is to the mass of blackberry bushes whose rapidly swelling berries send gusts of sweetness over his broad shoulders. He is dark-skinned, Indian-looking but not quite, over six feet tall, and a Communist. At least that is what I heard one of the younger fishermen grumble after the big man had spoken. "If you want to believe what a fucking Communist tells you. . ." he muttered, to which one of the older Greeks shrugged and said, "You can believe what the companies tell you if you want – it's your funeral."

I don't know what a Communist is, but I can sense it's something powerful and unusual, for I have never seen so many fishermen gathered together at one time, not even on the river, and I have rarely seen such a serious expression on my father's face. It frightens me, but I do not want to leave, even though I have gone beyond the range of my mother's red-winged blackbird whistle, calling me home.

The man on the fish box talks about the price of sockeye. He says that the companies' latest offer is an insult, that the fishermen can't work for those slave wages, that giving in now will make the previous weeks' efforts worthless. His voice is deep and strong and almost like a force of weather. The fishermen are restless and disgruntled, though. One shouts, "Yeah, that's what you said Friday," and there's a low murmur of agreement and a few burning cigarette ends blaze across the darkness. The man on the box, the Communist, shouts back something about unity, says that the companies always bank on the fishermen fighting amongst themselves, have been using that strategy for a hundred years. "Just a couple more days," he says, "Keep the pressure on. With all them Adams on the way, they can't afford this strike any more than we can."

The moon is out from the clouds. Its weak light falls over the assembly and reflects the metal buttons on several floater jackets. As if touched on the shoulder and asked to be quiet, each man lowers his head and seems to balance the moonlight like water on the sheet of paper before him. The river slaps the wharf. No one moves. Termites hover around the sizzling lamp bulb.

The explosion raises the still bodies as one, the dark heads and shoulders jerking up as if torn from their torsos, smoke and an acrid smell cutting rapidly over the scattered motion. Then, in the first few seconds after the sound has faded, a crazy peal of laughter flows up from the river, followed by the rip of an outboard engine starting up.

"Albert! You goddamned son of a bitch!"

My heart's beating so fast that I can hardly hear the shouts over the throbbing of the blood in my temples. But I see, in the swath of oily moonlight on the harbour, a hunched figure in the stern of a skiff, his head turned back over his shoulders, his face almost split in half by a grin. A cry of triumphant glee, a sort of cackling whoop, flies across the dark fathoms and joins the last shreds of the dispersing smoke on the wharf. *Hee hee hee.* And the outboard's throttle is revved, and the swath of moonlight, empty now, ripples its way back to calm.

"That crazy peckerhead," someone says, but there's admiration in the tone.

"Him and his goddamned seal bombs."

"Well, they're no damned good for seals anyway, he might as well use them for something else."

"I prittineer had a heart attack, that stupid bugger."

The tension's gone, the faces are slack, my father's smiling at one of the men next to him. I look for the Communist, but he's no longer on the fish box. My ears are still ringing and I realize there's no way I can hear my mother's whistle even if I was standing in our driveway. As the men mill about, shaking their heads and striking matches and smiling, I sneak away through the maze of legs, reach the openness of the dyke, and plunge headlong into the once-again moonless blackberry dark.

XXI

SUMMER BELONGED TO the river. Without flooding its banks, the Fraser seeped into the streets and through open porch doors and kitchen windows, it resurrected the past dormant in the eyes of the old and tugged at the dreams of children, waking them to a present that would shortly turn their flesh the colour of the current.

And the river belonged to the sockeye. For most of my life, I assumed the word *sockeye* had something to do with the salmon's impenetrable depths of darkness, that something had punched the light out of its gaze. That's when I considered the word at all, as a definition, for I knew well what it signified: a sleek, silver strength, an abundance, a richness of flesh, and a crackling electricity in the air below which it swam. The sockeye meant livelihood, and livelihood meant an acceleration of the pace of human behaviour. Even for the Coast Salish, the *sukkai* simply meant *fish*, in the same way that I called my Douglas fir "the tree." I grew up immersed in the question, "What are the sockeye doing?" exactly as if they were a people of will and character, a country whose internal politics so deeply influenced our lives that they might as well have been our country.

Though we were staunch federalists, the seat of government at Ottawa was foreign, often simply an unpleasant fact that had to be considered from time to time. The sockeye were something else entirely, a force of nature with its own means of dispensation, random and wild. Not like people at all, in fact. When my parents or other adults wondered aloud what the Americans were up to now, referring to some development in southeast Asia or South America or in their own burning streets, the implication and tone were very different. Even as a small child, I understood that Americans or the Arabs and Jews of the Middle East or Russians were unfortunate realities that you could only shake your head over in a mixture of amazement, disgust and pity; that they affected our lives was not questioned, but there was nothing soul-stirring or eye-widening about them, not even when they landed on the moon. No other person, not another fisherman corking you on the drift or even your closest family, was as palpable a presence as the sockeye in those few key weeks when they returned to the river. If we could have turned on our TV sets to an all-day, all-sockeye channel, showing nothing more than the silty-brown plume of the Fraser spilling into the green waters of the Gulf of Georgia, we'd have gone straight from the wharf to the living room couch.

The salmon with the highest oil content in its flesh and the deepest pink colour, normally weighing between five and seven pounds, the sockeye had been the most important commercial and native food and ceremonial fish since, respectively, the first cannery opened on the Fraser in 1869 and the glaciers retreated from the coast. Waiting for the sockeye to reach the river was like waiting for Christmas, with two significant differences: Christmas fell predictably each year on December 25, and no adult's stomach ever churned with the anxiety of what might or might not be under the tree for them. To predict the sockeye's behaviour and numbers was to predict a birth or death; each was undoubtedly on the way, but exactly how and when could never be foretold with reliable accuracy, even though one year in the four-year cycle was dominant, followed by a sub-dominant year, and two weaker years. These were merely ballpark guesses; the sockeye's life remained hidden. It was this nerve-fraying mystery surrounding them that gave the summer its peculiar, thick flavour of anticipation and heightened its general flowing and shadowy atmosphere, all burning coal-oil lamps and sudden splashes in moonlight and a sun-dazed languor that made your own hands watery as a mirage.

Albert Wigglesworth, more than anyone else, was of the summer and the sockeye, the one person who, when he touched the salmon, touched the muscle in his thigh and the sweat on his brow. Like the First Nations' Coyote, the trickster, except not even myth could include him, Albert turned Thomas and William Ladner's Victorian pre-emption into a timeless stretch of earth and water much more volatile and uncontained. Where the pioneers planted orchards, he raided them, where they built for the future, he exploded the present, where they stood over the scows of dead salmon, he pulled each fish, living and frenzied with desire, from the side of his own body. Everything about him was other, except for his relationship to the river and its creatures.

He did not even live in Ladner, unless you could say that a gull or a muskrat or a sturgeon was a resident. His home was on a twenty-eight-foot gillnetter as smoulderingly black as one of J.M.W. Turner's locomotives and moored on the far bank of the harbour channel among the oldest, most rain-eaten netsheds and the mossy skeletons of hulls. Albert came and went from his unadorned cabin to no schedule but his own, which was erratic even during the fishing season. I often marvelled at how he could be at anchor while even the calm and gentlemanly Prairie fishermen were anxious to set their nets. Did he care about money? Enough to go north after the salmon, which he did, again, to no discernible pattern. He never left or came back with the rest of the fleet. I suspect money was never what called him; the excitement did, the opportunity to test himself against the elements wherever they were wildest.

Wigglesworth, an old English name, described him accurately, for he was never still, probably not even in his sleep. If you managed to hold him in your gaze for a minute or two, you immediately noticed that his pupils were quick as tadpoles and that each eyeball was, like the earth, always moving even when it didn't appear to be. He wasn't a tall or powerfully built man, but he was what my father described as wiry and as strong as a bull. His strength, in fact, was legendary. When drunk, he was known to take on all comers, no matter how big or how many, and toss them about like chunks of bark. Yet he also looked after the abandoned rabbits who proliferated in the marsh after Easter, and had, as his boon companion, a small, stub-tailed, deer-gold mutt named Bullet whom I never once saw out of Albert's company – on that night of the union meeting, when the seal bomb exploded and the skiff full of manic glee crossed the moon's path, I'm certain Bullet was perched on the bow, his mouth pulled back in that joker's grin so common to dogs. When I think of Albert Wigglesworth, I often see him in his drab, green canvas coat, standing up to his knees in bulrushes, a palm full of sunflower seeds extended for the chickadees, a sort of St. Francis of the lower Fraser, though one who had never heard of God except as a curse word.

Jeff and I spent many hours of many days tracking Albert and Bullet, but they were fog always at the instant of burning off. Sometimes it seemed the man wasn't even real, that we had dreamed him up out of our desire for adventure and that his dog was simply an extension of every boy's inability to imagine a solitude so complete it could not be leavened even by an animal. But then, Albert would toss a seal bomb into a crowd of fishermen and their curses fleshed his phantom out, or else he'd do something equally unexpected that stuck like a tiny coho bone in the throat of propriety.

Here's a Sunday morning in August. Jeff and I have just come along the dyke after spending several hours catching bullheads on the float near where my father ties up. It's quiet, warm, the sun's marmalading the sun-swollen blackberries thick as flies on the bushes where the end of Georgia Street climbs into dyke. A group of eight ladies, a few girls, and the tall, grey-templed minister of the Anglican church push their way carefully into the prickles, seeking the juiciest and fattest fruit. Suddenly one of the women screams. The minister rushes over. He waves the ladies back, a grim look on his face. Jeff and I run up and, in the confusion, manage to see around the minister's blocking body. There, in full view, buck naked as the day he was born – though considerably larger and hairier – lies Singing Frank, one of the jungle bums. For a moment, I wonder if he's dead. But his lips purse out in a half-snore and I know he's just sleeping off another Saturday night bender. Beneath his considerable paunch, his wizened scrotum and limp cock seem fragile as a sparrow's nest, but no sparrow's nest ever caused such a fluster of red faces, herding motions and, in at least two of the women, hands-over-the-mouth titters.

"Go on, boys, back away now," the minister commands with a scowl, then looks down at the morning's unexpected glory with evident confusion. He has no article of clothing with which to cover up old Frankie, but no doubt feels he can't just leave the man there. And shaking him awake would only make the nakedness more alarming. As we step back a few paces, and the minister hovers in his dilemma, a familiar peal of laughter flows off the dyke, a hunched figure scurries by, dog at its side, and tosses an expanding octopus of clothes in our direction. *Hee hee hee.* And the fog burns off again.

Later that day, or another day, or another summer, the harbour's alive with the roar of outboard engines and shouts and laughter and curses, as Albert and a gang of teenaged river rats engage in a fierce, dangerous, skiff-to-skiff water fight. Bullet barks from the bow, a bucket of slimy bilge-water hits its young target square in the face, a skiff almost collides with another, the channel churns, and above the howls flows the season's and my childhood's unsettling yet never frightening sizzling wick of delight.

He was as dark and weathered as the cover of our family bible. His nape-long hair was oily and dark, his small eyes were fluid and dark, his full beard was dark and had the apparent consistency of an SOS pad. Even his white T-shirts were dark – with oil, grease, blood, fish-slime, mud and long use. About the only colour he wore was the red of his thick lips; it was somehow vampiric, a gruesome lipstick he must have put on by drinking blood straight from the sockeye's knifed-open belly. The most common expression that fell from these lips might have been dark if there wasn't always a hint of levity beneath it: *goddamnya.* Usually he spoke this rapidly joined trio of words twice in equally rapid succession. *Goddamnya goddamnya.* But god and damnation didn't come into it, and so the darkness kept away. Never have I known such a fluid, versatile meaning to shelter in so few syllables. Perhaps he picked up the importance of tone from Chung Chuck's daughters, with whom he had an enigmatic relationship. Likely Albert's own sense of being an outsider, combined with depths of kindness and generosity rarely found in more civilized quarters, fostered this unusual friendship between the wild son of an English immigrant and the three bulky, almost slave daughters of a Chinese potato farmer. Or maybe something more complicated was involved? No one knew for sure.

I understood this much, however: through his behaviour, speech, and associations, Albert Wigglesworth, like Chung Chuck, Rod Beveridge, Homer Stevens, and a dozen other characters of my childhood, the living and the ghosts, was different, and probably the most different of all. Who speaks of the loss of diversity in our kind? Ten thousand salmon stocks, a thousand varieties of apples, and at one time, just as much difference in every pair of human eyes raised off the river and the earth. The unique black of Albert's figure stepped straight out of the trunk of the Clapp's Favourite pear tree blooming faithfully in our yard after a century, whose dark grew out of the black inside the carcass of a spawned-out sockeye. Childhood itself is an eclipse of reality, a weirdness, a wonder. Sometimes I have to put my forearm, like a piece of smoked glass, against my eyes to see that world. The flesh of the cherry and the sockeye, the black roe on the bushes, the red light of the sun spilling and filling in its still slough: so brilliant is the past that I must step to the side of my own life, like Albert in the life of our town, and attend to heartbeats which belong to no one else, no other child, no other man, yet which are made of the common blood – these heartbeats, fluttering up from the sediment at the bottom of the river, to witness and record.

XXII

NO ONE'S ABOVE US but Albert. His nameless boat's engine has just shut off at the top of the drift, and the absence of sound immediately deepens the silence of the early evening. The heat of the day has dropped, and with it the frenzied pitch of violence. For most of the day, the sockeye catch was good, starting out in the morning at near a hundred, dropping by half on the next set, then tapering off by a dozen each set after that before finally dropping to a handful by late afternoon. On our last set we'd picked up three, and judging by the lack of action on our corkline – which lies in loose coils on the slowly moving current like the backbone of all those fluid python folds changing their bright skin for a beaten metal – this set won't be any better.

I'm sitting on top of the cabin, my bare legs dangling over the narrow doorway, which is fine with my father as long as I don't move around too much. Idly, I slap at a mosquito buzzing by my ear. There's nothing much to look at. A few harbour seals glide along between our corkline and Albert's, their haunted Munch eyes and cartoon whiskers striking the usual contradictory response in me. They are comical and playful and appealing, but they tear the fish from our net, and when the numbers of sockeye are low, no fisherman finds their presence amusing; most shoot at them or toss seal bombs their way. My father doesn't, though. He's lost his taste for shooting. In any case, when the fish are plentiful, when the catch has been good, there's no harm in letting the seals have a few easy pickings.

For a while, I watch the limpid surface of the river and try to predict where a seal will pop up next. Dad has told me that there are seals in the river as far as the Fraser Canyon, that it's quite a shock to see them when you're driving along the highway so far from the rivermouth. I keep watching and predicting. But before too long I lose interest in this game. I sigh, then draw in a long breath. The air's richly braided – mud, poplar leaf, willow frond, the first ripening blackberries and, nearer, the salmon slime and blood in our stern and on our deck: all these scents can suddenly give way to a sweet whiff of cut pea-vines or the pungent chloroform of steer manure when the wind blows off the delta farms to the southwest. It's a slumberous hour. Somewhere below us, Rick will be listening to his transistor radio, Mr. Beveridge will be having tea, my Auntie Pearl will be knitting. The current laps at our hull. A slumberous hour, but soon the sun will be red flesh dripping off the cottonwood branches.

I look to Albert's boat. It's black as a cave mouth. Suddenly, he darts from the cabin, like some sort of hermit in the rocks who has renounced his solitude at a sign from God. And because Albert is there, the black I see next appears to come out of his body, as if a dark shoulder blade has been yanked from his flesh. For one delirious instant, perspective gives him a charred wing, and then sound draws my eyes back across the water to where the seals have vanished in three quick blips.

Something's wrong. I look at my father. He's holding his burning cigarette in his right hand and staring upriver, but he's not moving. Whatever's happening can't be so bad, then.

The black rapidly separates from Albert's body and forms into a dorsal fin, a very high dorsal fin. It slices along the far bank, behind Albert's stained scotchman, then cuts towards us, gaining speed by the second. I can't open my mouth to speak. My father's moving now, almost leaping into the cabin. Our engine bursts to life. Just as Dad emerges, a white bubbling whorl, a tight braid of bubbles about eight feet long, rises in front of the fin and spreads quickly. Dad spins around and grabs me under the arms and plunks me behind him on the deck. His body's not so wide, however, that I can't see the whale's head as it surfaces, glistening black, a patch of white to each side, the lower half of the great gaping jaw also white and lined with large, conical, interlocking teeth. The whole looks as satiny as the inside of a casket. But the sight lasts for seconds only, is soundless but for a whoosh of air. The head goes under. With sudden clarity, I see the six-foot fin: the tip is pointed but there's a slight bulge below that, and a fair-sized indentation, almost a large nick, just above where the fin connects to the back. A greyish patch, scratched white like scrimshaw and perhaps a yard long, starts at the base of the fin.

For another few seconds, which seem to last an hour, the fin hovers in the dying daylight, water trickling like clear blood down its sides. It's only a couple dozen yards from our boat when, suddenly, it stops and turns back the way it came. When it too goes under, softly, as if a plough has sunk into a wet furrow and kept right on going, the silence is different. It takes a long time for the mosquito drone to reach my ears. I can't take my eyes off the surface of the river. But nothing breaks it, not even a shadow crosses over. Then, just as I'm about to turn to my father, the fin resurfaces near the far bank, rounds our scotchman, and stops, oddly, in a series of short jerks. Finally, it makes a wide circle below our net and heads back upriver, past Albert's scotchman and the end of his boat, shrinking as it seems to go into the North Shore Mountains. In a snapshot image, it hovers like a burnt gull at Albert's head. Then, at last, it's gone.

With a slightly trembling hand, my father lights another cigarette and flicks the match into the current. He smiles at me. I feel the deck swaying slightly from the last of the whale's wake. "How do you like them apples, Monk?" my father says before he stoops into the cabin and shuts the engine off. The deeper silence is like a cry that has left my body without my knowing. Inside it, the whale has found the deeper water of the main river, while we drift with our net out and struggle to return to ourselves.

* * *

In the early 1970s, killer whales, "blackfish" to west-coast fishermen, *Orcinus orca* to science, or grampus in Rod Beveridge's English memory, were just beginning to be understood as something other than voracious predators of warm-blooded prey and a threat to salmon stocks. Most fishermen tried to shoot them (25 percent of live captures of killer whales in BC waters had gunshot wounds). And they had the government's full approval. In 1960, for example, under pressure from sport-fishing lodges in and around Campbell River on Vancouver Island's east coast, the federal fisheries department ordered a land-based machine gun to be set up at Seymour Narrows for the purpose of keeping killer whales away from the area. Killers deserved to be killed, after all. But who defines a killer? As my mother would say, now there's a case of the pot calling the kettle black. Except the kettle isn't really black, or at least not all black.

As it turns out, only some killers are, in fact, killers, in the way we generally use the term. Using the whales' dietary habits as evidence, scientists have defined two distinct groups: residents and transients. Residents, of which there are a northern (upper Strait of Georgia to Queen Charlotte Sound) and southern population (the San Juans and the southern Gulf Islands), eat a mostly salmon diet. Transients, which have been described as "the motorcycle gang of orcas," prefer mammals – sea lions, seals, porpoises, belugas, sea otters, and several bird species, including cormorants, grebes, geese and loons. Recently, a third group of killer whales, the offshores, has been identified, but little is known about them, for they are rarely seen in protected coastal waters. It is believed, however, that the offshores also favour a fish diet.

To summarize, no killer whale fancies a human snack. Indeed, no authentic accounts of orcas attacking and eating humans have been recorded, though in the Antarctic, they have bumped into ice floes on which people were standing, perhaps mistaking the shadows for seals, which they have been known to knock into the water.

Did my father think of this as the fin accelerated towards

our boat? Perhaps. More likely, he just didn't know what to expect. Killer whales were uncommon visitors to the Prairie Drift, to put it mildly. But Dad knew about them. Several times each summer, he'd pause while picking out a third or fourth large spring in a row and say, "the blackfish must have gone by." And it's true: for the most common killer whales of the inland waters of BC, the spring salmon is the preferred prey.

Therein lies the problem the whales face: as the salmon become harder to find, and as the engine noise and general disturbance of whale-watchers forces the whales to work harder and sucks away energy they need for foraging, they become weaker and more susceptible to diseases affecting their immune systems. Sadly, these immune systems have already been compromised by the same pollutants that are helping to destroy so many other species on the coast, including the salmon. The damage is so great, in fact, that the beautiful, awe-inspiring killer whale, one of BC's most characteristic images (why, it's even found on the sweaters of the Vancouver Canucks, who are owned by a company called Orca Bay), is now the most toxic marine mammal in the world.

But just as there's a natural web of life, there's an unnatural one of our design, and the strands reach everywhere. As top-level predators on the food chain, killer whales ingest a wide variety of industrial pollutants in their diet, the most toxic of which are PCBs, dioxins and furans. PCBs are so toxic, in fact, that we've banned them in our region (and we don't ban anything easily), but they continue to leak out of old storage sites into the marine habitat. Even worse, PCBs are not banned in most Asian economies, so we still get them on the tides and in the rainfall. The world's fastest growing economies? China and India. Ah, but we can't slough off the blame on foreigners. Until very recently, local pulp mills were pumping all kinds of dioxins and furans into the sea as part of their chlorine-based bleaching process. At the same time, believe it or not, Neil Armstrong and Buzz Aldrin were spending eighteen days in quarantine out of concern that they might bring back poisonous microbes from the moon.

So, we humans continue to pollute with some horribly toxic substances, even after we've banned their use (that's how toxic they are). And the molecules of these chemicals work their way up the food chain, from plankton to fish to marine mammals. At each higher level, the toxic concentration increases through a process known as *bioaccumulation.* In other words, there's not so much poison in one salmon (unless it's farmed, of course), but if you're a harbour seal who eats many salmon, the fat-soluble poison will build up over time in your blubber, and if you're a transient whale who eats many harbour seals and other marine mammals, you'll soon be a swimming toxic dump site. As for resident killer whales, the toxic buildup in the blubber takes longer if you eat a fish diet. However, if you can't find enough salmon to eat, and turn to scooping up bottomfish, you'll accelerate the process, because bottomfish, down there with the industrial runoff and the nasty gook from salmon farms, have higher concentrations of toxins. Consequently, the resident killer whale population of the inshore southern BC waters has been declining rapidly over the past six years. In 1999, there were ninety-nine whales. Today, there are less than eighty.

But to return to the lone killer whale that surfaced on the Prairie Drift before my moon-wide eyes thirty-five years ago: it was probably a transient who had chased some seals up into the main river, then somehow made a wrong turn or else hadn't adjusted its remarkable memory to fit in with how our dredging and logging and dyking constantly alter the depths and flow of the rivermouth. Finding the water too shallow along the bank, it made a burst towards our boat as it found deeper water, then, after a surfacing peek, decided it better try another direction. When that direction, too, proved shallow, and resulted in the jerking motions of the fin as the whale scraped the silts, it decided to turn back.

When I think of this now, in light of all I've been learning about my coastal home, I realize it's perfectly apt that a transient whale should emerge from out of the dark figure of Albert Wigglesworth, then disappear beyond him as well. For there are creatures near to us whose lives we can never fathom, creatures who walk our streets, or once did, who might just as well swim in the depths of the ocean. And as the wild salmon and the killer whales begin to disappear in larger and larger numbers, so too do the humans that not only lived among them intensely, but in their own secretive migrations, mirrored them.

It's raining and the killer whale at the top of the totem pole outside the Ladner Museum grows darker, prepares to breach. I look away from it, my eye catching a shadow slipping out of the pub across the street. There he is! I follow with all the stealth I can muster, jumping into the doorways of the little shops along my side of the block. In the tongue-soft last light of a summer evening, under the whispering rain, he's only a dark, slightly crouching blur. I must run to keep up. Where's he gone? Around the corner of Magees' secondhand store, heading for the wharf – Bullet, as always, a dark patch at his legs. Hurry! Hurry! I begin to sprint. I race around the corner and . . .

"Boo!"

My heart is flung upward like a startled pigeon. I almost fall backwards.

"Hee hee hee. Got you that time."

And he's gone, still snickering, up the dyke and down to the river, while I stand blinking in the rain and smile, thinking, as always, I fell for it, why didn't I know better?

But I never know better, nor does anyone else, child or adult, who engages in any kind of play with Albert. He is the master of camouflage, his dark the dark of the air, his speed the speed of the river, and somehow Bullet never gives him away.

I go home, beaten but exhilarated by the triumph of my defeat. After all, who wants to know what each moment will bring, who wants to believe in their own mastery of the flux of life?

The killer whale leaps off the pole and into the depths and there's no one there to watch. But it happens, each night. Because the earth is always such a brave new world and there are still such creatures in it. Because our capacity for awe is our only defence against our terrible, killing certainties. Because I saw, a long time ago, the transient wild and the transient wild cross briefly in the long shadow of the mountains, as if making a solemn pact. Because I make this solemn pact with myself.

XXIII

THE MOON SETS INTO the Prairie Drift without a sound, like the bone inside the whale's head. Now it's so dark I cannot see my father's face, only the burning end of his cigarette. Where are the corks? The engine's idling, we're about to pick up. But I can't see the corks right behind the boat. Wait. Here they come, one, two, three – ten of them. We must have hooked a snag. Yet we're still drifting. A deadhead? Probably. There go the corks again, slowly, as if a woman is taking off a pearl necklace.

A deadhead is trouble. If it's not clean, if it has roots or shredded sides, it can tear holes in the net as it turns. Then it might have to be cut loose.

My father, though, isn't acting as if it's a deadhead. He's just waiting, watching. I step carefully alongside the drum and into the stern. The river smells even muddier than usual. Again, the corks surface slowly. We're not drifting fast. Maybe my father's just hoping the deadhead will work its own way out.

After another moment, he steps on the drum pedal.

"Come here, Monk," he says quietly.

He lifts me up in front of him so that I can see clearly over the rollers. There's a faint white glow below the black surface, but it isn't the corks or moonlight. And the smell floating up is so thick that I immediately swallow hard. This is something new.

The glow and the smell keep rising. My father holds me a little tighter. Something's alive down there, it's almost at the surface. The white's washing out to a dark greenish grey, and a long body, serrated along the top . . . there's a violent splash, the corks plunge. My father tenses, I pull back into him. Seconds later, the corks pop up again, as if some vertebra's been ripped from the bottom of the river. My father lets out his breath. In a relieved voice, he says, "I'd rather not have to take him, if I can help it. Be like cutting down an old tree."

There's no creature so old in or on the Fraser River. At least I'd still like to believe so. Once abundant but never counted, the giant white sturgeon, half shark, half catfish, the largest freshwater fish in North America (the record catch of twenty feet long and two thousand pounds occurred near Lillooet in the 1950s) is almost certainly close to extinction. Current estimates put the Lower Fraser's population at an encouraging fifty thousand individuals, but less than two percent of these are over three feet long; most are sexually immature juveniles. The breeders, the huge adults, are almost gone.

But not yet extinct, though their habitat, and the juveniles' habitat is so diminished and polluted that it's unlikely any will have a chance to reach the size of their ancestors. Typically, out of a greed masking itself as conservation, the BC government has started an aquaculture program to grow white sturgeon. Again, typically, the viruses that attend artificial breeding programs threaten to wipe out the wild sturgeon stocks (what crawls on the other eyeball of Alexandra Morton's daughter must be little men and women in business suits and lab coats). But these are not salmon we're talking about. The sturgeon, while a part of aboriginal myth and culture, are not so loveable. Given their prehistoric appearance and general invisibility, not to mention the commercial value of their tasty flesh and their roe as caviar, it's a wonder that the white sturgeon remains at all. Somehow, the mysterious bottom-feeder survived a rapacious fishery on the Fraser River between the early 1890s and the first years of the twentieth century. By the end of 1894, the total sturgeon catch on the Fraser was 452,000 pounds. In 1897, over a million pounds of sturgeon was harvested, which as Terry Glavin points out, is roughly the weight of seven thousand people, the population of New Westminster at that time.

Century-old fish were dragged out of the river like great cedars (in British Columbia, then and now, even the bottom of a river can be clear-cut). Finally, by 1902, only 33,500 pounds of sturgeon was taken. The slaughter was quick and devastating, but not without precedent. In 1892, 5.5 million pounds of white sturgeon was dredged out of the Columbia River and railroaded east. Naturally, many of the sturgeon harvesters on the Fraser were enterprising Americans looking for fresh sources of supply. This sort of brutal exploitation of natural resources reminds me of what a good friend told me the other day.

We were discussing the diminishment of the splendour we'd known as coastal children, and my friend – who'd grown up on the banks of the same mist-shrouded North Vancouver creeks along which my father had played truant several decades before – said: "There's this guy I grew up with, I bump into him every now and then on Lonsdale Avenue, he's very high up in one of the logging companies, CanFor I think. His job is to sit in an office with these high-tech computer maps of the province and search for the best areas to clear-cut. You ought to hear him talk about it. He's so proud, and his language is unbelievable, hardly recognizable as English. The thing that gets me is, he was once just this sweet kid. I wonder what the hell happened to him?"

North America happened to him. The nineteenth century happened to him. It looks through his eyes just as the first freshwater year of a sockeye's life looks through the salt fathoms of its approaching death. We are the inheritors of a creation that was a destruction. As the pioneers built, they tore down. As I was given a childhood along the Fraser, the sturgeon was driven to near extinction. As my children and yours are given their lives, the wild salmon have theirs stolen from them. This is our cycle, and to believe or say otherwise is simply false.

But there is mystery left down deep in the river. The giant white sturgeon is believed to favour the deepest channels for its habitat. It lies there, vacuum-like snout always pointed upriver, against the current, sucking up mostly fish – bullheads, crayfish, migrating oolichans, spawned-out salmon, even smaller sturgeon; the feeding is ironically akin to the appetite of the only thing that still feeds on them, which is us, for there is considerable incidental catch. Just as the sturgeon is a bycatch of the salmon gillnet fishery, almost anything is a bycatch of the sturgeon's hoovering appetite. There is something of the spider's patience involved, something of the snake's gorging, something of the prehistoric creature's irreducibility of time. For the sturgeon is an ancient fish, its recognizable fossils going back 64 million years to the end of the Cretaceous Period when the dinosaurs were just about to disappear (or morph into songbirds, as some paleontologists now believe). Scale-less but rough-skinned, its skeleton cartilaginous, its eyes black and tiny, its back and sides rowed with sharp-pointed bony plates known as scutes, the sturgeon lends itself to a kind of repulsed horror from which legends grow, especially for children.

You've heard of urban myths? These are river myths up close to an urban centre that does not pay attention to them. What might not be found in the gut of a great sturgeon? Anything that bumps along the riverbottom could conceivably find its way into that unfathomable blackness. As a boy, and one who'd read of the steadfast tin soldier found in a fish that was caught and opened, returning the toy soldier to the very child who'd lost it, I sometimes deliberately dropped an old, not very special toy off the boat. If any fish ever returned it to me, it would be the sturgeon. It didn't matter that we never took sturgeon home and gutted them; somehow I overlooked that detail. I knew Mr. Beveridge pickled the flesh of the sturgeon, and that his grandchildren sucked on the marrow, known as "Indian candy." Maybe he'd find my toy. Ah, but lost toys were minor compared to other legends.

Once an old murder case had been solved when a human skull turned up inside a great sturgeon captured near Mission. They identified the victim through dental records while the sturgeon hung from a hook above a wharf where an autumn bloodlight stained the capillary branches of the bankside poplars. I believed this, or I wanted to believe this. To think of a skull grinning its way out to sea and then upriver to

Mission – *I knew him, Horatio* – is beyond Shakespeare, beyond literature. Never mind finding inside a sockeye a toy soldier, or the wedding ring that had gone down the sink while you were washing dishes. Imagine the detective called out to the murky edge of belief, imagine the men gathered around that terrifying grave in the universe with their own fates laughing back at them. Then imagine being a child hanging over the stern of a gillnetter on a river that contained such creatures. Or once did.

Happily, the fate of the giant white sturgeon, even if it's as dismal as can be expected, judging all we've done and are doing to its habitat, remains unknown. The sturgeon eludes us even as we wipe it out. There's a poetry in that which not even a poem can articulate. But let's try a few scientific facts on for size.

Like the salmon, the white sturgeon is anadromous, with a mysterious saltwater migration and a freshwater spawning. Unlike the salmon, the sturgeon does not die upon spawning, nor does it live only a few years. Some of the giants are believed to be over 150 years old. That means there could be something down there in one of the sloughs off the Prairie Drift that hatched from an egg before the Ladner brothers even set eyes on the marshy delta, before British Columbia or Canada existed, before the American Civil War, before the West was won. And because the sturgeon can live so long, it does not reach sexual maturity until the age of fourteen in males, possibly even twenty-six in females, which means that they have to be left alone, in a habitat with enough prey (and human skulls, dioxins, and toxic plastic Atlantic salmon aren't much sustenance), long enough to reach reproductive age. Which means we can't continue to dyke and drain away and pollute the lower Fraser, which means our current annual population growth of five percent must be curtailed, and our destructive practices must stop, we must learn to love the earth and . . . I know, I know, quit dreaming and get back to the big fish.

Anglers love them. Whoo hoo, they cry, there's nothing like hooking onto one of these half-ton monsters! The really big ones, they say, will leap right out of the water like a killer whale. Too bad we can't bring them in and weigh them anymore, otherwise somebody would set a new world landed record.

Yes, the sturgeon must only be caught and released on barb-less hooks. There's even a Fraser River White Sturgeon Conservation Society, run mostly by men who like to catch them on a rod. This is just like Ducks Unlimited, the pretty organization that wants to conserve wetlands so that they'll have somewhere to go hunting.

But I digress. And besides, my family has killed more than a few dozen white sturgeon in our day. That we did it to live and not to play no longer matters. The question is, can we only protect something for our own purposes and not for the simple glory of being and diversity? Is each salmon only a chunk of cash to be divvied up by bureaucrats? Are killer whales useful only if we can capture them on videotape? Do we leave some old-growth forests upright because we want to go and stand under the trees and recapture the sense of awe that our society kills in us every waking moment of our lives? I'd like to think we can leave things alone, just let them be. Why not? It would be a change, at least.

Of course I know why not. We need to make money, we need to have a thriving economy. And that means using other forms of life for our purposes, seemingly benign and barb-less or otherwise. We were granted that right a long time ago. It's in the family bible my mother keeps in her hope chest. Dominion over all living things. Let's move this along.

The largest white sturgeon I've ever seen in the wild, at least wholly, was five feet long, just over a hundred pounds, not a very big one. But I remember it well for other reasons. My brother and I caught it in our gillnet in 1994, in the second summer of the great sturgeon deaths. Well, we didn't exactly catch it. The sturgeon drifted lethargically into our corkline and just lay there, alive but motionless, a victim of some inexplicable cause that would see dozens of twelve-foot long, six- and eight-hundred-pound fish wash up on the banks of the Fraser throughout 1993 and 1994. No one really knows why these century-old giants died, but if I was the detective called out to begin an investigation, and I had to make up a list of prime suspects, I wouldn't put "Avenging Bullheads" or "Old Age" at the top. I'd start with "Poison" and look my human face in the mirror.

That hundred-pound sturgeon was dying, and so we delivered it to Vic and Rosie on the *Maureen G.* Commercially at that time, if a sturgeon was over three feet long, you could kill it for money. As late as 1994, no government had enacted restrictions based on the knowledge of the sturgeon's breeding age. To kill everything over three feet long is to kill the species. Anyway, by 1994, my brother and I would have let the fish go if it had had any energy left to survive.

As a boy, I saw and handled dozens of white sturgeon, most of them juveniles, though occasionally one was a "keeper" and paid more per pound than dogs and pinks. A twenty-five-pound sturgeon meant about thirty dollars, and my father couldn't afford to throw back thirty dollars, even though he happily watched twenty times that amount kick free of his net.

Even small, they were unsettling. To stare at one was to stare at an earth without any human eyes staring back. And all sturgeon possess a remarkable capacity for living long periods out of the water. How often on a dark night, standing in the stern, have I jumped back at the sudden thrash of a sturgeon caught several hours earlier. How often have I shone a light onto that toothless mouth in its rictus cry of a very old woman on her deathbed, and swallowed hard. How often have I seen that skull gliding in the church-beam length of glimmering phosphor. No wonder the Sto:lo people of the Fraser, whose very survival had often depended on a sturgeon fishery, believed that people who fell from their canoes and whose bodies were never found became sturgeon, or lived among them. No wonder the armour-plated, anvil-shaped head, with the four long whiskers known as barbels and that gasping, protruding mouth still rises like a submerged moon into my consciousness. I cannot think of the white sturgeon without thinking of the dead body whose arm Jack Brophy tore away and of the little boy who rode his tricycle off the government wharf and disappeared and of the teenager who tried to swim home from one of the silt islands and was swept out to sea. Nor can I think of the great fish without rage for its destruction. To what purpose was the species almost obliterated a hundred years ago?

There are the detectives huddled around the hooked giant, little Hamlets passing the human skull back and forth. Who's that with them? Ah, Tom, Tom Ladner. I was beginning to wonder where he'd gone. He's standing on the wharf, on the landing, that bears his name, and he's looking into the sturgeon's tiny eyes. They make him shudder, there's no Christian god there, no family, only Darwin's miserable sacrilege. He turns and strides away. Up at McNeely's, there'll be cards and laughs and – he smiles – a dram of the old Tam Ladner, as it's called all along the river, the whisky coming in bottles shaped like his own girth. Or maybe he'll have a beer. Something, something to take the chill off.

What's going to take my chill off, Tom, the chill that comes from knowing the white sturgeon was driven to the point of extinction because its gas-bladder linings were used to make isinglass to clarify the draft beer tapped at McNeely's and every other drinking establishment on the coast?

Nothing. I huddle here and watch you walk where I walked, pushing your way past a hundred hooked giants as if you're struggling through some thick forest. Then the hundred hooks become ten million hooks dangling ten million wild salmon. It's a veritable Hall of Mirrors. Suddenly someone starts shooting at the flocks of wildfowl once so abundant on the delta that they darkened the sky, turned day into night. The mirrors smash. It's like *The Lady of Shanghai,* Tom. I might have seen that if the Ladner Theatre hadn't closed. Orson Welles. He was about your size. I wonder if you had any ladies of Shanghai slaving away in your cannery. I wish I'd seen that flickering on the side of the Atkeys' house. No, not the working intestines of your cannery, Tom, the movie.

But on second thought, we should have learned more about you and what you were really about, we should have seen the Chinamen in the China House in winter dying of scurvy, we should have seen the typhoid creeping up the throats of the sloughs, we should have been told that all your work and worries finally made you sick so that you lost two hundred pounds and nearly wasted away to a thin bookmark of sinew stuck in one of your children's cheaply produced memoirs of pioneer life. Christ, Tom, we ought to watch the film of your life and times now. Then we'd see that the skull is our own and that the body on the hook belongs to us.

Did you know, Tom, that scientists are studying the sturgeon in an attempt to better understand the condition known as a coma? I'm not making this up. I never lie; my father taught me to play up and play the game, as his father taught him. This is the game now. We're in a coma. We're on life support. Maybe the sturgeon, if we don't destroy them first, can save us. There's poetry in that, Tom. Tennyson for the deep's denizens. I'm something of a poet myself. But never mind that. What poets say is too easily dismissed by the world. I'd rather speak as a man who has come from one place and loves it, year by year, more than any other, even as he watches it disappear. Anyone can understand that, can't they, Tom? There were once halibut and humpback whales off the mouth of the Fraser. We killed them all.

This isn't revisionist history I'm writing, I'm not looking back with superior knowledge and shaking my head in condescension. Because you knew it was wrong, you and the other pioneers. When laws were put in place, you ignored them. Nothing was going to stand in the way of profit. It was illegal to blast rocks so close to the Fraser, but the railroad companies did it anyway. When the fisheries minister allowed Henry Bell-Irving twenty-six licences one year, he ignored the law and fished all seventy-eight of his cannery's boats.

And you, Tom, so saddened by what had happened to the herds of buffalo, could nevertheless stand on a scow surrounded by tens of thousands of sockeye that would never make it into cans, that would have to be dumped overboard rotten, and not see the damage you were doing? You were an intelligent man of your time, there were public protests about the terrible waste and greed of the salmon canners, and yet you continued on, building your private fortune, meeting with Ewen and Todd and Bell-Irving each year to plot how cheaply you could buy the fish from the fishermen, those who, as your son Leon put it so succinctly years later, *merely* caught the fish. They certainly weren't taking the train across the country to have supper with Sir John A. McDonald, as you did, Tom. They had no access to power then, and they still don't. Now a Vietnamese-Canadian fisherman, in desperation, blows up a van in front of Vancouver City Hall. Now a right-wing politician preys on the racism inherent in the fishery to earn himself his own expense account in the corridors of power. Now a middle-aged Caucasian fisherman wastes away on a hunger strike to protest the loss of his livelihood. Now the inheritors of your profit-first philosophy dine on tasteless plastic flesh after a hard day's work of looking for forests to clear-cut on computer maps. Revisionism? 2007 is 1880. Faulkner's right: the past isn't dead; it isn't even past.

I'm standing once more in the abandoned house at the south end of Georgia Street, looking out a window on the empty and cracked concrete swimming pool, a few morning-glory vines and blackberry prickles flung across the bottom like the green bones of the last swimmers. This was the house of H.N. Rich. He managed one of Tom Ladner's salmon canneries. Then he died. But before he died, he paid for the construction of the granite cenotaph in Memorial Park, a pear orchard away from the William Ladner House, where my parents, with their first baby, once rented a room from old Mrs. Ladner, an eccentric grand dame who wore a turban, smoked cigars on a long holder, and employed a Chinese houseboy (if the Ladner Theatre hadn't closed, and I'd seen Gloria Swanson in *Sunset Boulevard*, my young father as the young William Holden . . .). Mr. Rich paid for the cenotaph to be built because his only son had been killed in France. The father's grief didn't die with him; I soaked it up from the walls of the rooms in which he paced and wept and tried to go on. But it was no good; the wealth didn't matter. The swimming pool emptied of laughter and the house went dark. I stepped out of it to go to the park and watch my brothers play baseball and cheer if one of the balls they hit rolled up to the base of the cenotaph, for that usually meant a home run.

In this simple way we touch the past, and it's sad and beautiful enough, being human, not to continue to lay waste to the earth on which our difficult and cherished lives are played out. For they are difficult, and made of joy, and we degrade them by the narrowness of our material purposes, we do not learn. Revision! I could revise everything, say that the Ladners never founded Ladner, that Christ was a black man, that Napoleon won at Waterloo, and who could say with conviction that these changes would make any difference?

Slaughter is slaughter. Profit is profit. The pioneers on the coast knew. And we know. The splendour is diminished, and diminishing.

XXIV

I HATED TO GO to school. Why would I want to? The Hebrew poet Yehuda Amichai writes of his "hand that clutched the railing" when his time for school had come. How well I knew the feeling. Up to the fall of 1970, I was free. I had the company of those who loved me and the licence of the fields and streets, I had the muskrat's long brushstroke of the ditches and the heron's dripping canvas of its own blue period. Consider my foot, summer 1970. It's grass-stained and indented with tiny marks from the points of the crushed gravel in our driveway. There's a prickle scratch across the ankle, which is chestnut brown, like the rest of my body. The earth's what I stand on – no separation. Garter snakes slither near. The same silt that flows downriver settles between my toes. My foot is its own tiny animal among the animals. Ants contend with its presence. Cabbage moths and King Billy butterflies equally must assess the attraction of its stillness. Cats listen, dogs listen, pigeons and gulls listen. My foot smells of mud and blackberries, rain and sun, algae, creosote and cedar; it has flown over the earth, barely touching it, and then sunk into softness for surprising strings of minutes that aren't counted or even known (clocks meant nothing until school started).

And the foot is only the beginning. Look at the arms. They're full of the shadows gathered from lying on my stomach, full of the smell of wet dog and ripe plums. My lips? Powdered white from a plateful of Mrs. Demosten's pastries, pursed to spit into a spiderweb to try to trick the spider (who's never tricked). Behind one ear there's a seagull feather. In the pocket of the cut-off jeans, a dime, a shiny pebble, half a Jersey Milk bar, three Mountain Dew bottlecaps found on the wharf, a fish hook and a snarl of test. In one cupped hand, a grasshopper; in the other, the soundlessly blaring trumpet of the morning glory. On the elbows, grass stains. On the palms and wrists, sap from the towering Douglas fir across the street from our house. My nostrils quiver, sensitive to coming rain and cooking food and the smoke of the salmon's flesh in the smokehouses, the oil of the engines, the bleach of the hanging laundry, the salt tide in the form of a walking father or brother. My eyes are sky-blue and wide open. There's no limit to their openness. The Greek widows step lightly in, bringing their dead with them. Salmon strike there. A bough swings, heavy with cherries. And the tears hide, barely used, like understudies for the loss I won't know until the big doors shut under the flagpole and the bell's shriek ends and I sit, feet in laced shoes, in a desk for six hours a day, five days a week, ten months a year, while my blood eddies and fouls.

I cried then. Of course I cried. Think of all I loved, think of how little control I had over my ability to enjoy what I loved. My parents had no option. It was the law and the custom of the day. Besides, like so many Depression-raised children of poor backgrounds, they had an abiding faith in the importance of education and an unshakeable conviction that important things, great movements of the future, were learned at school. Or at least my mother did. My father had hated school himself, was regularly truant (I can just remember truant officers – how quaint they seem now!) so he could splash about in the creeks of North Vancouver (chasing the steelhead and salmon that aren't there anymore) and dive off its water tanks with the Indian kids. He probably would have ignored school until the authorities came calling, then he would have shrugged and relented. My mother, however, who had dropped out of high school in order to work in all the burgeoning industries of wartime, saw my love of reading as an encouraging sign that I'd enjoy grade one. Well, it's simpler than that. In 1970, every child went to school. Many cried, some were sick; the grief wore off.

But it never did for me, just as it never did for my father. His sense of loss pushed him into fishing for a living, mine pushed me into writing, two occupations that grant some freedom from authority and some access to the wild. How can I put this plainly? School cost me my heritage. Kept out of it, I'd have experienced so much more of the rich world into which I'd been born. Put into it, I learned how to raise my hand and how to sit still. And eventually I learned the cruelty and injustice of authority, lessons I wasn't supposed to use, lessons I'd have learned anyway. Given the choice, I'd have learned the world as a wild salmon learns it, senses first, in a flow of risk and change. Instead, I learned it in chains. There's no more accurate way to put it. I lost the streets, fields and river, I lost a world of adults and children not my exact age, I lost hours and hours of daydreams and solitude, I lost thousands of rainstorms and dozens of rare snowfalls, I lost thousands of sets on the Prairie with my father and untold hours of my mother's wisdom and my brothers' joy. Or rather, I had these things stolen from me. In return, I gained little I wouldn't have gained myself in a richer way. For the first six years of my life, I was wild. After that, I was farmed.

* * *

Even so, 1970 was a better year to be a child than 2007. Back then, grade one involved no homework, nor did grades two or three. After school did not mean daycare, another form of school; we were free at the last bell. There were no screens but TV to occupy us, and cartoons appeared only on Saturday mornings; there were no VCRs or home computers. Corporations did not spend 15 billion dollars annually on advertising that targeted us as a market group, nor did parents buy into the myth of widespread random abduction spurred on by a media with a fear agenda related to consumerist ideology. We could roam, we could sit fifty feet up in a Douglas fir in a fort we'd built ourselves of waste lumber and driftwood and found nails, we could let dusk settle over us and our town and let the stars give us back our unblinking gazes until a mother's whistle bid us home.

It was the childhood I had outside of school. I won't apologize for it, nor will I deny you your dysfunctions if you had them. And lest you think I romanticize the past . . . no, I won't even help you there. In my experience, those who rail against "romanticism" are really railing against the joy that is as real in memory as sorrow and pain are. Is drunkenness more true than sobriety? Who has the courage and the talent to write the great book of wildflower lore in this age of fashionable misery and addiction? I wish I did. Perhaps, if I live long enough, I'll win back enough of the wildness of my first six years to write a song of praise for the earth. Perhaps, on my deathbed, the salmon will sing me over.

School did not teach me the songs the Coast Salish people once sang on the Fraser when the sons of Thomas Ladner rested from their self-described slave labour (see, the past was not always idyllic for children) of chopping wood and hauling water and herding cows to listen to the strangely soft, as if made of rain, language of place. And I never heard an Indian sing to anything. They did sing, though, at one time. Perhaps they sang like the Kwakiutl of northern Vancouver Island who, over the season's first salmon, would begin:

Welcome, friend Swimmer,
We have met again in good health,
Welcome, Supernatural One,
You, Long-Life Maker,
For you come to set me right again
As is always done by you.

Always done by you. Fifty-seven salmon-producing streams once flowed into Vancouver's False Creek. They were all paved over long ago. Is there any reason to believe that the wild salmon will always exist to set us right again? What does a member of the Coast Salish say? Do they still sing the old songs? Do they still return the bones of the feasted-on salmon to the water so the fish can reassemble? Though I fished alongside Lloyd and Rocky Wilson in Canoe Pass, and own one of Lloyd's cedar salmon carvings, I can honestly say I've never heard a Coast Salish Native of the Fraser River delta speak a word in his own language. And I certainly never saw one let a fish go. Then again, there just weren't that many Natives around; just like the salmon on which their culture was built, they paid a devastating price for European settlement.

During the first century of contact, smallpox and other diseases wiped out 90 percent of the Coast Salish. The Tsawwassen people, whose name comes from a word in their Halkomelem dialect, *Stsewothen*, meaning *towards the open sea*, were thousands strong before those Spaniards arrived in 1791. By 1860, the permanent winter village site consisted of only seven longhouses, each containing three families. Twenty years later, a government census recorded fifty-two people, only fifteen of whom were children. When I was a boy, the few Natives I knew did not want to be regarded as such; most, in fact, had chosen to relinquish their status and live off the reserve, as white folks. Families who made that choice likely had no desire to retain their Halkomelem dialect, so it's little wonder I never heard even a single word of it spoken. In my forming British Columbia consciousness, especially once I started school, an Indian was Iroquois or Sioux and involved in colourful events a long time ago, events from which they emerged dead. Today, the process of cultural assimilation is gradually eroding all the Native populations of North America.

But the Tsawwassen remain for now, crammed into their reserve at the old winter village site, where they have built a luxury condominium complex on the beach, an act of "if you can't beat 'em, join 'em," which is part of a larger movement that's spawned several Native-owned, government-supported casinos in the Lower Mainland. All this begs the question: if the Halkomelem dialect is still spoken, does it even have words for "board meeting," "power lunch" and "venture capitalism"?

Ladner, once a mosquito-filled marsh the Tsawwassen paddled through on their way to hunt deer in Burns Bog to the east or to pick berries on Lulu Island to the north or, of course, to fish for salmon on the Fraser, today reflects its aboriginal heritage with a lone word of Halkomelem, an anomaly whose existence defies history every time someone's tongue trips over it. The word is *Chilukthan*, and it refers to the broad slough at whose mouth Thomas Ladner placed his farm and where the pioneers finally laid out a townsite. But no one knows what the word means, just as no one in Tsawwassen knows that their communal face is pointed towards the open sea (actually, it's pointed towards the open mouth of the George Massey Tunnel leading to Vancouver, but Bedroom Community, BC, doesn't sound as nice).

Residents do know, however, that the Tsawwassen band, like all the other Salish people from the rivermouth upstream to Yale – a larger grouping defined as the Sto:lo, or "people of the river" – receive unfair privileges to catch salmon. In the age-old clash between the haves and have-nots, have-not white fishermen have been conned into trying to dispossess the dispossessed, as they themselves have been dispossessed. It's the kind of sadly bizarre human psychology that Dostoevsky understood so well. If that brooding Russian was on this coast today, he'd pick up his manuscript of *Notes from Underground* and retitle it *Notes from Underwater*: corrupt bureaucracy, alienation and gloom, that pretty much defines the salmon fishery now. Meanwhile, the herons on the blackened pilings slouch in their frayed Gogol overcoats and the czars count their money. If England is a nation of shopkeepers, and the business of America is business, and Ladner was founded mostly by English and Americans, how could things be otherwise? Every scale of every salmon shows a president's or a monarch's face, and all that's been sung to the catch for 140 years is anthems.

XXV

LADNER IS RAINFOREST without the forest. Lowland. The flats where, at one time, you could buy salmon in the round off the wharf. The river drops and shows its ribs. But even as this happens, the rain falls and turns my childhood town into the moon, the streets and fields pocked and cratered with puddles. Walk there and you won't leave any footprints. You might leave your boots behind, but no prints. I do not know of any scientifically measurable link between growing up in a wet climate and a melancholy temperament, but I have long suspected that the link exists. When your landscape is forever appearing and disappearing, when you come to knowledge on the margin between the solid and the flowing, when water surrounds and encloses you, often for weeks at a time, how can you not feel the beauty of the ephemeral nature of life, and enter into that state the Japanese call the *slender sadness*?

Melancholy, in my definition, simply means a constant attentiveness to what has been. Some people – and most poets – live with this degree of attention. And some places give themselves freely to a sensibility open to their past, which is also their present and future. Just as a salmon depends on a specific place to be fully itself, so I depend on Ladner to teach me my own human story and, in a sense, to complete it. At twenty years old, for example, I could walk Thomas and William Ladner's original townsite and not see myself as connected to their time. At thirty, I could catch salmon and still not touch the ice of the retreating glaciers. Now, at forty, though I can't even say what knowledge I lack, I know that Ladner will give it to me if I'm patient enough and attentive enough. The *slender sadness* is its own ample reward.

* * *

It's raining heavily. The Douglas fir hisses like a soldering iron plunged into a vat. High up in the pencil-faint boughs, two boys perch, staring through their wet bangs at the richness that belongs to them. They watch the earth below with the intensity of eagles. One of the boys is me, but I can't hear what I'm saying. History has flooded in. I know the human child's eye contains a hunger for the earth that's as fierce as the eagle's hunger for the delicacy of the salmon's eyeball, and so I cannot hear anything but the roar of the past and the roar of the future. In the Fraser Canyon in 1913, ten miles of salmon stretched from Hell's Gate to below Hope, waiting to go home. But they couldn't make it. That summer, there were so many dead fish that the eagles, crows and gulls didn't even have to turn them over to pick out the other eyeball.

Those boys in the great fir are forty-year-old men now. And the earth is a clouded eye, almost blank, looking skywards and gravewards at once. But a child, your child and mine, will always turn it over, even after we've stopped hungering, even after we've been sated with the knowledge of our killing ways. That's the definition of hope. The truth is, I can hear what those boys are saying, I can hear myself. Let's look for Albert, let's find some beer bottles, there goes Tessie, if it keeps raining and then gets cold maybe there'll be ice on the river, come on, let's make a time capsule.

And they do. We did. Into one of the rotting root cellars in the overgrown backyards of one of the abandoned houses, we placed a few valuables in a paper bag: a shiny chestnut, a comic, some aggies, a hockey card, a jackknife, a pack of gum, a nickel. Then we carefully, solemnly, wrote a note and pinned it with rocks to the surface of the dirt-filled root cellar. Not to be opened until . . . until when? In 1969 or '70, the year 2000 possessed a magical futuristic aura. How different things would be!

And they are, though not in the ways we had imagined. We don't travel to work in jetpacks, we don't have aliens as friends, we haven't put an end to war. But the world is different. Over the years, we must have made dozens of time capsules, and probably we dug them all up. Though if one remains, if one was forgotten when the note blew away, I hope we put some salmon bones in it, a bullhead or two, a great blue heron's feather, a fir cone, an oolichan, a wooden cork, a jar of blackberry jam, a tape recording of a seal's cry and of an old drunk singing "Goodnight Irene" and of a Greek-Salish man cursing the goddamned companies. I hope we took some mud from the riverbank and some silt from the current and some rain from the grass. And I hope we looked at all these things a long time, seeing only what they are, the familiarity and naturalness of them, our faith in their endurance, the pleasure we took in sharing their world. But we were children, and we didn't see the path of diminishment we walked on.

XXVI

IN THE CAPITAL CITY of Alberta, in the years leading up to the Great War, my paternal great-grandparents and their four children kept bees. This was much more than a hobby: they were the city's premier honey sellers, producing thousands of jars from hundreds of hives, a product my grandfather and his brothers delivered to customers by bicycle. One of my most cherished family heirlooms is a little, privately printed book, not much more than a chapbook really, entitled *The Bee and Me.* It was put together and written by my great-aunt Gladys, who is today best remembered in Edmonton as the wife of Merrill Muttart, a wealthy lumber baron who left as his legacy to the city a curiously beautiful quartet of large glass pyramids known as the Muttart Conservatory. Each pyramid houses a different vegetation zone, with desert and rainforest being the extremes. Needless to say, the Bowling family workers would find a bonanza of nectar in the rainforest pyramid. But there are no bees inside, and no apiaries along Jasper Avenue either. That past is past, for my family and the city.

In *The Bee and Me,* however, it is still present. There's a photograph of my great-grandparents and my grandfather as a small boy, standing amongst the boxed hives, their faces veiled with heavy mesh, their arms padded, their gazes directed towards the camera. Around them, faint as rain, hovers a loose cloud of bees. There is something disquieting about the image, something ominous. I think it is the palpable sense the image gives to the viewer that the past is always mostly hidden from us, and to bring it into clearer focus, we risk exposing it to the poised stingers of the world and time. And yet, I'm proud too of the calm inhabitation of the wild my ancestors possessed, and I can't help but see in these few yellowed pages and grainy photographs born of a northern place beyond the salmon's range the origins of my own life with the salmon's special kind of wilderness. After all, the bee, like the salmon, constructs its brief time on a cycle of leaving and returning, and its returning is a rich sustenance for us. In this way, the hands that reached into the black swarms reach also into the black fathoms. My grandfather's boyhood spent delivering jars of honey to customers connects directly to my childhood of carrying jack springs up Georgia Street to Grandma Atkey. And the faith of my great-grandparents, who routinely kept hives in their basement through Edmonton's long, severely cold winters, is the faith of my parents who awaited the salmon's annual return.

Poets live on such connections, we dangle on fragile ropes over dark, rushing water and build our flumes of words to carry something on beyond ourselves. The heart that motors the breath that forms the language moves to a cycle not dissimilar to the bee's and the salmon's. And the fuel for that motion is a continual sensitivity to association, otherwise known as a metaphor-making spirit. I can see something of my life as a writer, for instance, in the poignant image of my elderly maternal grandfather tramping up and down Yonge Street during the Second World War, an employee of Underwood Typewriters, his job to change ribbons and make simple repairs to the machines in dozens of offices. That same English-born grandfather, who died when I was two, appears at eighty years old in a rare series of photographs taken of my father's first boat, the *Rona.* There he is, a small, thin Torontonian in a dark suit and fedora, sticking up through the hatch in front of the cabin. How strange it must have been for him, a city-dweller all his long life, to visit his youngest child, one of only four survivors from his fifteen-child brood, a child who had become a gutter and cleaner of salmon and pheasants!

And how much stranger, perhaps, for my parents to have visited me, a worker in the guts of language, in Edmonton on the occasion of my first child's birth. Often our lives seem simply a matter of recognizing cycles, one within another. That recognition is the poet's task, as much as archivism, celebration and honesty. In some ways, as a wonderful counter to North American society's youth obsessions, age makes the poet's job easier, for with age the patterns grow clearer. I lived in Edmonton for ten years and did not realize that my great-grandparents were buried there. I looked for the old house in which the bees had been kept warm through the winters, but it had long since been razed. I did not, however, seek out the graves of the Bowlings, graves that not even my hometown possesses. When I do return to find them one day, I'll breathe a different air, just as the salmon undergoes a change from salt water to fresh and survives long enough to guarantee its future.

* * *

"I built the hull right here on the kitchen floor," Uncle Earl says with a twinkle in his blue eyes.

Auntie Pearl shakes her head. "Yes, and I said to him, 'Earl, those nails aren't going into the linoleum I hope.'"

His smile widens. "'Oh no no no, don't worry, Pearl, I know what I'm doing.'"

They look at each other across fifty-plus years of marriage with such obvious love and affection that I'm pained by the knowledge of the imminent separation one must have from the other.

"Well," he says, "darned if I didn't go to pull the hull up and. . ."

"Right into the floor," she finishes for him, and I'm struck with the sudden thought that perhaps Noah's wife made her husband build his damned ark out in the yard.

The hull in question was the hull of the *Queen Bee*, so named because my uncle inherited the family gift for beekeeping, a gift reawakened by his father-in-law Newt McCullough, himself a salmon fisherman who near the end of his long life, hired my brother Bruce as a deckhand one summer (the bees go out, the bees return, the salmon go out, the salmon return). But Bruce, as I've mentioned, would carry on the family history in the plumbing trade, keeping that cycle alive.

It was Newt, as well, who guided my uncle through the backyard building of what is affectionately referred to as the *Queen*. And the blueprints for that particular design? They came from Rod Beveridge via his son-in-law Jim Robertson, which means that the *Queen Bee* and the *Thunderbird* shared more than the same drift of the river – they shared their skeletons.

Boats built at home, practical knowledge handed down from generation to generation and family to family, husbands and wives growing old together and teasing each other for the insignificant mistakes of the past, the bees to their hives, the salmon to their streams. It doesn't matter, in the end, who we blame for our losses; we have to live with them. And there is a social price we've paid and are still paying for the diminishment of the wild. When we no longer live with it and by its rhythms, we are also diminished. *In wildness is the preservation of the world,* declared Thoreau. And I know that my uncle, who fought in Holland during its liberation and returned from that horror forever changed, found a form of personal preservation in his work with the salmon and the bees.

Where will we find our preservation now? Recently, beekeeping has been banned in Ladner. The fishing fleet is almost permanently moored. And the *Queen*, the beautiful, homemade queen of the Prairie Drift, is wrecked and rotten on the banks where the canneries blacken year by year. I'm wearing the heavy mesh over my eyes, my arms are padded, the past is coming home.

XXVII

My mother, Dorothy Jean Stevens Bowling, was born and raised in Toronto, the last of eighteen children, ten of whom died at birth or in infancy. At eighteen, in 1944, she married a sailor she'd met while he was on leave in Toronto from his minesweeper stationed at Halifax. The sailor was from a far-off place called Ladner, way at the other end of the country. It took days to get there by train. When the war ended, and my mother was set to leave Toronto to join my father and start their life together along the Fraser, my grief-ridden, heavy-set, Irish-generous grandmother begged my mother, her baby, to stay at home just a little longer, at least for Thanksgiving. My uncle George, who would be killed a decade later driving into a train (he'd fallen asleep at the wheel, exhausted from working two jobs to support his large family), took my mother aside and said, "You have your own life to live, Jeannie, you must live it, you must go."

My mother went. A month later, my grandmother died in her bed of a massive coronary.

Although she has always been a huge-hearted woman to whom people are drawn for her innate warmth and generosity, my mother is attended by a sorrow more faithful than any servant. Her stories always have about them this fundamental darkness borne out of darkened parlours and rental houses wreathed with black to let the neighbours know of the latest tragedy. As she says about her mother's life, "The midwife was coming in one door as the undertaker was going out the other." As she says about her own life, "We coped."

I do not mean that there was a lack of laughter and joy in my childhood home, quite the contrary. My mother's great strength has always been built on an optimistic spirit that, at various times in my life, has shamed me and made me painfully aware of the nasty smallness of worldly ambition. But she is the product of her time and history, of urban poverty in the Great Depression, of war, of rigid domestic roles, and of the guilt and sorrow that come from the inevitable severances of the adult's from the child's world. She did not stay for that Thanksgiving and she never saw her mother again, not even in death, for she could not afford to return for the funeral. None of this was her fault. Yet she has always given the sense that everything sad or wrong is her fault. I do not know anyone who carries in their eyes so much of the weight of being human, and in their heart so much generosity, and in their arms so much tenderness and faith. The very songbirds she whistles each day to the feeder outside the large plate glass window of the house on Georgia Street must feel the survivor's impulse in her presence; it not only crosses, it eradicates the species. But to be a survivor means you have endured. My mother's endurance, as much as my father's work, is the beginning of history and poetry.

She arrived at the central train station on Main Street in Vancouver in the pouring rain and no one was there to meet her. She was nineteen, a city girl raised in a city of snow and cold. The only other people in the station were elderly East Indian men in turbans. She'd never seen this race before, nor heard the language. She waited. The dark autumn rain blurred the windows. A train departure was called out. Had she done something wrong? Did she get off at the wrong station? The longer she waited, the more she doubted herself.

But finally, after a fretful hour, there came my handsome, blue-eyed twenty-two-year-old father and my stogie-chomping, iron-willed yet soldier-on-leave casual grandfather. It turns out they'd gone to the wrong station. Now everything was back on track. The rain fell harder, but as they crossed a series of bridges, the sun kept breaking through the grey clouds. The water below the bridges was ocean and then it was river, and on the river floated booms of logs the colour of dried blood. Great plumes of smoke rose out of mills. My mother, sandwiched in the front seat of the plumbing truck between the two men, felt at once secure and vulnerable. Again the rain pounded the windshield and the black wipers seemed about to fling off the glass.

Through the brief clearings, my mother saw the flat delta, and the muddy last surge of the Fraser in its main channel going past Lulu Island. The river was coffee-coloured and boiling with the violence of the rain. There was no tunnel linking Vancouver to the south side of the river until 1959, so the little plumbing truck sat in a colourless lineup, waiting to board the small ferry to Woodward's Landing, a two-minute drive east of the townsite of Ladner. I imagine my grandfather spoke to several people on the ferry (everyone knew everyone else then), and if he introduced them to his new daughter-in-law, she would have smiled politely and said hello quietly. She was shy, insecure and, despite her excitement, oppressed by the drab marshes and bony sandbars and lowering sky. Here was her new home, as different from downtown Toronto as she could have imagined.

At the very top of the Prairie Drift, which neither she nor my father knew by name at the time, the little ferry turned east into the channel to Woodward's Landing. Were there boats fishing for dog salmon then? She doesn't recall seeing any, but in those days, fishing was almost a full-time job. And many men returning from the war were looking for jobs that would free them from taking orders. At the very least, on the Fraser delta in 1945, dog salmon still spawned in the marshes, giant sturgeon still wound through the sloughs, muskrats still lived in ditches along the main street of Ladner – just behind my grandfather's plumbing shop, where my parents would live at first in a shack at the back of the property. My mother, accustomed to spartan and poor living spaces, must nonetheless have felt a drop in her spirit at the sight of her new home. But then, she was nineteen, she was very much in love, the war was over and people – at least those not still grieving their losses – were palpably grateful and hopeful.

Ah, but the Fraser delta is a terrible place to be homesick. When I think of my mother in 1945, especially after she'd learned of her own mother's sudden death, the face of Edney Booth Ladner rises before me, wild-eyed, pale, tear-streaked. And it turns into the younger face of Mary Parr, Thomas Ladner's second wife who in 1910, after years of insisting, got her wish: the old boy finally agreed to move to Vancouver. Ladner's pioneer history – perhaps every pioneer history – is almost the history of men longing to be there and women longing to escape. Consider the wet and the dark and the absence of company! In those days, men and women spent eight months of the year in gumboots. The drudgery of daily work was relieved only by a rare house- or barn-raising bee; in winter, there were quilting bees, and in summer there was the considerable undertaking of a picnic in the bog. Otherwise, as T. Ellis Ladner so succinctly puts it, *Time hung heavy on the early pioneers.*

It hung heavy on my mother too. She didn't know anyone and it wasn't easy for a shy young woman to make friends. Her husband, who liked to shoot pool and play cards, often left her on her own at night. Her in-laws were kind, but no one could call them warm. And then after a month, my mother's mother, a woman so warm she would always – including at the height of the Depression – give the iceman or milkman a bite to eat even when it meant she would go without, died. And my mother's loneliness took on the weight of the sky.

Only now, in my fifth decade, am I mature enough to imagine her stepping out of that little shack, tears on her face, her long, full black hair flowing behind her, and walking along Thomas and William Ladners' first dyke, where she'd repeat endlessly, *I should have stayed for Thanksgiving, why didn't I stay, if I had only stayed, maybe she'd be alive, I should have stayed, it was only another week.*

From Edney Booth Ladner's arms around her dying child to my mother's mother-empty arms to my own first few fatherless hours on the wharf by Thomas Ladner's original farm at the head of Chilukthan Slough – this is the only significant education I've had in my life. Above all else, it is this history – not the names on the cenotaph but the hearts breaking over the midnight speaking of them – that the abandonment of one generation's wealth prepared me to learn. Walking those few blocks of the original townsite of a Fraser River town, carrying the stories of a Toronto childhood and a dead grandmother's expressions in my heart, I was a seedbed for poetry. All I needed was the salmon, and in 1945, they were already on the way to me.

"H-E double toothpicks, this thing isn't worth a tinker's darn." Sighing, my mother wrings out the torn, tatty dishcloth and puts it on the counter. She rummages in a drawer and pulls out a clean cloth, then returns to the sink full of dirty dishes.

I'm on the floor playing with hockey cards. My sister is doing homework at the kitchen table. My father and my eldest brother are fishing the Prairie Drift. The refrigerator hums softly, the sun-clock ticks, the dishes lightly clatter. I'm the marble between two cards, one is the past and one is the future, one is Toronto and one is the Fraser, one is the dead and one is the living, both are human. Now I'm holding the marble in my hand. It's the full moon before anyone has stepped on it, it's the earth before diminishment, it keeps growing, it's the eye of the salmon, larger than anything, and it's looking at me. My father opens the door. River, salmon, brine, blood, blossoms, earth. The eye is looking at me from two sides of shining silver. Surcease of sorrow. My father's hands, my mother's heart. Life is a two-way mirror and we cannot break it.

XXVIII

ONLY ONE MAN EVER called my father by his given name. Harold Savage, a Westham Island farmer for whom my father drove a tractor over potato fields each autumn for several decades, would enunciate the name in his curious laconic drawl with what always struck me as an affectionate civility. *Har-old*, he would say, emphasizing the syllables. Perhaps he called my father by his proper name because it was the same as his own, or perhaps simply because, being his part-time employer, he actually knew it. Everyone else, my mother included, called my father *Heck.* This caused some confusion, as many people – Vic Gerard, the packer, for instance – took *Heck* to be an abbreviation of *Hector.* It says much about my father's personality that he never bothered to correct Vic or anyone else. He would just wink at me and say, "Call me whatever you like, just don't call me late for supper."

My father seemed to attract nicknames. "Heck" was simply the only pronunciation of Harold that his sister Bunty (itself an inexplicable nickname for Lillian) could manage. For some reason, it stuck. "Ghost," on the other hand, never really caught on, but it did accurately reflect my father's curious social invisibility, just as it foreshadowed the general sadness that has come to define the old rural sense of community now diminished along the Fraser's mouth. The spectral nickname rose out of my father's annual absence at the charity fundraising softball game between the local women's team and a team affectionately dubbed "the Pioneer Oldtimers" (between 1965 and 1980, if you were over forty you were an oldtimer, and proud enough of it to wear the name on your back). This team drew its talent basically from the farming and fishing community. The games themselves, played in Memorial Park at the very end of summer, were always fun, crammed with balls hidden under caps and other sneaky tricks, not to mention stolen kisses and sometimes mock lewd flirtations. I attended most of the games, and was never bothered when the public address announcer, reading out the lineups, asked for Heck "Ghost" Bowling to step forward. The crowd chuckled appreciatively, and the festivities moved along.

In later years, Rick, known as "Pigger" in softball circles, served as the good-natured ump. It was a logical choice, and preserved some reputation for the family's community involvement. Logical because Rick knew everyone, of course, and who else wore a T-shirt showing chicks emerging from eggs with the slogan *I Just Got Laid* written boldly beneath, who else owned a pair of red Christmas underwear on which was written *Ho Ho Ho, Welcome to the North Pole*? Yet my brother was an acorn who did not fall so very far from the tree. "Ghost," as the weekly *Delta Optimist* called my father once a year all through my childhood, liked to kid around, but often in quieter ways. If my mother asked him what he'd like for dessert, a piece of apple or a piece of pumpkin pie, he'd answer, "Yes please," and grin at her "What I have to put up with" eye-rolling. Whenever anyone used the common expression, "Look at it this way," he'd screw his mouth up so that the top lip almost touched one nostril and the bottom lip almost reached his chin. It was such a famous response that, the moment you'd said, "Look at it this way," you knew your argument was lost. But you didn't mind. My father's good nature was its own irresistible current.

He had a particular fondness for the punning humour of Wayne and Shuster, a once-famous Canadian comic duo who hold the record for most ever appearances on *The Ed Sullivan Show*, and I well remember as a small boy delighting with him in the silent films of Buster Keaton and Charlie Chaplin. Mostly, though, he enjoyed hearing and telling the local stories, such as the time the game warden, Slim Cameron, was disarmed and tied up by a passing-through-town John Dillinger, or the time Albert, ticked off at some fisherman, stole the man's seine boat and ran it up into the marsh, or the time Big Dick (a name whose double entendre I didn't understand then), a new engine battery in his arms, stepped off the wharf, missed his boat, sank, but walked up the muddy bank still holding onto the battery. "Damned thing cost me too much," my father reported Dick saying. "I wasn't about to let go of it."

My father's shyness melted away whenever we had a visitor to the house, which wasn't often. Sometimes Uncle Earl and Auntie Pearl dropped by, or my mother's friend Helen Maxwell, and Dad would stretch out on the chesterfield, joking and teasing. Occasionally – and this was in keeping with his instinctive fondness for the outcast – he would bring a guest home for supper unannounced, which naturally didn't sit well with my mother. But she possessed enough of her own mother's generous Irish spirit not to show her displeasure, so the evenings always went smoothly.

One fairly regular guest was Albert Wigglesworth. How well I remember him sitting in an armchair, rubbing his woollen-socked feet together so vigorously as he spoke that I almost expected a fire to start. Both my father and my uncle made a point of befriending Albert, I think because they respected his remarkable practical knowledge and disliked the way some people dismissed him as a useless wharf rat. Whatever the reason, Albert sat many times in our living room, his body giving off a strong but not rank odour of mud and oil, his black eyes darting weirdly around at the somewhat genteel surroundings like the eyes in the large ancestral portraits of bad horror movies.

But even his presence was not as unusual as that of Mr. Beveridge's, who came at Christmas time with a bottle of homemade wine and terrified me with a graphic, deliciously told version of *Sweeney Todd, the Demon Barber of Fleet Street.* The massive frame of the renegade Englishman, his smouldering pale grey eyes and broken-toothed smile, the way he leaned forward and slashed the air with his arm as Sweeney Todd dropped another customer through the barber chair into the basement: little wonder that I could not eat a meat pie for weeks lest I find a fingernail in it, or that I crossed the street when passing Mr. Holloway's barbershop.

My father, a ghost in the community outside the waterfront, made a point of being sociable in unexpected ways. There was the summer, for instance, he invited the tramp to stay at our house. I would have been about eight, my father not quite fifty, and the tramp fifteen years older than that. His name was Jim, from the States, and he'd been wandering around North America for years. None of that was particularly interesting, except for one thing: Jim was as black as Shamus, the Lab next door. In those days, though, days of civil rights riots on the news, Jim was not so much black as he was a "Negro." There weren't many Negroes in Ladner. To meet one down at the waterfront, therefore, was akin to encountering a killer whale on the Prairie Drift. And if you could believe what you saw on television, a Negro was every bit as unpredictable. Moreover, this one was a self-proclaimed hobo. Don't let his soft Mississippi drawl fool you, I could hear my visiting aunt from Ontario thinking (she had lived among Negroes, she said, and knew all about what they were like) as my mother took another plate down from the cupboard.

But Jim wouldn't eat with us, nor would he sleep in the house. Grizzled, his broad face sedimented with wrinkles, and his hands so long and tapered they resembled iconic carvings in candle wax, he raised his river-brown eyes and said slowly, "Thank you no, Ma'am, I be plenty comftahbul in the yard."

And in the yard he slept, for two nights, on the swinging porch under the Bartlett pear tree, while Aunt Irene shook her head and tut-tutted and said, "We'll be lucky if we aren't all murdered in our beds." No one believed her, least of all my father. He just seemed to like minorities more the more other people were ungenerous towards them. For this reason, the daughters of Chung Chuck always shouted "Hello Mr. Bowling!" when they rode past him on their bikes, and the non-English-speaking female Chinese farm workers employed by Harold

Savage would point at my father's eyes and say "blue, blue" while he smiled in return and said, *Chucka mucka hi fungayo,* a supposed series of curse words that always made them giggle and cover their mouths. Not surprisingly, my father wasted no time on those who ran the Indians down. "I used to play on the reserve," he'd explain to me, referring to his boyhood spent in North Vancouver during the thirties. And that was all; no more need be said. His tolerance and my mother's charity set the tone for my formative years.

What did my father and Jim talk about? Mostly the latter's travels. He'd been everywhere, picked up what work he could, just liked to see new places, meet new folks. He couldn't have been, in other words, more unlike my father. But the connection existed, as it so often did between my father and others, in a shared resistance to the mainstream culture's materialist values. Jim had no truck with owning things, he just gloried in the bounty of the world.

So a wandering son of Mississippi who played a Jew's harp bonded for two summer days along the banks of the Fraser with the high-school-dropout son of the North Shore Mountains who in his twenties, in the early years of World War II, played trumpet for a dance band that made some good money in the Vancouver clubs. My father even took Jim out on the boat and paid him a little something, something he couldn't afford to pay, for his unnecessary help. Then the Negro was gone, on the road, and I would think of both him and my father every time I read Langston Hughes' poem "I've Known Rivers." For beyond the shyness and the removal from the world of getting and spending, my father's character touched on the character of the river, mingled with it, became, like the river, larger than itself. I'm glad his ashes will go into that current.

XXIX

I DON'T LIVE IN the past, the past lives in me. The eyes through which I witness my homeland's diminishment received their blue from my father, so when I stand on the banks of the Fraser and look at the 20 percent of the estuary that survives from pre-European settlement, I look both forward and back. This is done, of course, not physically but through the mysterious process of memory. The salmon's vision is of an even stranger kind. It can look forward with one eye, backward with the other, simultaneously! Fish in general have a broad range of vision, almost 360 degrees, though they cannot see far. The absence of light under water inhibits them, of course, but in most cases their sense of smell more than compensates for the murkiness of their environment. Some runs of salmon are so genetically attuned to their home streams that they can smell a bear's paw in the water. No hatchery-bred fish is going to inherit that subtle a tool. In many cases, when we try to help the salmon, we are nonetheless harming them.

On the Columbia River, for example, dedicated conservationists carry out a bizarre spring ritual of literally barging juvenile salmon past the river's many dams in order to save them from the slashing turbines. But juvenile salmon, for some unknown reason, swim to sea backwards. Doubtless this seemingly odd behaviour helps to imprint on their brains the path they must take to return home, or else it has something to do with their amazing transformation from a freshwater to a saltwater fish. Therefore, removing them from the water, keeping them in buckets, and frantically barging them past certain destruction might just be a different signature on the death warrant.

And yet that human desire to help, as strong as our desire to destroy, is itself a bond with the salmon's history through the commercial period. Whenever I think of those American barges carrying juvenile salmon, I see a couple of white men and a group of Natives carrying fully grown and ready-to-spawn salmon over the rocks at Hell's Gate. At the same time, I can see no salmon at all. Forward and back. Simultaneously. But if I walk away from the bank of the river without turning around, I'll only trip and hurt myself. We have no choice: we must turn and face our lives if we are going to make it, if we are going to give successive generations a chance. No one's going to barge us past our manufactured death. The eyes have to open and stay that way. Like the salmon's.

* * *

No, I don't live in the past. I own a computer, I'm typing this on a laptop, I work with editors and publishers over the internet. This isn't 1969 or '70. No one even walks on the moon anymore. But the past is just like the wild salmon; it remains in shivers, associations, hauntings.

Yesterday, for example, when I conducted a search for white sturgeon on Google, I hesitated at the word "Google." Wasn't there . . . yes, I think so.

Later, to confirm, I phoned my brother and asked him.

I could hear Rick's smile through the phone. "Oh sure, Barney Google. He was an odd duck. Always wore a straw hat and never wore socks. Quite the experimenter. Don't you remember his old boat? It had an Easthope in it. Cough, cough, cough. One time I came up the drift and saw Barney's net rolling in, except there was nobody in the stern. I figured, oh oh, something's happened to the poor guy. I came up alongside, and there he was, flat on his back, pedalling away."

"Pedalling?"

"Sure. He'd rigged up a system of wheels and chains, like a

bike, so he could lie down on the job. Whenever a fish flopped over the rollers, he stood up and picked it out."

"But what if there was a big spring just hanging on by a tooth?"

Rick laughed. "What did he care? He was strange. Barney Google, you know. It was some goofy cartoon character from the old days. One of the oldtimers must have given him the nickname. Yeah, he was strange, but nice enough. I think he came from Saskatchewan. Must have gone back there, I guess. Probably got tired of the Gibbies sneaking up at night and pulling his net around in a circle behind his boat."

And I'm there again, on the lost coast, stuck for days at a time, even as I function as a husband and a father of three and a worker with bills to pay. *What a piece of work is a man! How noble in reason!* . . . which isn't the whole story of Ladner. Actually, there's probably more Falstaff there than Hamlet. Ah, why dissemble, the lost coast *was* Shakespearean. It deserves, at the very least, a final turn on the stage.

XXX

THE MORNING WHEN I set out to break the law is cool, with that hint of rain just coming or just ended. The windshields of the cars parked along Georgia Street are dew-dampened and dripping – sides of salmon lifted from the river seconds before. It's a Sunday and despite all our efforts over the past thirty years to make every day of the week the same – a congregate of clock ticks for commerce – still not a working day for most people, and therefore still quiet. I walk slowly towards the dull light of the streetlamp near the lower Buckerfields building, and my shadow stays tight to me, as if trying its best to keep our business unobserved.

Soon we're on the dyke, and I'm surprised to hear a forklift running inside the cannery building. White lights blaze on the outside cement platforms. Briefly, I consider turning back. I had expected the waterfront to be the graveyard it has been all summer as a result of the fishery closure. I still can't seem to remember that wild salmon are trucked down from Alaska to be processed in Ladner. I can't seem to remember it's 2007, not 1970. It's a new world, or at least a variation of the old world of government complicity with concentrated wealth, and no matter how many ghosts and regrets I carry with me, I can't turn the clock back. However, like Gatsby, I'm sure as hell going to try. And while I'm trying, I'm going to believe I can succeed.

I have it all planned. This is no spur-of-the-moment crime. I've been preparing for months. I found a chunk of fall net in a dark corner of the shed in my mother's backyard – leadline, corkline and corks. Only a few dozen fathoms, most of which were snag-torn, but I also found a plastic needle and half a ball of dusty mending twine. It didn't take much to patch the worst holes. Nor did it take much to borrow a skiff from an oldtimer. I just want to row around the Prairie a bit, I said, and knew he'd commiserate with my nostalgic mood.

That was all. The only risk, apart from the slim one of getting caught by a fisheries officer on the river, was leaving the skiff tied up for one night at the moss-weighted, collapsing float in my father's old tie-up spot. It wasn't much of a risk, however. There aren't many people in Ladner Harbour these days. A few yachts and kayaks drift by, but the people navigating them see mostly a charming decay, a perfect stretch of river in which to observe a great blue heron hunched in his shabby raincoat. To the resident tourists that we've all become, what's another time-blackened skiff in an already cluttered postcard from the past?

I edge along the humming, clattering cannery, then turn sharply past the chain-link fenced area piled head-high with plastic fish totes. Immediately I'm enclosed by a mulchy rich, tan-coloured and dew-beaded tangle of blackberry bushes and grasses. Before me, in bold black letters against a vivid red background, are the words: *Private Property No Trespassing.* Just one more law to break.

A path narrower than my body leads through the blackberries towards the river. I follow it for fifteen metres, then emerge into thick riversmell and a hush so familiar that my bones ache with remembrance. The river is directly below me, brown, still, reflective as a smoked mirror. Only time, nothing but time, stands between me and the pure source of who I am.

I keep going. The old gangway is gone, a loosely roped, unribbed plank leads to the mossy floats. These are so tipped and precarious that they resemble a stretch of spring breakup on some northern river. But the tall yellow grasses sprouting like sloppy sheaves of wheat from the original blood- and oil-stained wood and the shaggy layers of green and yellow moss attest to the temperate climate. I proceed cautiously, the past in my arms, like some forgotten Native clambering over the rocks of Hell's Gate in the first year of the Great War. The smell of mud and Alaskan-caught salmon thickens the damp air as I step over and around a blue nylon tarp, an oily coil of rope, and several stacked bundles of blond, glistening lumber – someone is clearly using the wharf as a storage site for a future building project. I doubt the floats are slated for repairs.

The harbour is empty of boats on this bank, except for the skiff I stand beside, exactly in the spot where my father and I stood beside the *Rona* and the *Nola J* nearly four decades earlier. Across the slumbering channel, the same dark green and ochre netsheds, a few with corrugated tin roofs, remain. Several gill-netters are moored before them, two or three thick in places. The bare, black, and darkly dripping branches of eighty-foot-high cottonwoods appear as spiderwebs that have trapped the entire harbour as prey – I can almost hear the blood being sucked out of the life of the old town. I *can* hear it.

No, that's the gurgling and trickling of the river, the ten-thousand-year-old dialogue between the fresh and the salt that repeats *stay-go, stay-go,* endlessly, sometimes in a whisper, sometimes in a shout. For the Fraser is still North America's most savage river, even though here at its delta and all along its valley, over a century of dyking and dredging and draining has compromised its natural tendencies to spread and flow across a much larger area. In fact, if not for the dykes, Ladner would be entirely underwater at extreme high tide, a great sturgeon could swim through the severed roots of my beloved Douglas fir, the salmon could advance alive up Georgia Street instead of dead in my father's or brother's hands. It is a strange knowledge to possess that the cherished place of your memories is itself unnatural, a recent product of Victorian industry and stubbornness, and even stranger to understand its Atlantis-like fragility.

The nature of the Fraser River delta, despite human interference, is constant change. When I was a boy, the silt island behind the harbour netsheds was much smaller and almost tree-less. When the original townsite of Ladners Landing was being laid out, there was no island at all, and the main deepwater channel roared straight past the foot of Thomas

Ladner's farm. Massive flooding in 1894 and '95 shifted the channel and, to a great extent, the economic benefits of the salmon-fishing industry, to the north bank of the river's south arm where Steveston – even now Canada's largest fishing port – slumbers amongst proliferating foreshore condominiums built where the great canneries once flourished. Meanwhile, the still powerful thrust of the river – which begins 1,368 kilometres away in the Rocky Mountains near the Alberta border and drains an area one quarter the size of the province – shoots a silty plume forty-eight kilometres out into the Gulf of Georgia and extends its delta seaward nearly nine metres a year in some areas. The river, miraculously free of dams on its main stem (the Columbia, by comparison, is almost made of cement), remains impressively potent. At Hope, 185 kilometres upstream from Ladner, the flow at spring freshet is an astonishing ten thousand cubic metres per second.

But this is November, and I'm in the rapidly silting-up backwater of Ladner's dying harbour, stepping across the bodies of my father and Rod Beveridge and thousands of anonymous men and women of a dozen races into a cabin-less wooden skiff. It might as well be an open grave, except that Ladner, as I've written, is too soft for graves. So I take the dew-damp oars into my writer's soft-skinned palms and begin to row.

I'm glad the harbour's empty, for it takes me a while to get into the rhythm of things. At first, I resemble a great blue heron that's been shot with a pellet gun. And, naturally enough, the awkwardness raises anew the doubts about what I'm doing. All my life I've been law-abiding, more law-abiding than the esteemed railroad promoters who built this country, more law-abiding than the current premier of the province, more law-abiding than Thomas Ladner, Henry Doyle, Alexander Ewen, J.H. Todd and all the other pioneer salmon canners. My record is clean. Even when Jeff Bemi shoplifted candy from the Dairy Dell and Kin's, I demurred. No poet in North American history, not even Wallace Stevens, has been so uniformly on the accepted side of the law. What wildness I possess is of a different kind, manifested in decisions not to eat meat, not to send my children to school, not to watch television, not to read newspapers, not to own property – a very unsexy form of rebellion, free of drug convictions and legends of drunken and/or womanizing behaviour. Dull as ditchwater, straight as an arrow, yet nonetheless in opposition to nearly everything my culture values and upholds as worthy of reverence. This majestic Fraser River plume shooting out into the ocean is actually, as Alan Haig-Brown describes it, a smokestack spewing sewage and industrial waste into a poorly ventilated room – and the major contributors to this pollution have broken, and are breaking, more laws than I could break if I lived a hundred lifetimes.

None of this information helps me much as I finally assume control of the oars and slide past the grey-black hulk of the Buckerfields warehouse and the new government wharf built in the 1980s on the north bank, no people in sight anywhere, the whole fleet tied up, gillnetters and seiners crammed together like the impounded boats of the Japanese after the attack on Pearl Harbor. You can't arrest me, I hear myself saying, my father fished this stretch of river in the 1950s. You can't arrest me, I'm a poet on a mission of communal reclamation. *Tell it to the judge, son.* The judge who owned shares in a seiner during the seventies and eighties when the federal government made it easy for the wealthy non-fishermen to skim off the cream of salmon profits, the judge who sits on the board of the Salmon Farmers Association and works tirelessly behind the scenes to remove farmland from the Agricultural Land Reserve – a freakish anomaly of preservation made law by a social democratic provincial government in the mid-seventies – so that the prime real estate of marshy Atlantis-in-waiting can be subdivided and sold to people who will rarely even notice the Fraser River as they drive under it and over it on their way to their jobs in a city proud of its collective lack of interest in heritage.

Bitterness won't help me either. I know that. And besides, the rivermouth is still so beautiful on a quiet morning, the natural and social heritage still vivid enough even in decay, that I'm only seconds beyond the *Native Dawn* and the *Evening Star* and the *Nordic Gold* before all my negative emotions have sifted out of me the way rock is sifted to silt by the river. The condominiums placed where the backfield of tall grass and majestic poplars once stood don't upset me. Nor does the yacht basin filled with half-million-dollar pleasure craft where Chung Chuck's ramshackle float homes once blackened the bank inspire any nostalgic flights of United Fishermen and Allied Workers' Union rhetoric. Eventually, one tires of the relentless human struggle for justice and simply lets the earth's splendour fill the eyes and veins. I'm drifting down a great river where I was once a boy standing in the stern of a boat beside my father. It's no wonder T.S. Eliot described rivers as strong, brown gods, for the holy is more palpable here than in any church, the flow of the silts more humbling and inspiring than the flow of any saviour's blood.

As I dip my shoulder, almost in homage to the ghost of Rod Beveridge, whose property I've just passed, and begin my ascent of the Prairie Drift, my resolve strengthens, I feel 130 years of rowing in my muscles, eight thousand years of paddling. Yet there is no past or future, it is all moments of presence, one after the other, timelessness. The sky is heavy, the grey of a castle wall. I work hard against the current, then, resting briefly, look up to see a heron perched on a deadhead – the very proof that time has lost all privilege here. For the bird is only itself in this setting; it has flown off the postcards and the condominium signs and brochures and doesn't resemble a gargoyle or a person hunched in a raincoat or a porcelain vase or a broken umbrella or any of a dozen other desperate attempts to capture its peculiar essence. Now, here, the great blue heron is simply the brother of the great white sturgeon, the one gliding and resting above the water, the other gliding and resting below, both inviolate – promises of something we can't understand made to someone we lack the power to imagine. The bird in its ragged plumage does not mourn the diminishment of its habitat, does not live with the depressing fact that we are finding high levels of poisons in its eggs. Leave it alone, let it be, I tell myself, remembering Walt Whitman's words: *I think I could turn and live with animals, they are so placid/ and self-contained.*

The heron moves its head slightly. Its long neck and sleek body shape into an *S*, a miniature of the giant *S* the Fraser imprints on the province as it winds its way from the mountains to the sea. There may be a brief escape from the human on the river, but not from the salmon. It is the defining presence, always, of this place, and it will continue to be even in the ghostly form of its coming extinction. We are powerful enough to diminish our own lives, but the earth is not our possession. Ultimately, the damage we do is self-damage, we are too small and weak to diminish the spirit of what has never belonged to us. I look into the heron's eyes as I once looked into the salmon's. The same inexhaustible mystery and glory look back. Then, as if its wings are stone slabs on which no death date will ever be written, the bird labours skyward and vanishes into the grey above the tan bulrushes.

I resume rowing. By the time I reach the towhead, my back is aching and my arms light and trembling. My heart beats fast, the damp of the air mingles with the sweat on my brow. Above the sound of my blood flow I can hear the heavy traffic descending into the George Massey Tunnel, a dull, steady hum. But that sound fades; it doesn't belong here, it never will. When I turn my head and look across the drift at Wilkies Island, I realize I'm not alone.

Suddenly it's dusk, and everyone, everything, is coming out for the dark set. The *Thunderbird* is percolating up the drift, the *Rona* and the *Nola J* alongside, my father at both wheels, here's my aunt and uncle in the *Queen Bee,* Barney Google on his back, pedalling away, my brothers and sister on the *Driftwood,* a soft, slurred singing rising off the deck of the *I'll Be Damned.* Here's Mrs. Hatt and Grandma Atkey, floating on the air out of the slough mouth, the town behind them a flickering image on a grey screen, here's Tessie Demosten with her son Archie at her side, and Jeff Bemi paddling a raft of bark. They're all coming out, one last time. My mother's there, and the river flows out of her open arms, a river teeming with life – salmon, oolichan, sturgeon the size of fir trees. Albert Wigglesworth walks through the marsh, his eyes black and wide open as the salmon's, he's grinning, a killer whale rises beyond his shoulder. They're coming out for the dark set, but nothing will be killed that will not survive, they're all coming, the Chinese and Natives dead of homesickness and disease, their hearts are full, their skin unscarred, Edney Booth Ladner drifts down off the sternwheeler's deck, she's with her daughters, whole, bright-eyed, she's surrounded by the tenderness of a promised life, she's smiling at Mrs. Bemi who paints her portrait on each drop of the rain just beginning to fall. Everyone, all life, the muskrats gliding out of their mudbank homes, the seals with their spindrift gazes, great bucks plunging into the current, the Prairie Drift becoming a carved totem pole of fluid motion. The dykes are gone, the streets and farms, the pulp mills and factories and malls, the ruins of the houses and the orchards and the canneries. There's only eelgrass and silt and the river.

I set the net. By hand. It could be 1870. I could be my brother in 1970. *Time*, as the saying goes, *is a river without banks.* The corks drift on the dark surface, which rises and falls slightly as if breathing. I wait for the sound I first heard as a five-year-old and last heard a decade ago. To my surprise, it's not long in coming, just a few moments. A muffled splash, action on the corkline, the corks bobbing. Immediately I begin pulling the heavy fathoms in, my muscles straining. Rain blurs my glasses, pocks the river's surface. It comes to me as a sigh from the lives gathered around me, as a song I've never heard before. It's on my children's lips, for they too have come out for the dark set. Here they are, as adults, on the deck of the *Rona*, holding the hands of their own children, who stand close against my father's hip. Now my wife is pulling the net with me. I can't see her, or anything else now, my eyes are open to receive the first salmon and the last. The river's taking us down. All of us. This will never happen again.

"Welcome, friend Swimmer," I say, and stand at the corner of Georgia and Chisholm, in the streetlamp's glow, middle-aged, empty-handed, grateful and free.